Classmark: HD 1411 Mit

Accession no: 282319

Location:

SWANSEA UNI

LI

D0717472

£10.00

D

LONG LOAN

Items must be returned by the last date
stamped below or immediately if recalled.
To renew telephone 01792 295178.

J.C.
RETURNED
UWS LIBRARY
- 8 JUN 1999

BENTHYCIAD HIR

Dylid dychwelyd eitemau cyn y dyddiad a
stampiwyd olaf isod, neu ar unwaith os
gofynnir amdanynt yn ôl.
I adnewyddu ffôn 01792 295178.

TERMS OF TRADE
AND
CLASS RELATIONS

Other books
CALCUTTA DIARY

Terms of Trade
and
Class Relations

An Essay in Political Economy

ASHOK MITRA

FRANK CASS

First published in 1977 in Great Britain by
FRANK CASS AND COMPANY LIMITED
Gainsborough House, Gainsborough Road,
London E11 1RS, England

and in the United States of America by
FRANK CASS AND COMPANY LIMITED
c/o Biblio Distribution Center
81 Adams Drive, Totowa, New Jersey 07512

Copyright © 1977 A. Mitra

ISBN 0 7146 3083 7

*All rights reserved. No part of this publication may be
reproduced in any form or by any means, electronic,
mechanical, photocopying, recording or otherwise, without the
prior permission of Frank Cass and Company Limited in
writing.*

Typeset by Preface Limited, Salisbury, Wilts.
Printed in Great Britain by
T.J. Press (Padstow) Ltd, Cornwall.

UNIVERSITY COLLEGE LIBRARY SWANSEA

For those who have not

lost faith

Contents

Contents

List of Tables

Acknowledgments

This work was made possible by the award of a National Fellowship to me by the Indian Council of Social Science Research for the period 1972–75. A tenure as Visiting Fellow at the Institute of Development Studies, University of Sussex allowed me to revise the first draft during 1975–76.

Several friends tried, most of the time perhaps unsuccessfully, to educate me while the contents of this study were being discussed with them. Amongst those who helped in various ways, I must mention B. P. Adhikari, Amiya Bagchi, Nripendranath Bandyopadhyay, Amit Bhaduri, Krishna Bharadwaj, Sanjit Bose, Terry Byres, Nirmal Chandra, Nirmalkanti Chatterjee, Pramit Chaudhuri, S. C. Chaudhri, A. K. DasGupta, Barun De, A. K. Ghosh, K. S. Krishnaswamy, Tapas Majumdar, J. P. Naik, Dharm Narain, Deepak Nayyar, Prabhat Patnaik, Utsa Patnaik, S. K. Rao, Joan Robinson, Ashok Rudra, Ranjit Sau, Amartya Sen, Asok Sen, N. P. Sen, Sunanda Sen and Manu Shroff. My debts are particularly great to Prabhat Patnaik and Amartya Sen.

The Appendix to Chapter Three has appeared, in a slightly altered form, in *Economic Theory and Planning: Essays in Honour of A. K. DasGupta*, Oxford University Press, 1974. Certain ideas from Chapters One, Eight and Nine are to be found in my Dr. John Matthai Memorial Lectures at the University of Kerala in 1973. A substantial part of Chapter Four was incorporated in the Romesh Chunder Dutt Lectures on Political Economy I gave under the auspices of the Centre for Studies in Social Sciences, Calcutta in 1975.

ASHOK MITRA

At a certain stage of development, the material productive forces of society come into conflict with the existing relations of production or — this merely expresses the same thing in legal terms — with the property relations within the framework of which they have operated hitherto. From forms of development of the productive forces these relations turn into their fetters. Then begins an era of social revolution.

Karl Marx, *A Contribution to the Critique of Political Economy*, Moscow, 1970. Introduction, page 21.

CHAPTER 1

Economic Theory and the Class Question

Consider the state of economic theory even as late as on the eve of the Second World War. By and large, it was the domain of peaceful-looking geometrical curves, representing either indifference surfaces or technical transformation possibilities; first- or second-order derivatives of the tricks of calculus contributed their mite, and occasional footnotes acted as conductors of esoteric knowledge. In the lecture rooms, marginalism and perfect competition held sway. Since both Joan Robinson and E.H. Chamberlin had already produced their tracts, it would have been singular bad manners not to set aside a certain number of sessions to discuss imperfect market structures. The students were therefore told, in harum-scarum fashion, of those freak cases where the conditions of perfect knowledge, perfect mobility, infinite number of sellers, infinite number of buyers, *et al.*, failed to obtain, and where market forces accordingly came to rest at a point different from the arcadia defined as perfect competition. Following this somewhat breathless narration, the students were hustled out of the classroom and into the examination hall.

In such a pre-packaged navigation of the essential ports of call, little scope existed for deviationary drifting. There was an obvious absurdity in discussing the notion of market imperfection without relating it to the fact of mal-distribution of assets and incomes in society. The inconvenience was tackled in a somewhat roundabout way. Market realities, it was acknowledged grudgingly, do not always conform to the pattern laid down in the text-books; however — the reader would be assured — not much was, on balance, going to be lost by a failure to delve deeper into the mysteries of imperfect market structures, for the latter constituted only peripheral phenomena. True, a feeble group of protesters were already around — an occasional Joseph Schumpeter or a Paul Sweezy, a doubting Michal Kalecki or an Oscar Lange; but their collective voice did not carry very far.

Questions, such as what constituted the ingredients of market demand, or what determined the structure of supply, were therefore

1

taboo. Demand, as it expresses itself in the market, reflects the command over goods and services on the part of different members of the community. One was, however, not supposed to ask how the members of the community come to obtain their respective allotments of purchasing power which make the exercise of this command possible, or why such allotments differ from one another. There was evidently no time to spare for an enquiry into the law, if any, according to which the community's purchasing power is distributed, nor for one exploring the link between a given structure of asset holdings and the pattern of income distribution. The new generation of students were dutifully taken on a guided tour of the economic problems of socialism and were also told, in an aside, of the Keynesian prescriptions for tackling the scourge of unemployment. They were therefore vaguely made aware that income distribution, whether between persons or between factors of production, has a certain relevance to economic realities. But that it has a relevance to the distribution of property and the alignment of classes was carefully left unstated.

The cultural lag persists. While major qualitative shifts have taken place in economic theory in the three decades since the end of World War II — for example, the re-emergence of the issues of growth as a principal *quaesîtum* and the spreading disenchantment with the tenets of equilibrium analysis and the Pareto optimality,[1] little effort has been made to integrate the role of property relations and income distribution, as reflected in institutional and structural factors, into the corpus of theory. These continue to form disjunctive categories.

The organic relationship between the distribution of assets and incomes in society on the one hand and the structure of prices on the other has thus rarely been discussed in orthodox economic theory. The distribution of assets and incomes is a major determinant of prices, but prices too in their turn influence the distribution of incomes and assets. If one imagines a bartering community consisting exclusively of sellers (who are simultaneously buyers too), the division of the community's assets between its members determines to a large extent the *inter se* terms of trade between the groups who exchange commodities or services among themselves; but the terms of trade in their turn determine the allocation of real incomes between them, and over time therefore influence the distribution of real assets. Where the community is made up of one group exclusively of buyers and another group exclusively of sellers, a rise in the price level by a certain order would imply a shift in income distribution in favour of the sellers on *ceteris paribus* assumptions; to that extent, the relative income of the buyers would decline. If, on the contrary, the price level falls over a period, the distribution of income would, other things once more remaining the same, shift in favour of the buyers. One of the principal aims of all political activities in a class-ridden society is to influence not just the distribution of property, but also the structure of market prices, since, apart from confiscation or appropriation, it is only through an adjustment of prices that the relative shares of assets and incomes going to different social groups and classes are reallocable.

This becomes obvious once the role of the State is taken into account. Prices are then revealed as a manipulable category, which can be a major instrument in the hands of those who want to use the apparatus of the State for furthering sectarian interest. To ignore this fact is to ignore the basic relationship between the polity and the economy. Those who join the fray of politics do so with the object of capturing power. But the seizure of power is not to give vent to an abstract religious passion, nor is it an exercise in pristine aesthetics; it is to shift the distribution of assets and incomes in society in favour of those groups who support you — and to whom you look for support. Throughout history, assets have been commandeered by war, plunder, confiscation. The instruments for acquiring such a command, and thus effecting a redistribution of incomes and assets, today belong to the more common species of price policy, supplemented by policies which impinge on taxation and subsidies, borrowing and lending, and purchases and sales. All such policies have a direct impact on relative prices. Through a selective policy of, for example, taxation and subsidies, it is possible to lower or raise the prices of goods and services, as well as of capital assets, and thus affect the relative incomes of their buyers and sellers. Through the modality of borrowing and lending, it is again possible to expand or contract the output, as well as lower or raise the price, of a commodity or a factor. And certainly purchases and sales of commodities and services at different levels of prices have the profoundest effect on income distribution. The fact is usually slurred over in a milieu dominated by hypocrisy, but the entire frame of government operations is set up to ensure that groups who support the authorities add to their assets and incomes, while those ranged against suffer a loss.[2]

There is, quite clearly, an analytical gap here. At one end, we have the Marxian rubric which, in a vast historical sweep, delineates the process of transformation of human societies as a dialectical maturing of certain economic institutions; it analyses the organic link between property relations and the distribution of income and output at different phases of a nation's economic life. A sizeable literature has by now come into existence which discusses the implications, under varying assumptions, of the Marxian schematics for the pattern of growth of economies marked by particular social formations. This magnificent endeavour has left no perceptible mark on conventional economic discussions.[3] Marxian economics, to this day, remains the great outsider.

Largely as a consequence, studies concerning the impact of political institutions and class structures on the shaping of economic policy have been generally neglected. That economic decision-making is causally related to the political forces at work continues to be considered as a near-heresy in many quarters. Economists of the conventional school have grown accustomed to discuss the virtues and vices of socialist economies *vis-à-vis* those of the capitalist ones; but they have been chary to draw the logical conclusion that since differences in economic practices under the two systems mirror differences in political structures, the nature of the polity is itself the prime mover of the economic process.

The depression in the 1930s did cast a certain shadow. But only for a while. Once the crisis was staved off through the adoption of Keynesian prescriptions, and World War II intervened, economists in the West could get rid of whatever self-doubt was earlier engendered concerning their political and economic institutions. The species of economic welfarism expatiated upon in the Western countries in the past few decades has also not called for any detailed examination of the organic relationship between economic phenomena and the class basis of the State. Recent developments in most of these countries have brought the two principal contending groups — the bourgeoisie and the working class — to a state of relative equipoise. A stable pattern of income distribution is being taken for granted; both classes have seemingly concluded that it would be impossible to effect, either in the short or in the long run, any major shift in the balance of economic power. As no fundamental re-ordering of income distribution is any longer sought, the rationality of the economic structure is not questioned either. Only marginal adjustments are every now and then demanded by either of the groups; these are willy-nilly acquiesced in by the other.[4] A majority of practising economists have been drawn into this zone of tranquillity; enquiries pertaining to institutional issues have receded to the background.[5] The trend has caught on elsewhere, including in the under-developed countries. In these countries, the class composition of the economists themselves has been a contributing factor. The economists either spring from, or are in no time drawn into the folds of, the upper stratum of the community, who generally constitute the ruling class. Their attitude toward the establishment is not dissimilar to that of a family physician, quiet and unremonstrative. There are occasions when they find themselves in considerable disagreement with specific aspects of State policy. Even on such occasions, their recommendations are in the nature of friendly counsel. As a group, they have rarely, if ever, gone into the political and social roots of economic decision-making.

If issues concerning the structure are excluded from economic analysis, what remains is mostly either technical virtuosity or arid tautology, hardly able to keep away boredom. The desperate flight to mathematics of the second best to which the science has been reduced of late perhaps reflect this ennui. Economists find themselves in the state of John Osborne's anti-hero. There are no great causes lying in wait, no great challenges; one hurriedly escapes into a world of make-believe.

The present work is modestly conceived. It seeks to explore, in one general area, the relationship between political and economic realities. It argues that it is not possible to study the course of economic policy in isolation from the politics of class relations. A number of political biases influence the formulation of economic policy in every country. The biases are not accidental, but follow from the given structure of property and income distribution. This structure in its turn is affected by the apparatus of the State, which represents the interests of particular classes and groups. In so far as property relations are evolving continuously, the economic aspirations of the ruling groups are not always fully — and evenly — articulated through official policy. To that extent, the bias in economic decisions is characterised by shifts and contradictions. In other instances, decisions are influenced by political arrangements entered into by different economic categories who agree to a sharing — temporary or otherwise — of power. More specifically, the essay will examine the impact of one element of decision-making, namely, shifts in terms of trade between industry and agriculture, on the relative economic position of the different classes in society and thus on accumulation and growth. It is, of course, not the contention here that in the mutual interaction between class relations and product-cum-factor price, it is the terms of trade which constitute the dominating variable. The terms of trade effect on relative income shares neither supplants nor substitutes the crucial part played by property relations. It merely reflects — and extends — the process set in motion by the latter: the structure of class relations represents the stock, movements in relative prices are only a flow at the margin. Nonetheless, since over time the flow too does modify the stock, there can be a certain advantage in studying the relationship between income distribution and economic growth as the outcome of movements in terms of trade — movements which, it will be maintained, are engineered by developments in the polity.

The plan of the book is as follows. The discussion in the next chapter endeavours to show that the neglect of the class question is a relatively recent development in economic theory, and that the link between shifts in terms of trade and class interests had in fact been a major issue in classical political economy. This is followed by an interpretation of Rosa Luxemburg's model of accumulation and dwells on its implications for inter-sector income distribution and overall economic growth. The next chapter is devoted to an examination of the terms of trade models discussed in the Soviet Union in the 1920s. Some of Michal Kalecki's formulations which have relevance to the issue are examined in a subsequent chapter, followed by a neo-classical digression which sheds, albeit partially, further light on the problem. A schematics of class relations, based exclusively on terms of trade factors, is then suggested. The schematics is examined in the final chapters of the book with the help of Indian economic data; the hypothesis is offered that the quasi-stagnation in the Indian economy in the recent period is, to a principal extent, the by-product of political processes refracted through movements in inter-sector terms of trade.

NOTES

1   See, for instance, J. Kornai, *Anti-Equilibrium: On Economic Systems Theory and the Tasks of Research,* North Holland, 1971, and N. Kaldor, 'The Irrelevance of Equilibrium Analysis', *Economic Journal,* December 1972, pp. 1237-55.
2   State power serves the purpose of promoting a particular distribution of incomes and wealth by other means too, such as through legislation and direct administrative devices.
3   There is a strong ground for suspecting that this neglect of institutional issues was deliberate. The neo-classical opprobrium cast out not only the socialist writers, it also extended to such economists as J.A. Hobson whose formulations were marked by structural overtones. Savings, Hobson had argued, produce cycles of prosperities and depressions because savers invest promptly and thereby enlarge the productive capacity of the economy to a point where demand fails to keep up; as most savings are done by the relatively rich, the ultimate cause of cyclical disturbances, he pointed out, is the social inequality of income, a conclusion which could hardly be palatable to the orthodox school. See J.A. Schumpeter, *History of Economic Analysis,* 1954, pp. 1130-1.
   John Maynard Keynes does not seem to have read much of Marx beyond the latter's correspondence with Engels (see Keynes' letter to George Bernard Shaw, dated 1 January 1935, quoted in R.F. Harrod, *The Life of John Maynard Keynes,* Macmillan, 1951), but that did not deter him from using strong epithets ('a certain method of carrying on and a vile manner of writing'), epithets which could only be the outcome of class-biased prejudice. It is this prejudice again which must have goaded Keynes to refer together to 'the underworlds of Karl

Marx, Sidvic Gesell or Major Douglas'. (*The General Theory of Employment, Interest and Money,* Macmillan, 1949 edition, p.32). We have it on the authority of Roy Harrod that Keynes was most unhappy that the list of prescribed textbooks at the Honours School in Oxford included Marx's works! (R.F. Harrod, *op. cit.*, p. 327.)

4   The spiralling inflation since the early 1970s had led to a partial resurgence of trade union militancy in a number of the Western countries; but this does not contradict the central point stressed above.

5   A major exception in the writings of the so-called 'structuralist' school in Latin American countries.

CHAPTER 2

Class Conflict and Classical Political Economy

I

As far as classical political economy is concerned, the conflict of class interests was a basic condition of economic life. Adam Smith, in the Introduction and Plan of Work of the *Wealth of Nations,* promises to enquire not only into the 'causes' of the 'improvement' in 'the productive powers of labour', but also into 'the order, according to which its produce is naturally distributed among the different ranks and conditions of men in the society'. The moment one talks of 'ranks and conditions of men', one is, in fact, talking of classes. Consider also the following passage:

> As soon as the land of any country has all become private property, the landlords, like all other men, love to reap where they never sowed, and demand a rent even for its natural produce ... He [the labourer] must then pay for the licence to gather them; and must give up to the landlord a portion of what his labour either collects or produces.[1]

Is there the least doubt that landlords here represent a class, as labour does too, and that a relation of contradiction exists between the two? Later, in the chapter 'Of the Wages of Labour', Adam Smith reiterates, explicitly, the theme of class contradiction while discussing the formation of wages in the manufacturing sector:

> What are the common wages of labour, depends everywhere upon the contract usually made between those two parties [that is, masters and workmen], whose interests are by no means the same. The workmen desire to get as much, the master to give as little as possible. The former are disposed to combine in order to raise, the latter in order to lower the wages of labour.
> It is not, however, difficult to foresee which of the two parties must, upon all ordinary occasions, have the advantage in the dispute, and force the other into a compliance with their terms. The masters, being fewer in number, can combine much more easily; and the law, besides, authorises, or at least does not prohibit their combinations, while it prohibits those of the workmen. We have no acts of parliament against combining to raise it. In all such disputes the masters can hold

out much longer. A landlord, a farmer, a master manufacturer, or merchant though they did not employ a single workman, could generally live a year or two upon the stocks which they have already acquired. Many workmen could not subsist a week, few would subsist a month, and scarce any a year without employment. In the long-run the workman may be as necessary to his master as his master is to him, but the necessity is not so immediate.

We rarely hear, it has been said, of the combinations of masters, though frequently of those of workmen. But whoever imagines, upon this account, that masters rarely combine, is as ignorant of the world as of the subject. Masters are always and everywhere in a sort of tacit, ~~Silence.~~ but constant and uniform combination, not to raise the wages of labour above their actual rate. To violate this combination is everywhere a most unpopular action, and a sort of reproach to a master among his neighbours and equals. We seldom, indeed, hear of this combination, because it is the usual, and one may say, the natural state of things which nobody ever hears of. Masters too sometimes enter into particular combinations to sink the wages of labour even below this rate. These are always conducted with the utmost silence and secrecy, till the moment of execution, and when the workmen yield, as they sometimes do, without resistance, though severely felt by them, they are never heard of by other people. Such combinations, however, are frequently resisted by a contrary defensive combination of the workmen . . .[2]

Thus Adam Smith talks not merely of class contradictions; he also introduces the theme of class antagonism. In view of this, alongside the enquiry concerning how the national produce expands, how it is also distributed among 'the different ranks and conditions of men' ought to have, some may feel, commanded his equal attention. It did not happen this way. He, the inveterate optimist, was obviously waylaid by the notion of the 'progressive state', which, according to his contention, is 'the cheerful and hearty state to all the different orders of the society'.[3] A certain ambivalence creeps into his analysis. He feels confident about the positive impact of technical progress on wages: 'The wages of the labour . . . . . are never so high as when the demand for labour is continually rising, or when the quantity employed is every year increasing considerably.'[4] But while this may push up wages above subsistence in the short run, over the long range, the consequences could be different. In due course, stock accumulates 'in the hands of particular persons' and land becomes private property, and the three economic classes emerge with their distinct personalities: capitalists, landlords and workers. As technical improvements continue to take place and the productivity of land and labour goes up, the rent rises[5] in a developing society, while profit tends to shrink.[6] Despite their rising productivity, workers, Adam Smith appears to imply, are however unable to take full advantage of the situation, and become victims of the masters. In a society advancing through time, 'rent and profit eat up wages and the two superior orders of people oppress the inferior one'.[7]

Workmen can do nothing against this 'oppression'. Their awareness of class interests is yet to develop, they lack education, there are gaps in their information, they fail to combine effectively.[8] Thus, despite Adam Smith's optimism, the fate of labour remains somewhat indeterminate, and the answer to the query whether wages would rise above the level of subsistence is left to the realm of speculation. While rent as a category stands on its own, there is, in the *Wealth of Nations,* very nearly a nascent theory of conflict between profits and wages. But it is not quite brought out in the open.

Labour, being unorganised and weak, is an inert factor; the alienation of this class is not *effective* and is incapable of changing the reality of income distribution in society. However, what about a contradiction emerging between the interests of landlords and capitalists as national output keeps expanding? Adam Smith does realise such a possibility. Landlords are for greater competition and economic expansion, which raise rent; on the other hand, capitalists — 'dealers', in Smithian parlance — are for narrowing competition with a view to raising their profits. Adam Smith's sympathies are, quite obviously, against the dealers.[9]

Even in this instance, though, the theme of class contradictions is not pursued till the very end. Once Adam Smith comes to formulating his theory of distribution, the conflict between classes recedes to the background. The theory of distribution shades off into the theory of production; production and distribution are jointly determined. The price of a commodity is arrived at by the simple process of adding up wages, profits and rent: 'in every improved society, all the three enter more or less, as component parts, into the price of the far greater part of commodities.'[10] In the national dividend, since profits and rent are separately added up, they seemingly do not come into conflict; landlords and capitalists both prosper together, the prosperity of neither class is positively correlated with the adversity of the other one.

The Smithian analysis thus oscillates between two poles. The conflict between the interests of workers and their masters, as also between those of the 'dealers' and the rest of society, is alluded to, but Adam Smith's optimism intervenes in each case, and the conclusions are left hanging in mid-air.

It was left to David Ricardo to sweep away the ambiguity. In his schematics, the emphasis is in any event shifted in a significant manner; the 'principal problem of political economy' is no longer 'an enquiry into the nature and causes of wealth'. What was mute in Adam Smith — exploring 'the order according to which . . . produce is naturally distributed among the different ranks and conditions of men in the society' — becomes with Ricardo the principal *quaesitum*: to determine laws which determine the distribution of the produce 'among the three classes of the community; namely, the proprietor of the land, the owner of the stock or capital necessary for its cultivation, and the labourers by whose industry it is cultivated.'[11] The Ricardian theory of value and relative prices, in some sense ancillary to the purpose of explaining the income distribution between classes, vigorously casts aside the occasional Smithian notion of a harmonious complementarity between different class interests.

It is not really necessary to dwell at any great length on the course of development of Ricardo's ideas on class relations. Between the *Essay on Profits* and the *Principles of Political Economy,* there is a certain transition in Ricardian methodology, the analysis proceeds from the case of a single-commodity ('corn') economy to that of a many-commodities one, but the continuum of thought is not disturbed. Conflict, and not harmony, marks Ricardo's world. Labour remains the inert class, and its wages are still marked by subsistence — there is no escape from the Iron Law of Wages which later became associated with the name of Ferdinand Lassalle. The capitalists meanwhile have emerged as a formidable class; they have accumulated; they want outlets for their accumulation. But that other crucial factor, land, is scarce. The more the accumulatory urge on the part of capitalists, the greater is the pressure on land and the greater the opportunities open to landlords to mark up their rent. Increasingly with accumulation, the margin of cultivation keeps extending to inferior lands with lower productivity, while rent is steadily pushed up. With each extension of production, rent rises, wages remain constant (even though, since the price of 'corn' — or, more generically, wage-goods — increases because of rising demand and declining productivity, the *value* of wages goes up) and, as a result, profit shrinks. As national output advances over time, the share of rent (and also of wages) rises,[12] while that of profit falls. Technological advances could, for a while, stave off the impending doom, but, granted the assumptions of Ricardo's 'magnificent dynamics', a time is bound to arrive when rising rent would squeeze the rate of profits down to zero, drowning, once and for all, the capitalist urge to accumulate.

We are thus introduced, in no uncertain manner, to the phenomenon of class conflict between capitalists and landlords: as the economy moves through time and there is a deepening of accumulation, landlords gain, capitalists lose. What is noteworthy for our purpose is that it is possible to present the Ricardian formulation about class conflict as a movement in the terms of trade between agriculture and the rest of the economy. A consequence of the Ricardian process is obviously a shift in relative prices in favour of the landlords' commodity.[13] Irrespective of whichever way the debate over whether rent enters into cost is resolved, when rent rises, corn rises, and vice versa. The rising share of rent in national income can therefore be viewed as an aspect of the terms of trade effect, and the falling share of profit too can be interpreted as a by-product of the adverse movement in terms of trade against the service — or commodity — the capitalists offer.

With Ricardo, the struggle is joined between capitalists and landlords. Once we are permitted to assume that, in the given context, the capitalists represent 'town' and the landlords 'country', the Ricardian problem of income distribution then also emerges as a 'terms of trade' problem between town and country. Further, the famous controversy between Ricardo and Malthus over the Corn Law and tariffs falls into its proper place: a controversy over whether to shore up rent or not, whether to shift the terms of trade further in favour of the farm sector or not. Malthus, broadly subscribing to the cause of landlords, places himself on one side, while Ricardo, representing the rising capitalist class, drifts to the other side of the ideological barricade: the battle over terms of trade becomes the prism of class contradictions.

II

The Ricardo-Malthus debate is thus an important landmark in the history of economic thought; for the first time, economists are seen in this debate as proponents of their respective class interests. Orthodox Marxists have not considered it quite in this light. Marxists, beginning with Marx himself, have gone to great lengths to invite attention to the thematic contrariness in the contributions of the two scholars, both of whom lay claim to Adam Smith's ideological heritage. Marx pays accolade to Ricardo for recognising the capitalist mode of production as the most crucial instrument for growth and for his consistent pleading of the cause of accumulation. As viewed by Marx, the Ricardian analysis is driven by the single-minded objective of identifying the conditions which optimise economic growth: it is, so to say, a production model, with just the right stress on the virtues of an expanding capital-goods sector. It is a pure investigation; the stock-broker brings to bear a rare sense of detachment while tracing the historical-scientific law governing the 'development of the wealth of human race'; he is altogether indifferent whether the process of accumulation and growth destroys the property-owners, the workers or the capitalists themselves. In other words, Ricardo, Marx feels, was a neutral economist, who could abstract the problem of accumulation and growth away from that of the interests of the class to which he belonged. If, during the process of growth, the value of the capital stock owned by the bourgeoisie is reduced, or if the rate of profit tends to fall, it seemingly is not a matter of any great concern to him. Were development to affect the organic composition of capital in a manner which harms the capitalist cause, Ricardo is again indifferent. If his analysis appeared to have provided support to the cause of industrial capitalists, it was only because, during a certain phase of economic history, the interests of the capitalists coincide with the larger interests of the *economy as a whole*, since the capitalists, *at that juncture,* are the progenitors of growth. If, at any point of time, groups from amongst the bourgeoisie hinder the process of accumulation and growth, Ricardo — Marx appears to suggest — is as much against the bourgeoisie as he is, in other instances, against the proletariat at one end and the landed aristocracy at the other.[14]

In contrast, Marx has nothing but contempt for Malthus. A long and impressive array of charges is assembled against the 'parson'. Malthus draws from scientifically established premises only those conclusions which support the cause of the aristocracy as against the bourgeoisie or of both as against the proletariat; he is a 'vulgar' economist, who does not derive his economic conclusions by analysing phenomena in the sphere of production relations but travels to the sphere of circulation. Malthus's observations on protective tariffs and ground rent are motivated; their purpose is to defend the interests of the land-owning groups *vis-à-vis* those of the enlightened and progressive industrial bourgeoisie. It is again his class bias which leads him to come out in support of an out-and-out reactionary piece of legislation such as the Corn Law, placing as it did the interests of the aristocracy ahead of those of industrial capital — and of the nation. Marx has little doubt either that Malthus wrote his *Principles of Political Economy,* raising the spectre of an under-consumption crisis, mainly to throw a spanner in the works of capitalist accumulation, which cuts athwart the long-range interests of the landed aristocracy and the clergy, to whose fold he belonged.

Marx sticks to his prejudice with an astonishing ferocity. He admits that Ricardo was no particular friend of the working class;

the stock-broker regarded labour as mere beasts of burden, akin to commodities exchanged in the market place. Marx however has no complaints to lodge against Ricardo on this score: the Ricardian analysis is both objective and scientific, for, under the capitalist mode of production, labour is in fact treated as a commodity whose price is determined by the forces operating in the market place. Even though he travels via his own theory of value, Marx himself reaches more or less the same conclusion about the determination of wage-labour. Malthus's view in the matter is in essence no different; he too regarded labour as constituting a passive grist for the mill of production. But — and this explains Marx's wrath — where the demands of capitalist expansion reduced the landlord's rent or encroached excessively on the tithes of the Church, Malthus chooses wrongly, and, according to Marx, deliberately so. His concern for promoting 'the permanent increase of wealth'[15] is therefore a sham. Malthus opts to support those who place obstacles to the process of production. From Marx's point of view, there could be no greater crime committed by an economist.[16]

Could it be that this contrast between Ricardo and Malthus is overdrawn and both of them were prisoners of their respective class interests? As Marx himself has stated explicitly, the ideas of the ruling class are in every epoch the ruling ideas and the class which is the nation's ruling material force — that is, which controls the means of production and takes the key decisions affecting accumulation and output — is at the same time its ruling intellectual force too.[17] Accidents of birth and upbringing are just these, and it is not given to everybody to 'de-class' himself. It can certainly be argued that Malthus, as much as Ricardo, reflected the dominant thoughts of the class he belonged to. If this class — the landed gentry — worried in the first half of the nineteenth century over the phenomenon of short-period stagnation, and thus laid stress on ostensible consumption as a way out of the impending crisis, Malthus could have felt a social obligation to articulate these class views. Marx's ire against Malthus is again understandable, since the proposition that profits could be determined as much 'in commerce' as in the process of commodity production was anathema to his ideology. But once you grant Malthus his hypothesis, the deficiency of effective demand could be seen to emerge as a major threat to economic stability. The workers, according to Malthus, would be unable to find work beyond the point where their 'conventional necessaries' have been met. Industrial entrepreneurs too would weigh the utility of goods against the disutility of work. This consideration of weighing at the margin goods against leisure would, however, not apply in the case of those who subsist on 'fixed money revenue, obtained by inheritance, or with little or no trouble'; in other words, since these classes do not toil in raising an income, they would have no inhibition, Malthus asserts, to spend out of it. This may be fantastic logic in today's context, but did not perhaps sound altogether incongruous in the world of the early nineteenth century and provided a respectable enough rationale for tilting the terms of trade in favour of the land-owning aristocracy. Were income transferred to the idle rich from the industrial producers through taxes and other redistributive measures, the latter would then be forced — it could be argued — to increase their gross earnings so as to be able to maintain a given standard of living, and hence forced to expand their output. Finally, since aggregate output was the same as aggregate expenditure — which consisted of consumption and investment — consumption, as the only alternative to accumulation, could be considered equally essential for continuing 'uninterrupted' the 'motives to production'[18] — a remarkable anticipation of what John Maynard Keynes would say more than a century later.

Obviously, the Malthusian position was largely coloured by the parson's judgment about the operation of Say's Law in the short period; it was without question also afflicted by a particular class bias. Malthus was, quite frankly, espousing a sectarian cause. Even so, one must be fair. Was not the Ricardian rubric, too, influenced by a similar bias? Could not Ricardo be regarded as the intellectual compeer of the rising generation of industrial capitalists, and his model taken as reflecting the position taken by his own class against the aristocracy, the specific contradictions between the two classes having meanwhile come to the fore? The fact that the Ricardian and the Marxian views with respect to the process of economic expansion are, at least up to a point, parallel, is also explainable in terms of specific class biases. Despite the existence of fundamental contradictions between the interests of the industrial bourgeoisie and those of the industrial working class, both have a common stake in accumulation; since any factor — such as high ground rent — which militates against accumulation is to be reckoned as operating against economic progress, it was easy for Marx to support Ricardo against Malthus.[19]

The doubts therefore remain. Is Malthus the only one conforming blindly to his class interests? And is Ricardo as free from his? Where the interests of production come in conflict with the sectarian interests of the capitalist class, Ricardo — according to Marx — does not hesitate to come out in favour of the former and against the latter. It is, however, difficult to make too much of this proposition. Ricardo certainly preaches a message of gloom for the capitalists; certainly he analyses, with great meticulousness, the tendency toward a declining rate of capitalist profit. The conclusions he arrives at are seemingly against the interests of the class he belongs to; nor is he able to suggest measures that could avert the capitalist doom. He, however, does not derive any particular pleasure from his inability to offer prescriptions which could turn back the tide against capitalism. The process of accumulation is likely to lead to a situation where the capitalists would have to face the contingency of a stationary state marked by a zero rate of profit; the capitalists would nonetheless continue to accumulate: this Ricardian prognosis by itself at most indicates a streak of pessimism rather than that he was an exclusive votary of economic growth to whom the sectarian interests of the industrial bourgeoisie did not greatly matter. Were the Marxian theme of social alienation between the interests of the capitalists and those of the proletariat ever presented to him, Ricardo's vote, there cannot be any doubt, would have been cast with the capitalists.[20]

It was Malthus's advocacy of unproductive consumption even at the expense of accumulation that incensed Marx, who had no use for 'vulgar' theorems which relate value to circulation and make great play of short-period disturbances resulting from alleged lack of effective demand. Since the capitalist crisis is, in terms of his analysis, the outcome of internal contradictions arising in the wake of the accumulatory process, the Malthusian stance displeased Marx for more reasons than one. His own method of dividing the economy into two Departments should have perhaps persuaded Marx to explore, in greater detail, the possibility of short-period disequilibrium between supply and demand within each Department. The point somehow got lost in the mêlée. There is continuous reference in the writings of both Marx and Engels to periodic bouts of capitalist crises.[21] The theme is, however, not systematically developed and was left for examination to the Rosa Luxemburgs of later days.

III

The debate between Ricardo and Malthus over ground rent and the Corn Law marked the intrusion of the issue of class relations in classical political economy; the debate can even be interpreted as one which sought to define the role of terms of trade between 'town' and 'country' for serving specific class interests. One can suspend judgment on whether it was Ricardo or Malthus who won the battle of economic theory; but it was the former who emerged triumphant in the sphere of policy-making. The abolition of the Corn Law —

leading to a shift in the terms of trade against farm products — implied a signal victory for the capitalist class or, as Marx would say, for the cause of capitalist accumulation.

The narration, however, has to be carried forward. With Ricardo and Malthus donning their respective mantles, class conflict became a central theme of classical political economy. Marx completed the circuit by bringing to life that other — and, according to him, most important — factor of production, labour, which till now was a passive element among economic categories.[22] Everything in economic life, including the exploitation of nature and the accumulation of capital, hinges on labour; but, in capitalist society, there is a developing hiatus between labour and the means of production — labour grows increasingly alienated from the ownership of these means. Accumulation and alienation of labour proceed hand in hand. At the same time, accumulation means the emergence of increasingly larger scales of output, greater division of labour, and accelerated adoption of machinery and improved technology. The burgeoning growth of industry leads not only to impressive increases in the absolute size of the working class. As the bourgeoisie attempt to exploit them more and more, the labourers gradually learn to fight back, they combine in order to be able to offer effective resistance to the capitalists. In the process, the proletariat emerge as a distinct class, and the collision between the two classes — the bourgeoisie and the proletariat — becomes the dominant fact of economic life. From the Ricardo-Malthus nexus, a significant shift takes place. The scenario is no longer one where the principal *dramatis personae* are landlords and capitalists; landlords recede to the background, rent is subsumed under profits, the class confrontation is between the bourgeoisie and the proletariat, between capitalists and workers, between those who exploit and those who are exploited; the battle is over the distribution of national income between profits and wages. In this battle, avers Marx, the exploited will be avenged, they will smash the existing social institutions, they will throw away their chains and win a world.

Still, this denouement can take place only because of accumulation under the capitalist hegemony. Whoever and whatever stands in the way of capital accumulation must hence be opposed. Marx has no hesitation to run down even sections of the proleteriat who resisted accumulation and, therefore, in terms of his criterion, were against economic progress. The non-revolutionary elements from amongst the working people, he suggests, must be separated from the genuine ones. Small traders and manufacturers, shopkeepers, artisans, peasants, etc, belong to the former category.

They range themselves against the bourgeoisie and larger scales of output, and try to survive on the basis of small-scale operations. Despite their proximity to the proletariat community, by opposing accumulation and industrialisation, they are in fact attempting to roll back the process of history[23] and, objectively considered, are anti-working class. The bourgeoisie, on the other hand — and this explains Marx's admiration for Ricardo, the political economist who stood for the interests of the bourgeoisie — advance the process. They take the lead in hastening the pace of capital formation and industrialisation. Industrial growth allows labour to come together, and to pitch their demand for higher wages. It therefore cuts from under the feet of the bourgeoisie the very foundation on which they organise production and the appropriation of surplus value. They are thus their own grave-diggers. It is this potential in them for self-destruction which makes them such a welcome social category to Marx.[24]

Contrarily, almost any species of peasants is suspect. Landowners, who, by their aggrandizing behaviour, diminish the possibility of capital formation, are to be condemned. Even the impoverished peasant proprietor, who refuses the overtures of the bourgeoisie and tenaciously clings to his individual plot, therefore reducing the scope of higher output and larger capital formation, is to be excommunicated. To Marx, the so-called peasant problem was a non-issue. In his schematics, peasants do not constitute a distinct economic sector; rather, the general laws of production and exploitation are to apply in agriculture too. In the countryside, it is the landless peasants who are exploited by capital, just as, in the urban-industrial milieu, it is the workers who are exploited. The only difference is that the exploitation of the peasantry in the countryside assumes a two-fold nature. On the one hand, individual capitalists — perhaps capitalist farmers, perhaps absentee landlords — exploit individual peasants through the device of rent, mortgages and usury, while capitalists *as a class* — assuming they are in control of State power — exploit the peasantry *as a class* through the levy of state taxes.[25] The solution has to be analogous in the two cases: the misery of the peasantry can only be ended by smashing the machinery of the state which represents the exploiters.

The moment Marx hints at the possibility of capitalists *as a class* exploiting the peasantry *as a class,* he is in some sense reintroducing the Ricardo-Malthus theme of antagonistic relationship between landlords and capitalists.[26] The terms of trade question too makes a re-entry, for the fiscal levies he refers to can be considered as a device for manipulating the terms of exchange between 'town' and 'country'. Even were the general laws of exploitation in a capitalist economy applicable to developments within the farm sector, the particular production relations between the two segments of the economy, industry and agriculture, would still be a pivotal issue. Capitalists need to obtain foodstuffs as well as raw materials from agriculture; at the same time, the products of industry, in order that they may be fully absorbed, must be provided with an outlet in the farm sector. This problem of interchange between town and country is explicitly mentioned in *The German Ideology:* 'The greatest division of material and mental labour is the separation of town and country. The antagonism of town and country begins with the transition from barbarism to civilisation, from tribe to State, from locality to nation, and runs through the whole history of civilisation to the present day (the Anti-Corn Law League).'[27] The theme recurs in Volume I of *Capital,* but is not elaborated. While discussing the division of labour in industry, and in society in general, Marx draws attention to what he calls the Adam Smithian problem of 'exchange between spheres of production, that are originally distinct and independent of one another'. He then proceeds to insert the following comment: 'The foundation of all highly developed divisions of labour that are brought about by the exchange of commodities is the cleavage between town and country. It may be said that the whole economic history of society is summed up in the movement of this antithesis. We pass it over, however, for the present.'[28] There is an accompanying, rather tantalising footnote to the effect that Sir James Steuart is the economist who 'has handled this subject best'. Despite the half-promise in the text, there is, however, no return to the theme in the subsequent volumes of *Capital.*[29]

Accumulation does involve a realisation problem because of the specificities of industrial as well as farm output. Industry has to draw on agriculture, and a part of the industrial output would need to be disposed of in the countryside.[30] Whatever view one takes of the historical role of landowners, the significance of the original Ricardo-Malthus controversy over the rate of exchange between the products of land and of industry cannot therefore be assumed away: the size and pattern of accumulation is crucially dependent upon which way it is resolved. Even though history has rolled forward in many giant strides during the past century and a half, the problem remains, even though it has manifested itself in diverse forms in different countries. Developments in the Soviet Union beginning with the so-called War Communism followed by the New Economic Policy, and policy shifts preceding and during the five-year plans and stretching, for example, up to the programme of farm expansion in the Siberian steppes, illustrate the somewhat intractable nature of the equilibrium relationship between the industrial and farm sectors. Many of the economic difficulties experienced by the other East European nations in the post-World War II period have also stemmed from the necessity to extract a sizeable surplus from agriculture, a task which hinges upon the terms of exchange between the two main producing sectors. In the United States, the politico-economic questions linked to the determination of 'parity prices' for farm products have held the centre of the stage in the domestic sphere. And particularly for the large number of developing economies which have begun to step out of the fetters of both colonialism and feudalism, the determination of the appropriate rates of exchange between the products of agriculture and industry has assumed a grave significance, if only because it is for them a major *modus operandi* for raising a surplus for growth.

Obviously, an analysis of the terms of exchange between the industrial and farm sectors cannot abstract from the underlying production and property relations. Classical economists were aware of this. Between the two of them, Ricardo and Malthus posed the problem of 'town' versus 'country' in terms of class analysis; Marx, however elliptically, realised its significance no less. It is one of the grandest problems classical political economy has dealt with.

NOTES

1   Adam Smith, *Wealth of Nations,* Book I, Chapter VI, Everyman's Library edition, p. 44.
2   Adam Smith, *op. cit.,* pp. 58-9.
3   Adam Smith, *op. cit.,* p. 72.
4   Adam Smith, *op. cit.,* p. 230.
5   '. . . . every improvement in the circumstances of the society tends either directly or indirectly to raise the real rent of land, to increase the real wealth of the landlord, his power of purchasing the labour, or the produce of the labour of other people. The extension of improvement and cultivation tends to raise it directly. The landlord's share of the produce necessarily increases with the increase of the produce. That rise in the real price of those parts of the rude produce of land, which is first the effect of extended improvement and cultivation, and afterwards the cause of their being still further extended, the rise in the price of cattle, for example, tends too to raise the rent of land directly, and in a still greater proportion. The real value of the landlord's share, his real command of the labour of other people, not only rises with the real value of the produce, but the proportion of his share to the whole produce rises with it. That produce, after the rise in its real price, requires no more labour to collect than before. A smaller proportion of it will, therefore, be sufficient to replace, with the ordinary profit, the stock which employs that labour. A greater proportion of it must, consequently, belong to the landlord'. Adam Smith, *op. cit.,* p. 228-9.
6   'All those improvements in the productive power of labour, which tend directly to reduce the real price of manufacturers, tend directly to raise the real rent of land.

The landlord exchanges that part of his rude produce, which is over and above his own consumption, or what comes to the same thing, the price of that part of it, for manufactured produce. Whatever reduces the real price of the latter, raises that of the former. An equal quantity of the former becomes thereby equivalent to a greater quantity of the latter; and the landlord is enabled to purchase a greater quantity of the conveniences, ornaments, or luxuries, which he has occasion for.' Adam Smith, *op. cit.,* p. 229; ' .... the rate of profit does not, like rent and wages, rise with the prosperity, and fall with the declension of the society. On the contrary, it is naturally low in rich, and high in poor countries, and it is always highest in the countries which are going fastest to ruin'. *op. cit.,* p. 231.

7 *Op. cit.,* Book II.

8 ' .... though the interest of the labourer is strictly connected with that of the society, he is incapable either of comprehending that interest, or of understanding its connection with his own. His condition leaves him no time to receive the necessary information, and his education and habits are commonly such as to render him unfit to judge even though he was fully informed'. *Op. cit.,* pp. 230-1.

9 ' .... The interest of the dealers ... in any particular branch of trade or manufactures, is always in some respects different from, and even opposite to, that of the public. To widen the market and to narrow the competition, is always the interest of the dealers. To widen the market may frequently be agreeable enough to the interest of the public; but to narrow the competition must always be against it, and can serve only to enable the dealers, by raising their profits above what they naturally would be, to levy, for their own benefit, an absurd tax upon the rest of their fellow-citizens. The proposal of any new law or regulation of commerce which comes from this order, ought always to be listened to with great precaution, and ought never to be adopted till after having been long and carefully examined, not only with the most scrupulous, but with the most suspicious attention. It comes from an order of men, whose interest is never exactly the same with that of the public, who have generally an interest to deceive and even to oppress the public, and who accordingly, have, upon many occasions, both deceived and oppressed it'. *Op. cit.,* pp. 231-2.

10 *Op. cit.,* p. 44.

11 David Ricardo, Preface to The Principles of Political Economy, *Works and Correspondence of David Ricardo,* edited by Piero Sraffa, Volume One, p. 5.

12 J.R. Hicks ('Ricardo's Theory of Distribution', *Essays in Honour of Lord Robbins,* edited by M. Peston and B. Corry, pp. 160-7) suggests that the share of rent in the Ricardian schema can only rise under a special circumstance, namely, where the elasticity of substitution between labour and land is less than unity. However, aggregate rent rises in any event.

13 One implicit assumption here — not at all unrealistic — is that factor proportions are different between agriculture and the rest of the economy. In a single-commodity model, the terms of trade conflict would be between rent and profits; in a two-sector economy — consisting of agriculture and manufacturing — the problem resolves itself into one concerning the relative prices of farm and industrial products.

14 ' ... it is ... quite immaterial to him whether the advance of the productive forces slays landed property or workers. If this progress devalues the capital of the industrial bourgeoisie it is equally welcome to him. If the development of the productive power of labour halves the value of the *existing* fixed capital, what does it matter, says Ricardo. The productivity of human labour has doubled. Thus here is *scientific honesty.* Ricardo's conception is, on the whole, in the interests of the *industrial bourgeoisie,* only *because,* and *in so far as,* their interests coincide with that of production or the productive development of

human labour. Where the bourgeoisie comes into conflict with this, he is just as *ruthless* towards it as he is at other times towards the proletariat and the aristocracy'. Karl Marx, *Theories of Surplus Value*, Part II, Lawrence and Wishart, 1969, p. 118, original italics. Presumably what Marx has in mind is Ricardo's disapproval of conspicuous consumption on the part of the aristocracy, which could adversely affect capital accumulation. (In contrast, such consumption would have Malthus's approval.) For a different explanation, see Ronald L. Meek, *Marx and Engels on Malthus*, Lawrence and Wishart, 1953, pp. 120-1.

15   Thomas Malthus, *Principles of Political Economy*, John Murray edition, p. 330.

16   The venom of Marx's attack can be seen in this passage: '. . . . "parson" Malthus does not sacrifice the particular interests to production but *seeks,* as far as he can, to sacrifice the demands of production to the particular interest of existing ruling classes or sections of classes. And to this end he *falsifies* his scientific conclusions. This is his *scientific* baseness, his sin against science, quite apart from his shameless and mechanical plagiarism. The scientific conclusions of Malthus are "considerate" towards the ruling classes in general and towards the reactionary elements of the ruling classes in particular; in other words he *falsifies* science for these interests. But his conclusions are *ruthless* as far as they concern the subjugated classes. He is not only *ruthless;* he *affects* ruthlessness; he takes a cynical pleasure in it and *exaggerates* his conclusions in so far as they are directed against the poor wretches, even *beyond* the point which would be scientifically justified from his point of view.' Karl Marx, *op. cit.,* p. 120, original italics.

17   K. Marx. *The German Ideology,* quoted in Ronald L. Meek, op. cit., p. 123.

18   See Malthus's letter to Ricardo, dated 16 July 1821, in the *Works and Correspondence of David Ricardo,* Volume IX, p. 20.

19   In terms of Marxian analysis, accumulation, which is the function *par excellence* of the capitalist, is not to be looked down upon: it provides the major instrumentality of industrial growth and technological progress, allowing the working class the opportunity to come together.

20   The suggestion that, in their presentations, both Ricardo and Malthus were more or less reflecting the interests of their respective classes has sometimes been sought to be refuted on the ground that both derived the bulk of their earnings from a source which could not be identified with their respective classes. Thus while Malthus earned very little from his landed property, most of Ricardo's income came from his substantial investments in land. It is possible to turn this argument round. If Ricardo were to take his prognosis seriously — there was no reason for his not doing so — it was only rational for him to invest heavily in land; similarly, the meagre income he was deriving from his real estate could have provided an additional incentive to Malthus to oppose ground rent and support protective tariffs!
The following passage from his letter of 28 August 1821 to John Stuart Mill (*Works and Correspondence of David Ricardo, op. cit.,* Volume IX, p. 45) has been cited on a few occasions as evidence that Ricardo could rise above his own class interests: 'The only prospect we have of putting aside the struggle which they say has commenced between the rich and other classes, is for the rich to yield what is justly due to the other classes, but this is the last measure which they are willing to have recourse to. I cannot help flattering myself that justice will prevail at last, without a recurrence to actual violence: but if it does, it will only be because the event of the struggle will be so obvious to all eyes that expediency, the expediency of the rich, will make it necessary even in their view'. This statement is an indicator more of Ricardo's perspicacity than of his disinterestedness in class issues, even though his implied admission that 'justice' is 'due to the other classes' distinguishes him from the more crude apologists of sectarian interests.

21 *The Communist Manifesto* alludes to the 'growing competition among the bourgeoisie and the resulting commercial crises' and, later, to 'the commercial crises that by their periodical return put the existence of the entire bourgeois society on trial, each time more threateningly'. The Postscript to the Second Edition of Volume I of *Capital* includes the following sentence: 'The contradictory movement of capitalist society impresses itself upon the practical bourgeois most strikingly in the changes of the periodic cycle through which modern industry runs and whose crowning point is the general crisis'. There are also some references to the phenomenon of short-period disequilibrium in Volume II of *Capital*. But Marxist theoreticians ever since have by and large gone to great lengths to convince themselves and others that deficiency of demand would pose no standing threat to capitalist accumulation.

22 Ricardo had of course anticipated the problem of contradiction between the interests of labour and capital in his chapter 'On Machinery' in the *Principles*: '. . . the substitution of machinery for human labour, is often very injurious to the interests of the class of labourers . . . the same cause which may increase the net revenue of the country, may at the same time render the population redundant, and deteriorate the condition of the labourer' (*Works and Correspondence of David Ricardo, op. cit.,* Volume 1, p. 388). This contradiction was, however, not central to his theme of capitalist crisis.

23 'The Communist Manifesto', *Selected Works,* Part I, Moscow, p. 44.

24 *Op. cit.,* pp. 36-41.

25 See Karl Marx, *The Class Struggles in France, 1848-50,* in Marx-Engels, *Selected Works*, Volume 1, Moscow, 1955, pp. 216-7.

26 One should of course take care not to identify completely 'the peasantry as a class' with landlords but, in the particular context, it would be a case of 'country' being exploited by 'town'; the exploitation by some constituents of 'country' of some others remains a separate issue.

27 Karl Marx, *The German Ideology, op. cit.,* pp. 68-9.

28 *Capital,* Volume I, Moscow, 1954, Chapter XIV, Section 4, page 352. This particular sentence was quoted by N. Bukharin in his *Imperialism and World Economy,* but in the context of an implied international social division of labour: 'The cleavage between "town and country", as well as the "development of this cleavage", formerly confined to one country only, are now being reproduced on a tremendously enlarged basis. Viewed from this standpoint, entire countries appear today as "towns", namely, the industrial countries, whereas entire agrarian territories appear to be "country". International division of labour coincides here with the division of labour between the two largest branches of social production as a whole, between industry and agriculture, thus appearing as the so-called "general division of labour"'! (Bukharin, *op. cit.,* Monthly Review Press, p. 21.) A later analogy was presented by Lin Piao's famous 1965 formulation of 'the countryside', consisting of the socialist nations, encircling 'the towns', consisting of the capitalist ones.

The domestic economic issue was most sharply re-formulated — from the point of view of the landowning peasant — by N. Georgescu-Roegen in his famous essay, 'Economic Theory and Agrarian Economics' (*Oxford Economic Papers,* 1960, pp. 1-40.): 'That the interests of the town conflict with those of the countryside is by now a well-established fact. However it is not always realised that the price-scissors do not tell the whole story. For this story, we must observe that food is indispensable, whereas the need for industrial products is secondary, if not superfluous. To obtain foodstuff from the agricultural sector, and moreover to obtain it cheaply, constitutes a real problem for the industrial community. In the ultimate analysis, "cheap bread" is a cry directed against the tiller of the soil rather than against the capitalist partner of the industrial worker'.

In Georgescu-Roegan's view, therefore, the real class conflict is between the peasantry and the urban coalition of industrial workers and bourgeois capitalists!

29   There are, however, constant references to the theme in , for example, *The Class Struggles in France, 1848-50* and *The Eighteenth Brumaire of Louis Bonaparte.*

30   The problem finds no mention in the mainstream of Marxist literature; Rosa Luxemburg, however, perceived it, and sought to close the analytical gap through an extension of the Marxian system. In her formulation — which we discuss in the next chapter — the agrarian sector, which is representative of a primitive economy, is exploited by the industrial capitalists, who dump their products in the countryside at an unfair rate of exchange. It is of some significance that there is a not-altogether-faint echo of the Malthusian theme in Rosa Luxemburg, who sees the possibility of a structural maladjustment between demand and supply within the bourgeoisie-capitalist modality of production. Her treatment of the issue is, however, antithetical to Malthus's: the latter saw the solution of the problem of aggregate demand in turning the terms of trade *in favour of* landlords; the Luxemburgian schematics envisages capitalism solving the problem by turning the terms of trade *against* 'the country'.

CHAPTER 3

Rosa Luxemburg and the Theory of Unequal Exchange

Once the neo-classicals and the 'marginalists' had made their debut, the issue of an antagonistic relationship between social categories, so much to the fore in classical political economy, was ushered out of the limelight, and a process of atomisation set in: an individual unit of a factor of production became the focal point of analysis, classes lost their erstwhile pre-eminence. Moreover, each factor was supposedly paid according to its marginal product and the sum of such payments exhausted total output; the conclusion was thus drawn that there could be no divergence of interests among the different economic classes, since class conflicts were ruled out, and the state was seen as capable of regulating income distribution through, for instance, fiscal policy; tranquillity was the order of the day.

It was not so, as far as the Marxist school was concerned. Exploitation of one social class by another was central to the theory of surplus value; the terms of exchange between classes hence continued to be a matter of major concern for the Marxists. The concept of exploitation itself connotes an unfairness of exchange, an unfairness arising from the nature of production relations in a capitalist system. This theme never ceased to be the principal preoccupation in Marxian analysis, and a significant addendum was occasioned by the arrival of Rosa Luxemburg on the scene.

Can there be a category of exploitation separate from the one attendant upon the appropriation of surplus value in capitalist society? Exploitation reflects the phenomenon of non-equivalence in economic transactions. The value of a commodity, in the pristine world of Marxism, is determined by the content of socially necessary labour. Labour is, however, unable to appropriate this value in entirety; it is deprived of a part of its just share of the productivity contributed by it, whether directly or indirectly, and the consequence is the emergence of surplus value. Apart from this particular one, is it possible to conceive of any other mode of exploitation, or of non-equivalence in exchange, in economic life?

25

The problem did not occur to the orthodox Marxists. It was left to Luxemburg, the full-time political functionary and part-time Marxist theoretician, to stumble upon the issue. There could be hardly a more exciting instance of serendipity in the history of economic analysis.

Luxemburg's primary concern in her economic writings was to lay bare the nature of the forces that sustain capitalist accumulation. She invited attention to an apparent lack of emphasis in Marx on the problem of realisation of surplus value through sales in the market, a problem which she felt could indeed arise in a closed capitalist system. In the process, she wandered across to an exploration of the possibilities of non-equivalent exchange in the sphere of circulation.

Luxemburg has for long been a neglected goddess, if one can use that expression, in the pantheon of Marxism. This is no doubt largely the outcome of a rigidity in attitude within the Marxist school towards those who dared to suggest that not all questions concerning accumulation and capitalist development have been fully answered in the three volumes of *Capital,* or that Marx's position in the different volumes of the great work on a number of questions needed to be reconciled.[1] A kind of defence mechanism too has been at work: for a communist functionary to voice views, even if they be on seemingly abstract issues, which at least part of the way ran parallel to — or supplemented — those held by anti-socialist scholars such as Böhm-Bawerk and Tugan-Baronowsky was not considered in sympathetic light within the fold.[2] Rosa Luxemburg, after all, was keeping company with a whole line of non-socialist, as well as anti-socialist, academics in expressing the view that the Marxian system of expanded reproduction is not satisfactorily closed. This, to many orthodox Marxists, was heresy. Not surprisingly, her propositions were subjected to virulent attack: their most detailed refutation was by N. Bukharin in his *Imperialism and the Accumulation of Capital.*[3]

And yet, there can hardly be any question, Luxemburg was in her own manner merely annotating Marx. The bourgeoisie accumulate capital; this is what provides the ethos of the capitalist system. During the course of such accumulation, however, there is — she was more than convinced — a real possibility of a 'realisation' crisis resulting from the failure on the part of capitalists to realise the full value of their commodities.[4] To point out the specifics of this crisis was, according to her, the essence of scientific Marxism: she was but building on the edifice laid out by Marx — and strengthening it.

The genesis of the capitalist crisis, according to Luxemburg, lies in the rationale of capitalist accumulation itself. Surplus value is supposed to be realised in the market place. A part of this surplus value is used to provide for the consumption demand of the capitalists and their hangers-on; another part would, it is assumed, be invested. But what provides the inducement to invest? Will this inducement always be such as to absorb wholly the residual of the surplus value not used up in capitalist consumption? In a closed capitalist system, Luxemburg contends, this query cannot be answered unequivocally. Marx's reproduction scheme by itself fails to provide an adequate solution to the problem; it suffers from a number of lacunae. For instance, it does not quite deal with the issue of technical change, that is, that of an increase in the organic composition of capital, which could lead to a disproportion in the rates of expansion of constant and variable capitals. The interpretation of the nature of activities in, and exchange between, Departments I and II leaves many other similar loose ends. The major question concerns the sustenance of the urge to invest, which in turn depends upon the effectiveness of demand. There is no obvious mechanism by which the problem could be endogenously solved. Working with a numerical illustration of the Marxian model, Luxemburg[5] invites attention to an instance of disharmony between the rates of output of the two Departments: Department II throws up a surplus which cannot be absorbed in a closed system; that is to say, Marx's schematics is not self-contained; at the margin certain emendations are therefore necessary to ensure the smooth development of the capitalist economy over time; one has to go outside the system.

Rosa Luxemburg discovers the solution to the problem in the existence of primitive economies next to developing capitalism. The essence of her ideas is to be found in the famous Chapter XXVI of *The Accumulation of Capital,* and can be summarised here. The excess supply of the output of Department II can be taken care of — and capitalist accumulation sustained over time — by seeking markets outside the capitalist-worker two-class system. Capitalism can thus survive only on the assumption of the existence of an exogenous third market. The pre-capitalist economies which still survive — for instance, the pockets of feudal and petty-commodity production — provide this much needed exogenous market. It is through the invasion of these primative economies that predatory capitalism keeps its own activities going. By unfair trade, plunder and military conquest, the industrial bourgeoisie spread their tentacles over pre-capitalist economies, which become the dumping ground for the excess supply of the capitalist system. The problem of accumulation-cum-realisation is thus solved by going out of the system in this manner; the rising stream of industrial output finds an additional outlet in the primitive economies, which are forced to absorb that part of the supply of consumption goods which is internally in excess.

The existence of under-developed primitive societies serves two separate purposes. First, a crisis of accumulation within the capitalist economy, which could be linked to a possible deficiency of demand, is averted now that the produce of the consumption goods sector has a ready receptacle; this forestalls the threatened organic disharmony between Departments I and II. The availability of these external markets helps in a second manner too: it enables the capitalists to resist successfully the demand for a rise in the wages of industrial workers, a solution which might otherwise be vigorously pressed by ideologues and others to ensure an increase in the level of aggregate demand.[6] The external markets act as a receptacle; they help to augment the rate of accumulation for a given rate of internal exploitation. As accumulation is stepped up, further inroads are made into pre-capitalist economies. It is thus a dynamic picture of continuously growing penetration into those primitive markets, and the boundaries of exploitation are continuously extending outwards.

Luxemburg's 'third market' has often been confused with the notion of 'third persons', and suggestions have been made to the effect that she recognised the role of an intermediate 'middle' class for resolving the 'realisation crisis' encountered by the capitalists, The following passage is however unambiguous enough, and would indicate that such Malthusian notions hardly appealed to her:

> Apart from these two classes [that is, capitalists and wage labourers], there are a host of other people: the landowners, the salaried employees, the liberal professions such as doctors, lawyers, artists and scientists. Moreover, there is the Church and its servants, the Clergy, and finally the State with its officials and armed forces. All these strata of the population can be counted, strictly speaking, neither among the capitalists nor among the working class. Yet society has to feed and support them. Perhaps it is they, those strata apart from the capitalists and wage labourers, who call forth enlarged reproduction by their demand. But this seeming solution cannot stand up to a closer scrutiny. The landowners must as consumers of rent, i.e. of part of the surplus value, quite obviously be numbered among the capitalist class; since we are here concerned with the surplus value in its undivided, primary form, their consumption is already allowed for in the consumption of the capitalist class. The liberal professions in most cases obtain their money, i.e. the assignment to part of the social product, directly or indirectly from the capitalist class who pays them with bits of their own surplus value. And the same applies to the Clergy, with the difference only that its members also obtain their purchasing power in part from the workers, i.e. from wages. The

upkeep of the State, lastly, with its officers and armed forces is borne by the rates and taxes, which are in their turn levied upon either the surplus value or the wages. Within the limits of Marx's diagram there are in fact only the two sources of income in a society: the labourers' wages and the surplus value. All the strata of the population we have mentioned as apart from the capitalists and the workers, are thus to be taken only for joint consumers of those two kinds of income.[7]

And she proceeds:

Seeing that we cannot discover within capitalist society any buyers whatever for the commodities in which the accumulated part of the surplus value is embodied, only one thing is left: foreign trade.[8]

She in fact launches on a detailed rebuttal of Peter v. Struve's proposition that a category of 'third persons' could provide the mainstay of capitalist accumulation:

It is obvious that, if we categorically refer to consumption by the capitalists and the workers, we do not speak of the entrepreneur as an individual, but of the capitalist class as a whole, including their hangers-on — employees, civil servants, liberal professions, and the like. All such 'third persons' who are certainly not lacking in capitalist society are, as far as economics is concerned, joint consumers of the surplus value for the greater part, in so far, namely, as they are not also joint consumers of the wages of labour. These groups can only derive their purchasing power either from the wage of the proletariat or from the surplus value, if not from both; but on the whole, they are to be regarded as joint consumers of the surplus value. It follows that their consumption is already included in the consumption of the capitalist class, and if Struve tries to reintroduce them to the capitalists by sleight-of-hand as 'third persons' to save the situation and help to realise the surplus value, the shrewd profiteer will not be taken in. He will see at once that this great public is nothing but his old familiar retinue of parasites who buy his commodities with money of his own providing. No, no, indeed ! Struve's 'third persons' will not do at all.[9]

Obviously, the problem she had in mind was broader than the neo-Malthusian one of realisation of demand. If, à la Keynes, the problem was one of the-goods-are-there-but-where-to-sell-them, then 'third persons' — for instance, the clergy and such others Malthus was fond of referring to — who had a higher propensity to consume than the average for the nation, could provide a solution provided incomes were transferred to them. Luxemburg's 'third market' could not however be constituted by any indigenous category of 'third persons', for the latter do not have the answer to the organic difficulty afflicting accumulation over time.

From the very first day, Rosa Luxemburg's theory has been the target of strong criticism, as much by orthodox Marxists as by others. Her analysis is vitiated, it has been said, because, while discussing expanded reproduction, she retains the assumptions of simple reproduction, which is not permissible. Her solution for capitalists to get round the 'realisation' crisis, namely, dumping consumption goods in pre-capitalist economies, is, it has been argued, no solution at all, for trade cannot be one way, and capitalists will also have to buy from the primitive economies.[10] The latter point can, however, be countered: in case the exchange between capitalist and pre-capitalist economies assumes the character of non-equivalence — and this is what Luxemburg was arguing about — even a *seeming* balance of trade can be of advantage to the former.[11] Where the capitalist system is able to maintain an export surplus *vis-à-vis* primitive economies and colonies — and use this surplus for extending and strengthening the colonial arrangements — this particular caveat entered against the Luxemburg thesis in any case falls to the ground. Even when the export surplus is the other way round, an imperialist-capitalist system, by refusing to honour its obligations *vis-à-vis* a colonised territory, can achieve the kind of results Rosa Luxemburg has in mind.[12]

How far the Rosa Luxemburg propositions closely approximate to reality and whether, as Nikolai Bukharin asked, there was any necessity at all for her 'third market' outlet to explain the genesis of imperialism, are questions which need not directly detain us. Of particular interest for our purpose is the presence of the underpinning of a two-sector institutional mechanism in the Luxemburg model, which can be adapted for analysing the terms of exchange between 'town' and 'country'. All one has to do is to 'internalise' the third market, that is, the pre-capitalist economies. If the capitalist economy as a whole is assumed to constitute a single sector producing only industrial goods and the primitive economies, existing across from it, raise only farm products, then in terms of the model, capitalist accumulation of surplus value is accompanied by, and sustained by, primitive accumulation: the industrial sector survives and expands only because of its success in imposing a system of unequal exchange on the primitive sector; in the absence of such 'unfair' transactions, there would be an impasse over accumulation and effective demand, leading to the collapse of the industrial sector. More specifically, transactions between the two sectors could assume the following modalities:[13] (a) captive sale of industrial products to agriculture; (b) monopsonistic purchase of farm products against such sales; and (c) transfer of surplus resources from industry to agriculture which in turn ensures that the farm sector develops the infra-structure needed to fulfil its role under (a) and (b).

Such a reformulation of her model opens up a vista of analytical possibilities. One can, if one so wants, steer clear of the controversy whether her prognosis about a disharmony between the output of the two Departments is shot full of errors,[14] or whether — as maintained by Bukharin[15] — her 'third market' strategy, with stress on the necessary condition of imperialism, is a non-solution of the problem of capitalist crisis. For it is still given to us to abstract her analytical schema from the immediate issues which provided the stimulus for its construction. The passion of ideological debates which once raged against the Luxemburg thesis is now stilled; the rudiments of an exciting two-sector model of accumulation and growth nonetheless remain. The two sectors in the model can be taken to represent two social classes poised in an antagonistic relationship with each other, namely, the capitalists and the peasantry; the capitalists are in a position to force their surplus products on the peasants; what is more, the latter are compelled to sell their products to the capitalists at rates dictated by the latter; the terms of exchange established in these transactions between the two classes are 'unequal', for there is no free bargaining and the prices reflect the fact of the disparity in their holding of assets and the dissimilarity in their political circumstances. Through such unequal exchange, the capitalist class resolves its internal crisis. Wage-labour is employed in the alien farm sector, to be paid with the excess supply of goods originating within the capitalist sector; the products of wage-labour are then bought back, but under exploitatory terms, that is, the exchanges taking place between the two classes — the capitalists in the industrial sector and wage-labour in the farm sector — are 'unequal'.

Thus presented, the Luxemburg model in effect depicts the second form of exploitation of the peasantry — exploitation by the capitalist class — referred to by Marx in *The Class Struggles in France 1848-1850*. Its archetypal application would be where the industrial sector represents a colonial-capitalist hegemony and agriculture is the colonised sector, and capitalists belonging to the former come down hard on the peasantry who populate the farm sector. There is also an implicit issue of terms of trade whenever economic transactions are postulated between either two sectors of an economy — such as industry and agriculture — or between two classes, such as capitalists and peasants. The colonial power[16] in the model — in our formulation, the class of industrial capitalists — tries to tilt the terms of trade in its favour and against colonial agriculture (or against the peasantry). Luxemburg describes the resulting phenomenon as the 'struggle against the peasant economy', which manifests itself in non-equivalent exchange. There is no attempt in *The Accumulation of Capital* — or in her subsequent tract, *The Accumulation of Capital: An Anti-Critique* — to offer a measure of this non-equivalence. But she leaves nobody in doubt concerning the essential features of the process as she perceives it.[17] In her frame of analysis, exploitation in production and exploitation in exchange are additive and conjoint processes; both imply non-equivalence in transactions. The mechanism of exploitation too is analogous in the two cases. Capital cheats labour by offering it a *price* which is less than the *value* created by it. Similarly, in the sphere of circulation, the predatory power sells at relatively high prices consumer and investment goods to the exploited sector or class, and, *pari passu*, the latter is forced to part with foodgrains and raw materials to the predatory power — the industrial bourgeoisie — at relatively low prices.

Luxemburg, it will be noticed, does not stop to analyse the internal composition of the so-called primitive economy, which, in our formulation, is identical with the farm sector. Thus, wage-labour in the peasant economy is not distinguished from the rich owner-farmer; evidently, the capitalist farmer is yet to establish himself as a distinct entity. In the context of her model, therefore, no occasion arises for delving into the relationships obtaining between the capitalists dominating the industrial sector and the emerging capitalist-farmers belonging to the farm sector, or those obtaining between the latter and the alienated workers of either sector. By implication, Luxemburg distinguishes between the role of the capitalist and that of the alienated worker in the industrial sector; however, what she has to say in this context is mostly annotation of Marx. That there could be an analogous concept of alienation in the case of a primitive economy remains unrecognised: the latter constitutes an exogenous variable; it is as if one need not expend too much time or energy to investigate its internal working.

In a sense, therefore, while what is exciting about the Luxemburg model is its explicit, open frame of analysis, a certain latitude is called for in case it is to be applied for analysing an economy featured by expanded reproduction. One can scarcely get away from such facts as that, for most modern economies, the internal structure of agriculture has long ceased to be homogenous, or that production relations as they exist in an advanced capitalist system are also mirrored in agriculture once the processes of capital accumulation begin to permeate into it. Even before capitalism invades agriculture, the increasing alienation of small peasants from cultivable land could transform the sector into an arena of acute class antagonisms. This recognition inevitably necessitates changes in the assumptions of the *simpliste* model depicted by Rosa Luxemburg on the relationship between capitalist industry and pre-capitalist agriculture; the later chapters of this book will have occasion to concern themselves with this particular issue.

One aspect of the Luxemburg schematics is meanwhile worth noting. Suppose the industrial crisis is not one of non-absorption of consumption and investment goods; suppose it is actually the other way round, namely, one of capacity expansion, a task held back by an unsatisfactory rate of accumulation. Also assume that the primitive economy existing next to the industrial sector is not by any stretch a colony, but politically extremely powerful and, instead of being in danger of being plundered and annihilated by industry, is in fact itself scheming to put the squeeze on industry. Further assume that agriculture is dominated by a small number of big owner-farmers, while industry is completely socialised. In other words, suppose we retain Rosa Luxemburg's format, but the parametric values of the two sectors are thoroughly overhauled. This in effect was precisely what the state of the Soviet Union appeared to be to Evgeny Preobrazhensky in the years immediately following the revolution, and which led him to propound a law of 'socialist primitive accumulation'. Even though the resemblance between his 'law' and the Luxemburg schema has so far not been analysed in explicit terms, there can be no escape from the conclusion that what Preobrazhensky attempted was an 'inversion' of the latter. It is almost as if he adopts the Luxemburg model and transplants it to a different ethos and with a different intent. Historically, capitalist accumulation, says Rosa Luxemburg, *is accompanied* by primitive *capital* accumulation; given the problems faced by the Soviet Union in the post-revolution period, socialist accumulation, asserts Preobrazhensky, *must be accompanied* by primitive *socialist* accumulation. The tool of unequal exchange has a place in the framework of both: the *deus ex machina* for exploitation in Rosa Luxemburg becomes the vehicle for socialist progress in Preobrazhensky.

To an analysis of the specific economic issues, which provided the background to the Soviet debate over unequal exchange in the 1920s, we therefore now turn.

APPENDIX TO CHAPTER 3

On the Notion of Equivalence in Exchange

I

Economic activities are social activities, a large part — if not all — of which involve, or imply, exchange. Theories of value concern themselves with constructs for determining, under stated conditions, the rates at which exchanges take place, or ought to take place. A major implicit claim in neo-classical analysis is that these rates are not random occurrences, but a twice-blessed category like Shakespearian mercy, awarding with fairness either party in an act of exchange. While never quite expressed openly, the claim involves the possibility of a transition from an equilibrium rate of exchange to an equivalent rate of exchange. Alfred Marshall's famous cogitations over the nature of barter and the locus of the true equilibrium rate[18] reflected this anxiety to discover the content of fairness in exchange. The intractability of inter-personal comparability, however, cast its shadow; and Marshall's harping on the constancy of the marginal utility of money was in the nature of a desperate groping for a way out. Much of the subsequent expatiations in neo-classical demand theory, including the cardinalist escape hatch, has been similarly motivated.[19]

If for different reasons, a parallel concern over the equivalence or non-equivalence of exchange has been shown by Marxist theoreticians. This is only natural, for the concept of exploitation itself implies a disharmony in exchange: while value is determined by socially necessary labour-power, since labour nonetheless is exploited, a certain non-equivalence of exchange is embodied in the process. As we have seen in the present chapter, in Luxemburg's extension of the Marxian schema to the sphere of circulation, so as to cover instances of capitalist exploitation of the peasant economy and consequences of colonial expansion, there is again no mistaking the presence of an implied notion of non-equivalent exchange: the extraction of surplus value is an act of piracy, forcing the victims — be they the dispossessed peasantry or indented immigrants in colonies — to acquiesce in an unfair transaction. Luxemburg's idea reappears, even though in a considerably altered form, in the debate between N. Bukharin and E. Preobrazhensky on the problems of primitive socialist accumulation, pursued with vigour and acrimony, typical of the era, in the Soviet Union in the 1920s. In a manner common to all such controversies, extensive use was made of the term 'non-equivalent exchange', but the import of the expression was rarely, if ever, specifically spelled out.

A transaction in which either the buyer (the consumer) or the seller (the producer) is by implication offered a quantity of a commodity, or a service or money, as the case may be, less than what may be considered to represent a value on par can be stated to be a non-equivalent exchange. This, however, is mere tautology. All that such a definition suggests is that, as a result of a transaction of this kind, either the buyer (the consumer) or the seller (the producer) will have to concede a discount, or enjoy a premium, in relation to what can be regarded as the natural pay-off. But neither Preobrazhensky nor Bukharin enquires into the nature of this natural pay-off. The nearest thing to a definition of the term occurs in Preobrazhensky when he attempts to distinguish between non-equivalent exchange under capitalism and under conditions obtaining in the Soviet Union following the October Revolution:

> Under capitalism non-equivalent exchange between large-scale and small-scale production, in particular between capitalist industry and peasant agriculture, though forced to a certain extent to adjust itself in the price field to the value-relations of large-scale capitalist agriculture, is, in the sphere of purely economic relations and causes, a simple expression of the higher productivity of labour in large-scale production as compared with small. In the Soviet Union non-equivalent exchange is at present connected above all with the technical backwardness of our industry, the lower level of productivity which prevails in it as compared with the advanced capitalist countries, the higher cost of production of articles, and, finally, the historically and economically inevitable alienation, by means of price policy, of part of the surplus product of private economy for the benefit of the socialist accumulation fund. This means that as long as we have not caught up with capitalism nor completed the period of primitive socialist accumulation we shall inevitably have non-equivalent exchange with the countryside, owing both to the causes which condition non-equivalent exchange in world economy and therefore under normal conditions determine the maximum prices of our agricultural products, and to causes specifically connected with the conditions of existence of the Soviet system of economy. When the latter causes have disappeared the former will remain. This in the first place: but, in the second place, in so far as the development of large-scale and medium co-operative and socialist agriculture, and of the proportion of exchange of products between it and state industry, will dictate to non-co-operative agriculture (that is, for a long time, to the greater part of the countryside), non-equivalent exchange will to that extent not result from the undeveloped and backward state of socialist industry but on the contrary, from the development of the co-operative-socialist sector of agriculture and the growth of the productivity of labour in that sector. In this situation non-equivalent exchange will be merely the expression of the unprofitability of small-scale production compared with large. And, contrariwise, equivalent exchange, in these conditions, would only mean a tax on socialism for the benefit of small-scale production, a tax on machinery in favour of the three-field system, the wooden plough, and economic Asiaticism.[21]

Here is a concept of non-equivalent exchange significantly different from what is implied in the notion of exploitation in the labour market. If, under conditions of capitalism, the rate of exchange between two sectors is non-equivalent, that, according to Preobrazhensky, is largely because of disparate labour productivities in the two sectors; if the embodied labour has reached a higher stage in one sector compared to another, the former will enjoy an advantage in exchange over the latter. No doubt, the labour theory of value makes its presence felt in this judgment, but there is not a hint of any phenomenon resembling exploitation. And when Preobrazhensky describes the role of non-equivalent exchange as between different sectors of the economy for furthering the cause of primitive socialist accumulation, it is as if he is talking of a technique, of an apparatus of capital formation. The theme of exploitation is not at all brought in: the discussion on non-equivalence proceeds without equivalence being defined in the first place.

The confusion was compounded when, in the debate between Bukharin and Preobrazhensky over the terms of trade between agriculture and industry in the Soviet Union, normative opinions were expressed about certain historical trends. Here the approach was breathtakingly simplistic. If, over a number of years, industrial prices, for instance, had moved at a rate faster than the movement in farm prices, the conclusion was drawn that a situation of non-equivalent exchange had developed: industry had gained and agriculture had lost. An issue of substance was thereby reduced to a problem of index numbers.

II

It would therefore seem in order to persist with the enquiry: what is an equivalent exchange, be it exchange between persons, groups, or sectors? Could it be that those who innovated the expression had a particular kind of optimum in mind and wanted to define non-equivalence in terms of deviations from the idealised conditions underlying that optimum? What, for example, is the price relationship between agriculture and industry which may be described as one of equivalence? Could this norm be invariable, irrespective of spatial and temporal shifts, an abstraction continually marked by transcendental bliss?

The issue can be further explored by referring to certain limiting situations governing transactions between two parties. Following Alfred Marshall, one can say that in a system of barter, these limits will be set by the opportunity cost per unit. That point beyond which it is not possible for a producer or a seller either to produce the commodity (or service) or to offer it for disposal in the market, as the case may be, will set the nether limit for the exchange. This would usually be given by the sum of the unit cost of production (or distribution) and what is considered to be normal profits. The nether limit for one party in the exchange will naturally be the upper limit for the other one. Under barter, with two sets of producers (or sellers), two such limits will emerge, and we will encounter an intermediate zone of bargaining. This zone will be featured by extra-ordinary profits, to be shared by the parties participating in the barter. The point of equivalent exchange will lie somewhere within this range. An obvious case to consider is the point where the rate of extra-normal profits is the same for both the sectors. If, for example, it costs 0.25 unit of a standard industrial commodity to produce 1 unit of a standard farm product, and if 2 units of farm products are needed to produce 1 unit of industrial output, the point where 1 unit of the standard farm product exchanges for 0.375 unit of the standard industrial commodity may in terms of this definition, be described as the point of equivalence: a rate of exchange lower than this may appear to be adverse to agriculture, one higher than this adverse to industry. At the precise point of 'equivalence', the rate of extra-ordinary profits will be the same for all the parties, that is to say, the market will appear to treat them about 'equally'.[22]

Even so, the difficulties are hardly resolved. The notion of defining equivalence merely in terms of an equal rate of extra-ordinary profits, without regard to the relative economic positions, including the structure of technology in the form of fixed capital and the distribution of assets and incomes, may appear as altogether arbitrary. Besides, the specific technical relations between commodity and commodity, or commodity and service, obtaining in the market at any point of time cannot be abstracted from institutional factors. Technical relations are themselves the product of price relations, and the latter are shaped by history and institutions. The world hardly ever any more consists of barters of the primitive type, and there is no standard farm product and no standard industrial commodity. The nature of production and exchange in a modern economy is wide-ranging as well as complex; the range and the complexity both reflect the cumulative history of past price relations.

Perhaps because of this, the challenge of defining equivalence in exchange has had few takers. There has also been little endeavour to measure the equivalence or otherwise of exchange in terms of the relative movements in the rates of extra-ordinary profits — or in terms of any similar formulation.[23] For instance, in most of the discussion on the procurement crisis in the Soviet Union in the 1920s in the works of, for example, M.H. Dobb,[24] M. Lewin,[25] E.H. Carr,[26] Alec Nove[27] — which we deal with in the following chapter — the problem of the rate of exchange between agricultural and industrial products is analysed exclusively in terms of developments since the pre-World War I days. The allegedly harsh treatment meted out to the kulaks and middle peasants is sought to be established by some of these authors on the basis of the fact that the terms of trade between the two sectors appeared to have tilted by more than fifty per cent against agriculture between 1913 and 1923. While this certainly proved the point that the real income of the surplus-raising farmers declined over the decade, it would still leave open the issue whether, in the latter year, the exchange between farm and industrial sectors has assumed a non-equivalent form in the sense that the rate of extraordinary profits in agriculture had slipped below that in industry.

To answer this question more firmly, the structure of costs in agriculture as well as industry would have to be analysed, and a common measure of normal profits applied to the two sectors. Once this is done, it would then be necessary to compare the extra-ordinary profits obtained in the two sectors proportionate to their respective cost of production (including normal profits) in 1913. To complete the analysis, the level of extra-ordinary profits proportionate to cost of output in the two sectors would have to be worked out for 1923 too. Even though the terms of trade in the Soviet Union had moved against agriculture and in favour of industry over the ten-year period referred to, thus indicating a lowering in the level of aggregate real income for agriculture, extra-ordinary profits as a proportion of total cost might conceivably still have increased in agriculture at a rate faster than in industry. This could happen provided the cost of production (including normal profits) in the industrial sector rose at a rate faster than — or fell at a rate slower than — in agriculture.[28]

It is therefore not so much the movement in the terms of trade between two sectors (or groups or persons) which is relevant for determining whether the exchange has, over time, grown more or less equivalent, but the relative movements in what is essentially the Marxian rate of profit — that is, surplus value as a proportion of aggregate outlay — in the two sectors. It is only when the rates of profit obtaining in the two sectors have been disturbed from a position of equality that one can refer to the emergence of the phenomenon of non-equivalent exchange; a mere shift in the relative rates of profit would not by itself connote non-equivalence.

Certain other difficulties, however, remain. The rates of profit obtaining in the different sectors of an economy can, of course, change over time. One sector may experience a rise, or fall, in this rate of an order greater than in another sector. But where an increase or decline in the rate of profit reflects the fact of a variation in wage cost, it may be difficult to reach a normative judgment whether the rise or fall in the rate of profit, either absolutely or in relation to the rate of profit obtaining elsewhere in the economy, is to be socially preferred. The components of cost cannot be examined in isolation of historical circumstances; the state of technology, which often determines the rate of profit, is itself largely a consequence of elements which are shaped by specific market conditions. There could also be other factors to be taken into account. A rising rate of profit in a particular sector of an economy may not seem to subserve the interests of growth in case the profits are largely deployed for conspicuous consumption. On the other hand, if as a result of a development which outwardly takes the form of a trend toward non-equivalent exchange, a purposive transfer of resources takes place from a low-saving sector, thus stimulating growth, such non-equivalence could be considered socially worthwhile, as Preobrazhensky had done. But in case the process is accompanied by a fall in the level of aggregate consumption of the workers in the first sector, a judgment on the issue would evidently be more complicated.

III

On the conceptual plane, equality in the rates of profit could thus provide a criterion for defining equivalent exchange; the search for a satisfactory empirical correlate of the concept may nonetheless continue to be elusive. The measurement of surplus value cannot be abstracted from worldly realities. As we have just seen, movements in the rates of profit cannot be welcomed or frowned upon just on the basis of the sign of direction of the movement; one's social preferences have also to be brought in.

This in a way takes us back to the significance of the Marshallian quest for a true equilibrium rate, a rate at which equilibrium coincides with equivalence. Can this quest be divested from one's system of values? It should be obvious that it cannot be. For the problem which then emerges is one of exercising a value judgment from which there is no escape; it is a matter of choosing between alternative value systems, and, therefore, between alternative collective choice systems, which have their roots in altogether disparate categories of economic positions and social relationships.

The genre of the problem remains the same whether it is a question of exchange between individuals or sectors of an economy or, for that matter, different economic classes. Since economic classes and groups represent separate value systems, to subsume the problem of exchange between them under, for instance, the usual category of situations of collective choice and social bargaining found in the standard tracts on welfare economics will be an impossible assignment. It is futile to argue that, since transactions between different sectors and classes take place within a given economic and political framework, these should be amenable to the conventional analysis of neo-classical welfare economics. In matters of class bargaining, the fact that classes co-exist within the same polity may mean little. For it could be the ultimate aim of one of the economic classes to destroy the bases of a given society and to transcend the postulates implied in the latter. True, even for such a class, certain short-term goals — the so-called objectives of economism — may take for granted the existing institutional arrangements. These short-term considerations would still have an organic link with the long-range goal which the class sets for itself.

One cannot therefore but view with scepticism a frame of analysis which presupposes that the concepts of fairness, equivalence, neutrality, etc., are so uniquely definable as to make them acceptable to each of the confronting classes, sectors or groups in an economy.[29] What may be fair to, for example, the landowning community may not seem to be so to the rural proletariat; a decision which may appear reasonable to the industrial workers may be considered as arbitrary by the industrial bourgeoisie; a situation which satisfies agricultural producers may raise the hackles of the mercantile community; and so on. Disappointment may be in store even were one to attempt to arrive at a unique concept of neutrality, since it has to be defined in relation to either an historical circumstance or an idealized situation. That in this matter one's choice of historical circumstances can be excluded from one's values would be a difficult claim to sustain. Moreover, even a particular norm of equivalence that may be set — such as the one described above — could be a target of attack, and substituted by another one.

This should convey a not altogether unimportant message for those in search of the empirical correlates of equivalent exchange. Equivalence may be semantically an expression bereft of any bias, but the moment a corpus is sought to be added to it, the familiar problems of a value-loaded system crowd in. By no stretch of imagination can economic science be considered a neutral body of knowledge nurtured by, and entirely given to, formal techniques. The choice of the techniques itself often reflects a certain bias toward structures and institutions. Even were this particular point to be ignored, the techniques chosen are applied for the attainment of certain objectives. The choice of these objectives can be defined only in terms of one's system of values. In the Rosa Luxemburg-Preobrazhensky type of model, the concept of equivalence in exchange or its absence is by implication defined in terms of historical shifts in a set of variables. In the more generalised Marxian formulation, equivalence or non-equivalence is defined by the degree of alienation of the share of labour from total output; the extent of this alienation too is a determinant of history. Those who would contest the criterion of alienation of labour from gross product as a measure of equivalence will have a completely different system of values in mind.

The reason for Alfred Marshall's pleading the cause of constant marginal utility of money now becomes obvious: changing values militate against determinism in equilibrium, constant values do not. The condition for attaining the true rate of equilibrium Marshall was trying to stress in Appendix F of his *Principles* was that the stock of one of the commodities which is in the market and ready to be exchanged must be very large and in many hands; in other words, he was depicting an idealised picture of perfect competition under which exchange could be true and fair. Such an idealised picture, where sellers and buyers are numerous and therefore are in no position to influence.the decisions of the other participants in the market, belongs to the realm of utopia. In a milieu where bargaining between classes and sectors is carried out against the background of unequal holdings of assets and incomes, the reality is closer to the case with which Marshall starts his exposition, namely, barter between two individuals where the equilibrium arrived at is in the nature of an accident. The nature of this accident cannot be precisely analysed in terms of any formal model, not even one which pays due obeisance to the stochastic factors affecting social processes. The relative bargaining capabilities of different classes and sectors reflect a series of historical circumstances incapable of being captured in a generalised frame, unless of course it be a very broad one conforming to the tenets of historical determinism.

NOTES

1 Marx himself, however, would seem to have perceived — and anticipated — some of the issues which exercised Rosa Luxemburg. Compare the following passage: 'If surplus labour or surplus-value were represented only in the national surplus product then the increase of value for the sake of value and therefore the exaction of surplus labour be restricted by the limited, narrow circle of use-values in which the value of the [national] labour would be represented. But it is foreign trade which develops its [the surplus product's] real nature as value by developing the labour embodied in it as social labour which manifests itself in an unlimited range of different use-values, and this in fact gives meaning to abstract wealth', Karl Marx, *Theories of Surplus Value,* Part Three, Lawrence and Wishart, 1972, p. 253.

2 See Paul M. Sweezy, *Theory of Capitalist Development*, Dennis Dobson, 1952, pp. 206-7.

3 Translated into English by Rudolf Wichmann, edited with an introduction by Kenneth J. Tarbuck, Monthly Review Press, 1972.

4 For a detailed discussion, see Sweezy, *op. cit.,* pp. 157-213, and Maurice Dobb, *Political Economy and Capitalism,* Routledge and Kegan Paul, 1946, pp. 79-126.

5 Rosa Luxemburg, *The Accumulation of Capital,* translated by Agnes Schwarzschild, Routledge and Kegan Paul, 1963, chapters VII — IX; also see Joan Robinson's introduction to the volume, particularly pp. 24-27. Joan Robinson sums up the Luxemburg problem as follows: 'If . . . . the distribution of income between workers and capitalists, and the propensity to save of capitalists, are such as to require a rate of accumulation which exceeds the rate of increase in the stock of capital appropriate to technical conditions, then there is a chronic excess of the potential supply of real capital over the demand for it and the system must fall into chronic depression'. *Op. cit.,* p. 26. A controversy has been kept alive as to whether Luxemburg was more concerned with the problem of 'realisation' than with that of accumulation. Paul Sweezy, *op. cit.,* stresses the aspect of realisation and brackets Luxemburg with others belonging to the so-called 'under-consumption' school. It is, however, arguable that her prime concern was with-accumulation, and the issue of realisation came in only because it has a bearing on this.

6 See, for example, Maurice Dobb, *op.cit.,* p. 90.

7 Rosa Luxemburg, *op. cit.,* pp.134-5.

8 Rosa Luxemburg, *op. cit.,* pp. 135-6.

9 Rosa Luxemburg, *op. cit.,* pp. 294-5.

10 '. . . the imported goods absorb purchasing power just like those home produced and thus to the extent that exports are offset by imports they do not contribute to the expansion of the markets'. M. Kalecki, *Selected Essays in the Dynamics of the Capitalist Economy,* Cambridge, 1971, p. 152. 'It is not possible to sell to the non-capitalist consumers without also buying from them. So far as the capitalist circulation process is concerned, the surplus value cannot be disposed of in this way; it can at best change its form.' P. M. Sweezy, *op. cit.,* p. 205. For a summary of other criticisms of the Luxemburg thesis, see Kenneth J. Tarbuck's editorial introduction in the Monthly Review publication referred to above, pp. 22-23.

11 The issue here, as would be obvious, is analogous to the issue of *value vis-à-vis price* of production.

12 P. Patnaik ('A Note on External Markets and Capitalist Development', *Economic Journal,* December 1972, pp. 1316-23) suggests another solution: a country could have balanced trade with outside pre-capitalist economies, while, *within the country,* the capitalist sector could maintain an 'export' surplus with respect to a pre-capitalist one.

13 The following passage could as well refer to transactions between two sectors belonging to the same economy: 'Accumulation is more than an internal relationship between the branches of capitalist economy; it is primarily a relationship between capital and a non-capitalist environment, where the two great departments of production sometimes perform the accumulative process on their own, independently of each other, but even then at every step the movements overlap and intersect. From this we get most complicated relations, divergencies in the speed and direction of accumulation for the two Departments, different relations with non-capitalist modes of production as regards both material elements and elements of value, which we cannot possibly lay down in rigid formulae. Marx's diagram of accumulation is only the theoretical reflection of the precise moment when the domination of capital has reached its limits, and thus it is no less a fiction than his diagram of simple reproduction, which gives the theoretical formulation for the point of departure of capitalist accumulation. The precise definition of capitalist accumulation and its laws lies somewhere in between these two fictions'. Rosa Luxemburg, *op. cit.,* pp. 417-8.

14 See, Ernest Mandel, *Marxist Economic Theory,* translated by Brian Pearce,

Rupa, p. 362; Tom Kemp, *Theories of Imperialism*, Dobson, p. 55 and M. Dobb, *op. cit.*, p. 269.
15 N. Bukharin, *op. cit.*, pp. 238-68.
16 Even in the original version of Luxemburg, '. . . (the) "third" market does not necessarily imply *foreign* or overseas markets since they can often be found in the same country until quite late in the development of the capitalist economy'. Kenneth J. Tarbuck, *op. cit.*, p. 21.
17 The following is as good a formulation of what she has in mind as any:
      . . . capitalist accumulation as a whole, as an actual historical process, has two different aspects. One concerns the commodity market and the place where surplus value is produced — the factory, the mine, the agricultural estate. Regarded in this light, accumulation is a purely economic process, with its most important phase a transaction between the capitalist and the wage labourer. In both its phases, however, it is confined to the exchange of equivalents and remains within the limits of commodity exchange. Here, in form at any rate, peace, property and equality prevail, and the keen dialectics of scientific analysis were required to reveal how the right of ownership changes in the course of accumulation into appropriation of other people's property, how commodity exchange turns into exploitation and equality becomes class-rule.

      The other aspect of the accumulation of capital concerns the relations between capitalism and the non-capitalistic modes of production which start making their appearance on the international stage. Its predominant methods are colonial policy, an international loan system — a polity of spheres of interest — and war. Force, fraud, oppression, looting are openly displayed without any attempt at concealment, and it requires an effort to discover within this tangle of political violence and contests of power the stern laws of the economic progress.

      Bourgeois liberal economy has taken into account only the former aspects: the realm of 'peaceful competition', the marvels of technology and pure commodity exchange; it separates it strictly . . . from the other aspect: the realm of capital's blustering violence which is regarded as more or less incidental to foreign policy and quite independent of the economic sphere of capital. (Rosa Luxemburg, *op. cit.*, p. 452).

    This passage, while it describes the phenomenon of non-equivalent exchange, is still somewhat vague about the actual *measure* of non-equivalence. An attempt to correct the lacuna has recently been made by Arghiri Emmanuel in his *Unequal Exchange: A Study of the Imperialism of Trade* (Translated by Brian Pearce, NLB). Emmanuel distinguishes between a primary form of non-equivalence, marked by equal rates of surplus value but unequal organic composition of capital, and a pure form where the rates of surplus value are themselves unequal: 'Regardless of any alteration in prices resulting from imperfect competition on the commodity market, unequal exchange is the proportion between equilibrium prices that is established through the equalisation of profits between regions in which the rate of surplus value is "institutionally" different — the term "institutionally" meaning that these rates are, for whatever reasons, safeguarded from competitive equalisation on the factors market and are independent of relative prices'. A. Emmanuel, *op. cit.*, pp. 63-64.

    The primary form of non-equivalence may be regarded as an adjunct of technological development. It is what Emmanuel describes as the 'pure' form of non-equivalence, namely, where rates of surplus value are unequal, which is, however, more crucial. For a fuller discussion, see Appendix to this chapter.

18 Alfred Marshall, *Principles of Economics*, Book V, Chapter II, Section III, and Appendix F.

19 For a critique of the neo-classical position, see J. de V. Graaff, *Theoretical Welfare Economics*, Cambridge University Press, pp. 154-5 and 167-71.

20 See Chapter Four.

21 E. Preobrazhensky, *The New Economics*, translated by Brian Pearce, Clarendon Press, pp. 5-6.

22 Under competitive equilibrium, it may be pointed out, abnormal profits disappear for each and all; moreover, the rate of normal profits is the same everywhere, thus fulfilling the basic conditions of equivalent exchange. This is obviously the answer to the neo-classical prayer.

23 One must, however, refer to a number of recent attempts to quantify the extent of non-equivalence in trade between countries at different stages of economic or political development. See in particular A. Emmanuel, *op. cit.*, pp. 63-4.

24 M.H. Dobb, *Soviet Economic Development since 1917*, Routledge and Kegan Paul, pp. 185ff.

25 M. Lewin, *Russian Peasants and Soviet Power*, translated by Irene Nove, George Allen and Unwin, pp. 214ff.

26 E.H. Carr, *A History of Soviet Russia, The Interregnum, 1923-24*, Macmillan and Penguin, Part I.

27 Alec Nove, *An Economic History of the U.S.S.R.*, Penguin, pp. 93-6.

28 According to Strumilin, as quoted in Dobb, *op. cit.*, p. 162, such a development had indeed occurred in the Soviet Union during the period referred to.

29 One could, in fact, proceed further. Even if there were no conflicting classes or groups, it would hardly be easy to identify an 'objective' rate of exchange that is 'fair' or 'equivalent'. Witness the considerable debate currently on among the economists of the East European countries on the correct rates of exchange between such countries.

CHAPTER 4

Terms of Exchange and Accumulation : the Soviet Debate

I

The problem of exchange between town and country came to haunt, as nothing else did, the foster-comrades of the world's first socialist revolution. The switch in policy-making, back and forth, in the early years following the Revolution, from the days of War Communism to the improvisations of the New Economic Policy, and the subsequent — and often frequent — adjustments throughout the 1920s, were each rude manifestations of the crisis posed by the 'accursed' question. The polemics of revolution had to be substituted by the artifices of economic growth. It was an awkward transition, but had to be gone through. While grappling with the problems of transition, it was impossible for the leaders of the Soviet Union to abstract from the fundamental issue of extraction of surplus from the countryside, for it is only on the basis of this surplus that development could proceed on a wide span elsewhere in the economy. This, after all, followed from the tenets of classical political economy itself.

The difficulties were real and grave. Since agriculture remained the predominant economic activity, accumulation for growth had to depend primarily on the transfer of resources from the farm sector. The mechanism for ensuring this called for a satisfactory resolution of the so-called peasant question. The Revolution notwithstanding, the organisation of agriculture in the Soviet countryside was still largely dominated by the rich and middle peasants; in any case the bulk of the surplus grain was under their control. Should the State then follow the maxim Leon Trotsky had enunciated way back in 1909, and adopt an aggressive stance, but thereby also run the risk of alienating some of the relatively small peasants, who, presumably, had even supported the revolutionary cause in its initial phase?[1] Or could the 'class alliance', as Lenin had described it, 'between the proletariat, the vanguard of the working people (the petty bourgeoisie, etc.), or the majority of these' be maintained and strengthened? Could, in other words, a mutually satisfactory arrangement in regard to terms of trade be worked out between town and country?

The agony of the first dozen years following the Soviet Revolution was the agony of groping for a solution to this particular question. And it was over only with the launching of Stalin's great offensive against the kulaks in 1929.

Lenin perceived the underlying issues at a fairly early stage. In 1919, in the course of an incomplete article,[2] he had several interesting things to say on the process of transfer of grain from surplus holdings to where the need was greatest. Up to a point, he was in complete agreement with Trotsky: 'Peasant farming continues to be petty commodity production. Here we have an extremely broad and very sound, deep-rooted basis for capitalism, a basis on which capitalism persists or arises anew in a bitter struggle against communism. The forms of this struggle are private speculation and profiteering versus state procurement of grain (and other products) and state distribution of products in general'.[3] The problem of development, he went on to explain, was the problem of 'organisational reconstruction of the whole social economy', by a transition from 'individual, disunited, petty commodity production' to 'large-scale social production'. This transition, he however added — and those who are inclined to do so can here discern a shift away from Trotsky's position — must necessarily be a protracted process. It was no use trying to rush things: the transition would, if anything, be delayed and complicated by hasty legislation and administrative fiats. Growth could be hastened only through rendering such assistance to the peasant as would enable him 'to effect an immense improvement in his whole farming technique, to reform it radically'.[4]

Lenin thus introduces at one stroke the twin problem in agrarian planning: improving the technology so as to ensure a rise in farm productivity, but, simultaneously, reforming the general attitude of the peasantry. The problem of transferring the surplus, in other words, could not be divested from that of increasing the volume of the surplus itself, which was, in its turn, dependent upon technological shifts in the basis of farm output.

The second, and the more difficult, part of the problem, Lenin goes on to say, is the separation of the good from the bad elements amongst the peasantry: 'The proletariat must separate, demarcate the working peasant from the peasant owner, the peasant worker from the peasant huckster, the peasant who labours from the peasant who profiteers'.[5]

The genuine ties which stem from the contradictions inherent in peasant agriculture are, Lenin acknowledges, genuine. Since petty commodity production was linked to a low level of technology, the surplus available to a small peasant could not but be meagre. This meagreness of the surplus should normally help the peasant to identify his 'oppressors' and 'exploiters', and compel him to seek an alliance with the workers against the 'capitalist', as well as against the 'profiteer' and 'trader'. Yet the conditions of petty commodity production are such as to tend to turn him too, in a vast majority of cases, into a 'huckster' and 'profiteer'. Since he had so little, each attempt to persuade the peasant to part with a portion of the surplus grain set up in him a tremendous resistance. Nonetheless, if growth were to be accelerated, the 'peasant profiteer' had to be isolated from the 'working peasant'. Lenin has no doubt about their respective identities:

> That peasant who during 1918-19 delivered to the hungry workers of the cities 40,000,000 poods of grain at fixed state prices, who delivered this grain to the state agencies despite all the shortcomings of the latter, shortcomings fully realised by the workers' government, but which were unavoidable in the first period of the transition to Socialism — that peasant is a working peasant, a comrade on an equal footing with the socialist worker, his faithful ally, his own brother in the fight against the yoke of capital. Whereas that peasant who clandestinely sold 40,000,000 poods of grain at ten times the state price, taking advantage of the need and hunger of the city worker, deceiving the state, and everywhere increasing and creating deceit, robbery and fraud — that peasant is a profiteer, an ally of the capitalist, a class enemy of the worker, an exploiter. For whoever possesses a surplus of grain gathered from land belonging to the whole state with the help of implements in which in one way or another is embodied the labour not only of the peasant but also of the worker and so on — whoever possesses a surplus of grain and profiteers in that grain is an exploiter of the hungry worker.[6]

The peasantry, Lenin argues, occupies a half-way position even under the dictatorship of the proletariat. At one end, it represents a large mass of toilers united by the common objective of extricating themselves from the oppression mounted by the landlord and the capitalist. At the other, it is made up of 'disunited small masters, property owners and traders'. This delicate economic position causes it to vacillate in its quest of identifying class interests, between the proletariat and the bourgeoisie. This vacillation impedes the generation of surplus and, hence, of growth. The objective of economic policy in a socialist State should be to win over to the cause of the proletariat those sections of the peasantry who are willing and able to cut athwart this contradiction, and who would agree both to undertake technological transformation of their fields and to deliver ample quantities of grain to the State *at reasonable prices*. What are reasonable prices? What principles must be brought to bear to determine the rationality of price-setting? The experience of War Communism and the early years of the NEP proved that this was no longer an arid, academic issue, but a matter of life and death for the socialist state. Even as rapidly failing health compelled Lenin to withdraw more and more from the direct running of administration, the practical implications of enforcing a fair rate of exchange between the products of town and country came increasingly to the fore. Polemics began to shade off into actual policy-making. It was left to Lenin's immediate comrades and followers to interpret, against the background of emerging realities, his dictum about fair prices. By 1922 or thereabouts, the Great Debate over terms of trade was fully joined.

At the forefront, articulating Trotsky's 1909 *obiter,* was Evgeny Preobrazhensky. Lenin's problem, namely, how the terms of exchange affect accumulation, and thereby growth, became Preobrazhensky's grand *quaesitum.* He embellished the contemporary polemics with a theoretical structure, and in a manner which both dazzled and illuminated. Perhaps it would not be too much to claim that the analytical frame set up by him for analysing the problem has not really been superseded by any other subsequent model. His *New Economics*[7] is arid reading, but, for those who want to analyse the stark relationship between economic growth and terms of trade, there is no substitute for the Preobrazhensky tract.

II

Preobrazhensky the person was a typical product of the revolutionary ferment in nineteenth-century Russia, which led to the emergence, from ordinary bourgeois households, of an extraordinary galaxy of individual activists. These individuals lived through the Czarist repression and, as the Bolshevik Revolution succeeded, staked claims to participate actively in the building of socialist society. They combined combatant political work with intellectual tasks of a most substantive nature. Shooting into prominence both as a leading party person and as an economist, jointly authoring the *ABC of Communism* with Bukharin in 1919, soon differing violently with the latter over modalities of primitive socialist accumulation, remaining at the centre of the procurement controversy throughout the mid-1920s, Preobrazhensky disappeared from the scene in the middle thirties — when, one would have thought, Stalin's squeeze on the kulaks should have vindicated all that he had stood for in the preceding decade. The acceptance — howsoever obliquely — of his formulations did not, however, imply a rehabilitation of the person. Preobrazhensky's remains an unmentionable name in the Soviet Union.[8]

The problem of exchange confronting the leaders of the Revolution, Preobrazhensky felt, was basically an aspect of a broader issue, which concerns the sources and methods of what he described as 'primitive socialist accumulation'. Growth of the socialist sector depended upon the accumulation of capital on the part of the State. Foreign loans apart, the only other sources for such accumulation are : (a) the surplus output of the State-owned industrial sector (that is, the difference between the value of output and socially necessary labour), and (b) the exploitation of the small-scale private sector — mostly agriculture — by coaxing out of the latter a greater sum of values than was to be given to it in exchange. Given the immediate context of the Soviet Union, Preobrazhensky considered (b) to be a much more crucial source than (a). The formulation of a strategy which would help to alienate a major fraction of the surplus of private enterprise for purposes of the State thus became the central issue in his analysis.

Preobrazhensky's schematics has a certain straightforwardness. Following the victorious Revolution, the State had taken charge of the major units in the industrial sector. Industry, Preobrazhensky was convinced, had already begun to exhibit the symptoms of monopolistic behaviour: this was inevitable as well as desirable, since advantage had to be taken of the well-known economies of scale. The moment the State assumed charge of organised industrial units, it also thus came to exercise monopoly power in the sphere of industrial production. This industrial monopoly controlled by the State was confronting, at the beginning of the 1920s, the alien and supposedly hostile sector of agriculture. The farm sector was hostile — shades of Trotsky — in the sense that the bulk of the potential surplus in agriculture was in the grip of the upper strata of the peasantry, who were described under the generic name of *kulaks*. The majority of the agricultural labourers, that is, the peasant proletariat, should form a natural alliance with the industrial working class, who controlled the State machinery as well as the levers of industrial activity. But this was yet to be. Despite the Revolution, the agricultural workers continued to work as wage labour for the big and middle peasants, who decided what compensation was to be offered to them. Since opportunities for work had not yet expanded satisfactorily in the non-farm sectors, the kulaks were in a position to exercise the powers of a monopsony *vis-à-vis* the poor peasants. What was equally disconcerting, they even determined the terms under which surplus foodgrains and industrial raw materials were traded off with the State sector. The State was in the market to purchase both foodgrains and industrial raw materials — foodgrains to meet the consumption needs of the urban population, including those of the urban proletariat, and raw materials to keep pace with installed industrial capacity. In case the kulaks were unwilling to part with the required quantities of food and raw materials, the pinch was bound to be felt by the State sector. Were they to charge inordinately stiff prices for these commodities, then too they would place themselves in a position of antagonistic contradiction *vis-à-vis* State power.

It is in this context that Preobrazhensky introduces his ideas regarding rates of exchange between products of the State and private economies.[9] The primary purpose of public policy, he asserts, should be to further the interests of the State economy — under the conditions then obtaining in the Soviet Union, the economy of the industrial sector — at the cost of those belonging to the non-socialist milieu. Here was a direct exercise of what in the terminology of orthodox economics would be described as value-judgment. The non-socialist segment of the economy consisted, by and large, of profit-seeking kulaks, who disposed of their products to the State sector. To accelerate socialist accumulation, the State, maintains Preobrazhensky, should offer the lowest possible price to farm products raised in the private economy and, in return, sell products of the State sector to the kulaks at the highest possible price. The State sector enjoyed two built-in advantages for the successful pursuit of such a policy: (a) the nationalised industrial sector is aligned with State power, and (b) this State-owned industrial sector is a monopolistic, integrated entity, while the constituents of the private economy, such as the kulaks, are divided and scattered.[10] The objective of State policy must be to intensify what Preobrazhensky, lifting the term from the corpus of Rosa Luxemburg's writings, defined as 'non-equivalent' exchange, that is, the State must keep the terms of trade between socialised industry and private agriculture tilted continuously in favour of the former and against the latter. Relative prices must be made to move uninterruptedly in favour of industrial goods, turned out by the State, and against the produce of the farms, raised by the kulaks. The procedure would be akin to a kind of progressive impost on the kulaks. In formal terms, it would involve an increasing alienation, for purposes of the State, of the farm surplus from its legal claimants.

Rosa Luxemburg is thus turned upside down. While he borrows the idea of unequal exchange from Rosa Luxemburg, there is, it will be noticed, a change of context and perspective in Preobrazhensky; the respective roles of agriculture and industry are, so to say, inverted from the Luxemburg model. What Luxemburg says capitalist industry *does* to primitive agriculture, Preobrazhensky says nationalised industry *should* do to pre-socialist, private agriculture. Preobrazhensky's primary concern is to ensure a faster rate of production in the socialised industrial sector; it is the kulaks lying in wait in agriculture — and hampering the smooth development of industry — who are the predatory elements in his analysis. The specific mechanism of 'exploitation' and 'plunder' in Rosa Luxemburg — non-equivalent exchange — thus assumes a positive role in Preobrazhensky, it in fact emerges as a major instrument of growth. The term 'non-equivalent' sheds its erstwhile, somewhat unsavoury connotation, and is very nearly deified. It is the context that matters, or so we are told. Non-equivalence in commodity production, whereby labour is forced to yield — in value terms — more than what is offered to it, is exploitation; non-equivalence in the terms of exchange between a socialised industry and an agriculture dominated by the kulaks is, however, to be treated in a different light — it not only involves exploiting the exploiters, but also promotes accumulation, thus deserving support on both ideological and economic grounds.

Such a price policy tilted against agricultural products and in favour of manufactures, subsuming within itself elements of taxation, need not, in Preobrazhensky's view, at all affect adversely the level of incomes of workers and the rural poor. After all, it is not the rural proletariat who constitute the principal consumers of industrial output. The burden of high industrial prices would fall, by and large, on the rural rich. In case poorer sections of the rural community have to buy some manufactures and thus suffer on acount of the shift in terms of trade in favour of industry, it should be possible to calculate what they lose in real terms. Preobrazhensky suggests that an equivalent amount could be subsequently returned to the rural poor in the form of credit and subsidies. In so far as the urban proletariat were concerned, they too could be compensated for the increase in industrial prices following the shift in terms of trade, for instance, by offering them a *pari passu* rise in money wages: '. . . if as a result of an appropriate price policy the working class along with the rest of the population, pays to State industry say 50 millions, the State can easily return this sum to the workers by an increase in wages, while the money received from the bourgeois and petty-bourgeois consumers is not returned to them and goes to swell the socialist accumulation fund'.[11]

The early Soviet pioneers loved to dream in terms of wide vistas. Preobrazhensky was no exception; he too tried to generalise. Basing himself on the premises concerning the immediate problems of capital formation in the Soviet economy, he went on to articulate a rather ambitious 'fundamental' law of primitive socialist accumulation. There is an engagingly simple linearity in this 'law', and its main tenets are easily summarised: the more economically backward a country, the greater is its need for accumulation if the State sector is to expand satisfactorily; furthermore, the sources of primary accumulation are more limited for a country without colonies than for one which possesses them.[12] This being so, while launching on socialist accumulation, a country without colonies would be obliged to alienate a substantially greater part of the surplus product of the 'pre-socialist' sectors than would be necessary in the case of one which has colonised territories under its control. The suggestion that a socialist economy could develop without drawing heavily on the resources of the petty bourgeoisie and the peasantry was straightaway ruled out.

Even granted Preobrazhensky's premises, the major difficulty with his 'law' concerns the feasible area of its operation. In the practical world, one must know the limits beyond which the rationale of the model ought not — or might not — be stretched, an aspect of enquiry which did not at all detain the author of the *New Economics*. Even in terms of the conditions obtaining in the Soviet Union in the early 1920s, the important question to ask, one would have thought, was the degree of alienation the kulaks could be safely subjected to. At any particular point of time, the extent to which alienation by one class — even where this class was aligned to State power — of another class is to be considered feasible has to be assessed in terms of objective realities. Where, for example, the State sector was yet to complete alternative arrangements for the production as well as distribution of essential foodgrains, or for the raw materials needed for industry, it would obviously be awkward to tilt inordinately the terms of trade against private agriculture. On the other hand, if the rural proletariat had already reached a certain stage of organisational maturity and political awareness, and a perfect understanding existed between them and representatives of State power in the countryside regarding both policy objectives and operational procedures, it could then be a matter of indifference how far to carry forward the process of alienation. To put it still more bluntly, once the alternative institutional basis was firmly laid down, the issue would boil down to a decision on whether or not to liquidate the kulaks : such liquidation would *per se* affect the process neither of production in, nor of extraction of surplus from, agriculture.[13]

III

Even before the Preobrazhensky model was spelled out in any manner, attempts to introduce what in retrospect seems to be its quintessence had taken place in the Soviet Union during the phase of War Communism. The crisis in prices which disequilibrated the economy in 1922-23 illustrated the kind of situations that could arise if the terms of trade were pushed excessively against one or other of the major sectors of the economy, and no countervailing measures were adopted to soften the consequences of the act. In the course of that tumultuous year, even as the Central Committee of the Communist Party carried on the great debate over relative prices and Trotsky, with the help of diagrams and pointers, tried, for days on end, to explain to the dazed and befuddled members of the Committee the significance of the 'scissors' crisis, the terms of trade moved first against industry, then against agriculture.[14] It is the latter swing which caused much greater concern, and a dying Lenin provided the guidelines to the Thirteenth Party Congress on how to close the 'scissors'. What followed is the staple of economic history.[15]

Even if Preobrazhensky's basic prescription for capital accumulation were to be regarded as theoretically impeccable, the central problem therefore remains: how, and where, does one set the limits of non-equivalence in exchange? Lenin, the master pragmatist, saw during his last flickering days what the issues were. No sympathy need be expended on the residual non-socialist elements of the economy. Let the dictum of non-equivalent exchange be enshrined in statecraft. Nonetheless, it was important to discover how far, in the sphere of reality, non-equivalence in exchange could be pushed at any given point of time between the sector aligned with the State, and the one alienated from it. The constraints operating in the short run must be acknowledged, and the importance of not killing the hen that lays the as-yet-golden eggs taken into account. As long as no substitute was available for the hen, her foibles had to be put up with. While one might decide that the feed for the hen needs to be progressively reduced, care must be taken not to transgress the limits of tolerance. In other words, there was a level of 'subsistence' even for an exploitatory rate of exchange — in the particular context, for payments to be made to the kulaks. This level would in fact have to be significantly higher than what would be considered as living wages for the rural proletariat. Until alternative organisational forms are available for the pursuit of agriculture and trade, the kulaks and their friends must be humoured; this was part of the armoury of revolutionary tactics.

The period between the resolution of the 'scissors' crisis in 1924 and the launching of Stalin's onslaught against the kulaks in 1929 constituted an interregnum. This was the phase of transition for the Soviet economy, marked as much by intense debate on policy issues as by pragmatic shufflings of strategies. This was also the period when Preobrazhensky's views were opposed with vigour — and, shall one add, ferocity — by his former colleague and collaborator, Nikolai Bukharin. At the official level, Preobrazhensky's treatise was allowed to be published, read, but never altogether approved, even though there is not the least doubt that someone was making mental notes from its pages. As the period ended, Preobrazhensky was gradually pushed out of the limelight; oblivion claimed him; Stalin's great purge saw to his physical liquidation in 1937. It is ironical — or perhaps not — that while the essence of his thesis was rehabilitated — and put into operational use from 1930 onwards — Preobrazhensky himself was not. As he confronted the kulaks, Stalin more or less adopted the rationale of the Preobrazhensky model,[16] but the person who conceived it was being hurtled to his grave. The year 1929, it was emphasised in no uncertain manner, was not 1922. Enough care was taken to ensure that there would be no recurrence of the 'scissors' crisis. The decision was taken to get rid of the kulaks. Stalin had done his calculations; the basic economic functions hitherto performed by the kulaks were not going to be affected; the rural proletariat, through the co-operative and collective farms, and the authorities, through the State farms and the State credit and marketing organisations, would carry forward the tasks in agriculture. While Preobrazhensky had thought of soaking the private kulak economy as the source of primary socialist accumulation, Stalin's policy of collectivisation, it could be argued, went for the introduction of an altogether new 'mode of production' in place of kulak agriculture. In case the private sector of production were left intact, a mechanism of appropriation of the Preobrazhensky kind could conceivably not immunise the working peasantry against a scale of exploitation similar to that which obtained in Meiji Japan. Stalin, it could be said, wanted to avoid this danger.[17]

IV

Can one not, however, abstract Preobrazhensky's 'law' from its specific context of the circumstances obtaining in the Soviet Union in the mid-1920s and generalise it into a more ubiquitous model, as he himself desired? In order that this may be done, certain elements in it will need modification. For example, at the time *New*

Economics was written, the industrial and agricultural sectors were more or less being identified in the Soviet Union with the State and the private sectors respectively. In formulating his 'law', Preobrazhensky accepted this identification as basic. They need not be so in a changed context.

Of particular relevance for Preobrazhensky's 'law' was the characteristic attributed to the industrial sector. Those constituting the major decision-makers in this sector were also in complete control of State power and thereby in a position to influence at will the terms of trade between agriculture and industry. The degree of monopoly associated with industrial activity could hence be further strengthened through the instrumentalities of the apparatus of the State. In its original form, therefore, the Preobrazhensky model presents the case of an integrated industrial sector, featured by traces of oligopoly, confronting an agriculture, consisting of a large number of widely dispersed production units. In addition, those ruling the roost in the industrial sector wield considerable influence in the polity and play a key role in the determination of industrial and farm prices. Were the model to be extended or modified, one interesting issue to explore would be to find out how far the degree of monopoly enjoyed by industrial capitalists would be impaired if they ceased to be aligned with State power. Equally interesting would be to test the sensitivity of (a) supplies from agriculture for industry, and (b) the demand for industrial products from within the farm sector, to shifts in the intensity of monopoly power enjoyed by the capitalists. For it is indeed possible to imagine that if relative prices keep shifting in favour of industry and against agriculture, production rigidities might develop within the latter sector, leading to a tapering off of supplies. Alternatively, farm demand for industrial products might shrink abruptly. There could be an empirically conceivable point where the gains from moving the terms of trade in favour of industry are exactly matched by the losses following from the contraction of the demand for industrial goods because of both depressed incomes in the farm sector and the increasing reluctance of agricultural producers to part with their crops at deteriorating terms of exchange.

Further degrees of freedom can be introduced in the model once it is assumed to be an open economy. For then industrial products could be disposed of elsewhere than within domestic agriculture, for example, in a foreign country. Were the shift in the terms of trade to affect adversely the supply of raw materials and foodgrains, the maintenance of industrial output could cause considerable strain. However, given an open model, importation of raw materials and foodgrains from exogenous sources should become possible. What therefore assumes importance are specific parametric values; for instance, the terms for exporting surplus industrial goods to a foreign country, and those governing the import of foodgrains and raw materials from outside. It is when Preobrazhensky's law is presented in this particular manner that its linear descent from Rosa Luxemburg's theoretical construct becomes still more obvious. In the Luxemburg formulation, a sector exogenous to the economy is at the 'receiving end' of non-equivalent exchange — either a peasant economy cut off from the process of capitalist growth or a colonised tract which is a victim of imperialist aggrandisement. This exogenous sector is *internalised* in Preobrazhensky, and the underlying normative issues are muted.

In Preobrazhensky's as much as in Luxemburg's model, the crucial economic decisions are related to the nature of power exercised by the industrial sector. The binding alliance between the industrial bourgeoisie and the political authorities provides the driving force of primitive socialist accumulation in Preobrazhensky, for it is instrumental for the tilt in relative prices in favour of industry. If circumstances change, other forms of alliance might emerge. In one such alternative formulation, not the industrial sector but the surplus-raising farmers in agriculture could come to dominate State power; the movement in relative prices could then be altogether different from that envisaged by Preobrazhensky.

In terms of Preobrazhensky's specific model, the flash-point of crisis should arrive — as it actually did arrive in the Soviet Union in the 1920s — once the price scissors begin to part consequent to the terms of trade moving inordinately in favour of industry and against agriculture. Crisis of a contrary kind is conceivable where it is the affluent farmers who are aligned to State power and the industrial decision-makers are alienated from political authority. The degree of monopoly enjoyed by organised agriculture could then outstrip that enjoyed by the industrial bourgeoisie, and farm prices consequently pushed up over the years in relation to industrial prices. Other things remaining constant, such a development could provide a stimulus to farm production, while a crisis of output visited industry. First, with farm prices rising continuously, the unit cost of industrial output could rise directly because of the increased burden of raw materials. Second, rising levels of foodgrain prices could affect the level of money wages, so that unit industrial costs might increase further. In a closed system, such a course of events could, with a time-lag, adversely affect the demand for manufactured goods, especially since a larger proportion than before of money income would now have to be set aside for farm products.

The situation might be aggravated if rising incomes in agriculture were not evenly dispersed, but tended to be concentrated in the hands of a limited number of surplus producers. Were the over-all rise in farm production not reflected in the money incomes of small farmers and agricultural workers, large-scale distress might ensue among the latter, since they are net buyers of foodgrains. Many small farmers might dismantle investments; their land might be gradually appropriated by the surplus-earning farmers. The initial consequence could therefore be a strengthening of the trend toward alienation *within* agriculture. However, if money wages were not adjusted upwards for agricultural labour in proportion to the rise in the price of wage-goods, a shrinkage in labour input and a decline in efficiency could follow, and which could grievously affect farm output. Widespread unrest in the countryside need not be ruled out either. It might assume the form of a movement against existing tenurial conditions; pressures could develop for a more even distribution of land or for higher wage-scales. Whatever the particular pattern of the unrest, the likely consequence would be an abatement of monopoly power exercised by affluent farmers. This lessening of monopoly power could in turn lead to a re-alignment of relative prices between agriculture and industry.[18]

Speculations of this nature are always tentative. Suffice it to say that once Preobrazhensky's model is liberated from the specificity of economic circumstances obtaining in the Soviet Union in the 1920s, a wide number of analytical possibilities is opened up. Accumulation is pivotal for growth, and it was left to the author of the *New Economics* to lay bare, in almost brutal terminology, the link between terms of trade and accumulation. If a surplus needs to be squeezed out of the economy for ensuring economic development, the *modus operandi* has to be somewhat remorseless, and some particular class or classes in society made the victim of non-equivalent exchange. If this latter phenomenon was to be described as exploitation, Preobrazhensky could point out that the classes who would be 'exploited' had in the past themselves, for decades on end, appropriated the fruits of exploitation, for instance, in imperial Russia, by denying the rural proletariat their just dues. In his anxiety to rehabilitate himself with the party, Preobrazhensky tried, subsequent to the first publication of the *New Economics,* to withdraw some of the more extreme formulations of his law.[19] That does not detract from the quality of the remarkable analytical frame which his tract retains to this day.

V

But we must retrace our steps. For Preobrazhensky was only one of the dramatis personae in the Soviet controversy in the mid-1920s over terms of trade between industry and agriculture. To obtain the flavour of the then ongoing debate,[20] it is equally important to analyse the views of the man who adopted a stance furthest from Preobrazhensky's, namely, Nikolai Bukharin. For this particular follower of Lenin, the implication of the warning administered by the leader — that, in the period of transition, the peasant question must be resolved through a careful demarcation of the respective roles of the growth-oriented peasantry and the 'peasant huckster' — could not be clearer. The revolution had to be saved, and it could be saved only by an alliance of the proletariat and the peasantry, by forming a worker-peasant block, which would win over to the cause the progressive peasantry and isolate the reactionaries. In order that such an alliance could come about, had not Lenin suggested that peasants be offered 'reasonable prices' for their grains? What Lenin had really meant came to occupy the pivotal place in the controversy.

Bukharin's comments on the relationship between the agricultural and industrial sectors of the socialist economy signified the final transition of his political attitude. During the early phase of his career, his sympathies were with the extreme Left elements in the party. And it is thus one of those ironies of history that the two erstwhile party stalwarts, he and Preobrazhensky, proceeded to hold toward the end such sharply contradictory views on the peasant question. As earlier mentioned, they had jointly authored the treatise on the *ABC of Communism,* perhaps the most radical public declaration on what the Soviet Union should seek to achieve following the Revolution. At the time of his political grooming, Preobrazhensky was commonly regarded as one of the closest supporters and admirers of Bukharin. But, once the great debate was joined, Preobrazhensky gradually came to epitomise the left — or, as some said, the Trotskyite adventurist fringe; and Bukharin became the standard-bearer of the cautious and conservative right, the propagator of the celebrated slogan exhorting peasants to 'enrich' themselves.

The polemics came to a head only following the 'scissors' crisis of 1923-24. By then, Lenin had passed away. How to interpret the master, particularly in the light of the difficulties encountered in 1923, emerged as the dominant issue. In two articles published in the *Bol'shevik,*[21] Bukharin dilated at length on Lenin's statement that progress under socialism predicated a close alliance between the proletarian vanguard and the peasantry, which should therefore exclude Trotsky-Preobrazhensky forms of 'increased pressure on the peasantry for the greater glory of the proletariat'. In a subsequent pamphlet, *Put k setzialism i raboche krostyanski blok,*[22] Bukharin summarises his point of view on the peasant question in the Soviet Union: '. . . we began by collaborating in the villages with the batraks and the poor against the nobility and the kulaks. Then we switched to alliance with the middle peasants by granting them NEP. Now [in the summer of 1925] we are about to give the strong peasants and the kulaks the green light.' This, however eliptically put, was, for a Communist Party functionary of his stature, a remarkable statement to make, for it was tantamount to admitting that the kulaks were being accommodated within the system. And yet, once you grant him his hypothesis, it would not seem to be an altogether untenable position. It is not that Bukharin was all of a sudden veering away from the revolutionary principles enshrined in the dialectics of class antagonism, or giving up the dream of building Soviet society on unshakable socialist foundations. He was — his admirers would say — only following his own lights about the nature of the optimum arrangements for attaining rapid socialist growth. Rattled by the traumatic experience of the 'scissors' crisis, he was, by 1925, more convinced than ever that the antagonistic economic relationship between town and country was the most critical problem facing the Soviet Union, for it involved the basic issues of surplus and accumulation, on which depend the rate and modality of economic growth.

Whatever strategy was adopted for solving the key question must, according to Bukharin, be guided by one fundamental assumption, namely, that even though political power had already passed into the hands of the proletariat, for economic growth to proceed unhampered, the latter must nonetheless form a working alliance with the peasantry.[23] The working class no doubt had assumed the leading role in the economy following the Revolution and would determine the pace and pattern of material development. It must not, however, try to impose itself unduly on the peasantry, especially its upper echelons, since the foundations of the socialist polity could be greatly endangered if co-operation were not forthcoming from the surplus-raising farmers. In the final analysis, the relationship between the proletariat and the peasantry could not but be one of contradiction. Even so, Bukharin was at great pains to explain, this contradiction need not and must not assume an antagonistic form right at the start of the development process. An immediate showdown has to be avoided; this called for a certain measure of imagination as well as tact on the part of the working class, who must not forfeit the goodwill of the peasantry. For, as Lenin himself had indicated, in the formative years of socialism, the peasants, including even the landless ones — the bulk of whom were still politically backward — sway between two alternative poles of attraction, namely, the bond of proletarian fealty on one side and the lure of bourgeois living on the other. The great majority of the peasantry must be convinced of the great gains to accrue from proletarian unity and the emergence of the socialist State; this conviction could only come from direct experience. While the economic powers which the kulaks continued to enjoy in the countryside must be eliminated in due course, one should go about the task with proper circumspection. Violent means must be eschewed, and there must be no abrupt reduction in the level of real incomes for the rural population, including the kulaks. Peasants must not be scared off by Preobrazhensky-type edicts of non-equivalent exchange; rather, in the short run the emphasis should be on establishing the rule of 'equilibrium' prices between agriculture and industry. To try to force the issue would be — Bukharin did not have the least doubt — counter-productive, for this could reduce the flow of raw materials and foodgrains to urban areas, and thus affect the rate of growth of industrial output in the socialist sector. The State sector of industry could not, after all, develop by 'devouring' the private economy of agriculture, for it was the rural demand for manufactures which determined the pace of industrial expansion.[24]

Bukharin ventured to go further. The peasantry could be won over, and a smooth transition effected in the farm sector, only by exposing the rural development process to the laws of the market economy. In other words, the compromise, which the principles of the NEP already represented, should be further extended. Let the conditions more or less resemble the free market; this would ensure a fair price for farm products; the peasant, guided by self- interest as by the mild prodding of the State, would increase the scale of operations of his hitherto uneconomic — or at least low-yielding — holding. Once the 'free market' experiment was persevered with for some time, the small peasant-proprietor would on his own discover that his output could be enlarged, and the benefits of diversification reaped, if only he adopts co-operative methods. Co-operative purchases of inputs and sales of farm products would lead to a dramatic fall in unit costs; similar results would obtain from the extension of co-operative credit; co-operation would also bring to the fore the advantages of branching out into newer directions. Encouraged by the gradually unfolding experience, small peasants would proceed to collectivise their farms, thereby reaping further economies of scale. The help proffered by the State to collectivised farms in the form of supply of cheap power and other inputs, as well as liberal amounts of credit from the State-owned banks, would facilitate the drive towards collectivisation.[25] Once this process was sustained for a while, the small peasants in the countryside and the urban working class would begin to come closer, so much so that in due course the former would be fully integrated into the proletarian vanguard. Thus, exclusively through a system of voluntary experimentation and gradual spread of co-operative institutions, socialism would establish itself amongst the small peasantry, and the workers'-peasants' State would come to full bloom.

This still meant abstracting from the theme of class struggles and class alienations, for there is no explicit reference to the plight that was to overtake the kulaks even as the rural proletariat organised their co-operative units and expanded their collective operations. Bukharin had an answer to the particular query, even though, here too, his prescription leaned heavily on the possibility of a smooth transition. The kulaks and the rest of the bourgeoisie would be eliminated from the rural scene, Bukharin argued, again through the operation of market forces; let the flowers of economic competition bloom, the *euthanasia* of the kulaks would then be an inevitability. Alongside the small peasants, the kulaks too would, however, be at a severe disadvantage in competing with the co-operative institutions set up by the small peasants. This would be so, since the co-operative units belonging to small farmers and the rural proletariat would receive certain special dispensations from banks and other state-owned agencies which would be denied to the kulaks, such as pertaining to the terms and conditions of credit. The kulaks would soon begin to realise that, were they to maintain their separate identity, they would lose out to the co-operative units belonging to the small peasants; as this realisation dawned upon them, they would be anxious to cut their losses; they would join up with others and progressively merge their units with the State-owned ones. Thus co-operative units set up by the non-exploiting peasantry would vanquish the rural capitalists at their own game; the kulaks would voluntarily liquidate themselves; the transition to socialism would be complete in the countryside; the problem of antagonism between town and country would resolve itself.

How far can one agree with this approach? Without question, Bukharin's was an idealised solution. He assumed that the kulaks would be a passive element and merely look on even as the entire process of advance of the rural proletariat toward co-operativisation and collectivisation was unfolding. The resources of the State, he further assumed, would be available in such abundance to co-operative organisations belonging to the poorer peasantry that the rate of progress attained by the latter would be much higher than in the case of enterprises set up by the kulaks. Provided the rural proletariat were able to organise their activities in an efficient manner, that by itself, Bukharin held, would bring the problem of mutual relationship between town and country to a satisfactory conclusion; no conflict need arise over the terms in accordance with which the output raised by the rural proletariat was to be exchanged against the products of urban industry. In the Bukharin model, the problem of accumulation for growth — which is what makes the issue of terms of trade between farm and industrial products of such vital importance — is almost slurred over. The time factor is also not brought up: the implication remains that the pattern of rural transformation that was being talked was not subject to any constraints of time.[26]

Under conditions of comparative statics, and if no other forces were to intervene, the kind of development Bukharin had in mind might well come to full fruition. In the situation prevailing in the Soviet Union in the 1920s, this was clearly impossible. The progress of co-operative enterprise among the rural proletariat was only halting, and the link between the State sector — including the State-owned banks — and the small peasants was at most tenuous. Large segments of the poorer peasants continued to be under the economic dominance of the kulaks. Even where rural co-operative organisations were functioning, the extent of assistance provided to them by urban industry was meagre.[27] For example, very little power could be spared for the poorer peasants. Politically the kulaks were very much alive and kicking; since they remained strongly entrenched in the countryside, they could frustrate whatever good intentions the State and its agencies might have harboured towards the small rural co-operatives.

Bukharin's idealised model was therefore a non-starter. In the short run, for a brief couple of years between 1923 and 1925, it served its purpose by postponing major policy decisions and by helping to close the 'price' scissors. But only for a time. Inside the party the debate continued. As was to be expected, Bukharin's position was branded as a manifestation of revisionism; it was under strong attack from the Left, which was spearheaded by both Trotsky and Preobrazhensky. Even amongst those not belonging to the extreme Left, the dominant attitude was one of ambivalence, as much because of ideological reservations as because of a lack of clarity over the role of co-operative bodies and mutual aid committees. After some years of vacillations and stop-gap decisions, Stalin, who had been waiting and watching, finally took the plunge in 1929, and launched on what he considered to be the ultimate solution of the town-country imbroglio.

VI

Stalin thus completed a full circle. Earlier, in such tracts as *The Foundation of Leninism* and *The October Revolution and The Tactics of the Russian Communists,* he had inveighed against Trotsky's and, by implication, Preobrazhensky's, views on the peasant question. To put an excessive squeeze on the peasantry, as the Trotskyites were advocating, would be — so asserted the Stalin of *The October Revolution and the Tactics of the Russian Communists* — tantamount to flouting Lenin's theory of the dictatorship of the proletariat, and palpably wrong.[28] But that was more than half a dozen years ago. Trotsky had meanwhile been effectively removed from the scene and Preobrazhensky relegated to purgatory. It was also legitimate to claim that the objective situation had been transformed. The price scissors had closed for a time; but the problem recurred. The policy of relative benevolence towards the kulaks had begun to show diminishing returns. With the procurement crisis of 1928, Stalin's mind was made up. The time had come to rid the party and the Soviet government of the influence of 'Right deviators', such as Bukharin. In his *Problems of Agrarian Policy in the USSR,* Stalin unleashed a full-scale attack, deriding the so-called theory of 'equilibrium' between the different sectors of the national economy. Bukharin was not mentioned by name, but nobody could mistake who or what the target of the attack was:

> This theory [that is, the theory of the 'equilibrium'] is based on the assumption that to begin with we have a socialist sector — which is one compartment, as it were — and that in addition we also have a non-socialist or, if you like, capitalist sector — which is another compartment. These two 'compartments' move on different rails and glide peacefully forward, without touching each other. Geometry teaches that parallel lines do not meet. But the authors of this remarkable theory believe that these parallel lines will meet eventually, and that when they do so, we will have socialism. This theory overlooks the fact that behind these so-called compartments there are classes, and that these compartments move as a result of a fierce class struggle, a life-and-death struggle, a struggle on the principle of 'who will win'! It is not difficult to see that this theory has nothing in common with Leninism. It is not difficult to see that, objectively, the purpose of this theory is to defend the position of individual peasant farming, to arm the kulak elements with a 'new' theoretical weapon in their struggle against the collective farms, and to destroy confidence in the collective farms.[29]

Continuing, Stalin turns his gaze on the question of farm surplus:

> Can we say that our small-peasant farming is developing according to the principle of expanded reproduction? No, we cannot. Not only is there no annual expanded reproduction in the bulk of our small-peasant farming, but on the contrary, it is seldom able to achieve even simple reproduction. Can we advance our socialised industry at an accelerated rate as long as we have an agricultural base, such as is provided by small-peasant farming, which is incapable of expanded reproduction, and which, in addition, is the predominant force in our national economy? No, we cannot. Can Soviet power and the work of socialist construction rest for any length of time on two *different* foundations: on the most large-scale and concentrated socialist industry, and the most scattered and backward, small-commodity peasant farming? No, they cannot. Sooner or later this would be bound to end in the complete collapse of the whole national economy.[30]

The solution, Stalin explains, lies in the enlargement of farm units and in creating — and raising — the capacity to accumulate on the part of agriculture. This could be done either through the capitalist way — by handing back rural power to the kulaks — or by the socialist way, namely, the establishment of collective and State farms, via the amalgamation of small peasant farms and the deployment of machinery and scientific methods.[31] Bukharin's 'equilibrium' theory was an attempt to indicate a third way: but it was, Stalin comments, 'utopian and anti-Marxian', and patently beyond the realm of feasibility.

VII

Neither of the two great combatants in the terms of trade debate survived the procurement crisis. Along with Preobrazhensky, Bukharin too perished in the great purge of the 1930s. His model of the 'non-exploiting' peasantry gradually getting the better of rural capitalist enterprises is now rarely referred to. It nonetheless reflected a certain quality of analysis for appraising the problems of accumulation and development which deserves attention. For there are aspects of the Bukharin model which have relevance for countries waylaid by the problem of terms of trade between the products of town and country during the process of economic growth. In a way, the objective conditions in a number of countries belonging to the so-called Third World bear several parallels to the setting Bukharin had in mind: the problem of raising resources from the rural sector, and of an adequate level of procurement of foodgrains, were essentially the issues over which Bukharin battled with Preobrazhensky, and these are also what afflict several developing economies today. Of course, the basic differences with Bukharin's postulates need not be slurred over. In the Soviet Union, a socialist industrial sector had already emerged and representatives of the industrial working class exercised total control over the apparatus of the State. These conditions do not obtain in many of the Third World countries. Nonetheless, since Bukharin's was a soft model of growth, there could be a point of view that, while it had no chance of success in the Soviet Union — where class alignments had already got deeply frozen by 1923-24 — it could still have sufficient relevance for those underdeveloped countries whose political, social and economic institutions are marked by dualism. A major element constituting the satisfactory ending, if one can so describe it, in the Bukharin scheme stems from the prospects of a breakthrough in agricultural production, centring the activities of the co-operative farms, largely as a consequence of generous assistance accorded by the State industrial sector. Within the ambit of such assistance, Bukharin had in mind not only credit and inputs, including fertiliser, but also the supply of electric power. In line with Lenin's thinking, he too assumed that the availability of cheap power would have a tremendous liberating effect on the Soviet countryside. In addition, of course, he had the vision of a benign frame of terms of trade between agriculture and industry — a frame laid down by the State — which would ensure both rapid accumulation and inter-class harmony.

For nations currently struggling to break out of the rut of economic stagnation, the Preobrazhensky-Bukharin debate over the terms of exchange between town and country thus retains a relevance. The role of the State in influencing these terms of trade is also of equal relevance. There is at least one modern economist, Michal Kalecki, who perceived the significance of the underlying issues. In the next chapter, we discuss some of his formulations.

NOTES

1 '... precisely in order to guarantee its victory, the proletarian vanguard would be forced in the very early stages of its rule to make deep inroads not only into feudal but also into bourgeois property relations. While doing so, it would come into hostile conflict, not only with all these bourgeois groups which had supported the proletariat during the first stages of its revolutionary struggle, but also with the broad masses of the peasantry, with whose collaboration it — the proletariat — had come into power'. Leon Trotsky, *1905*, Preface to the first edition, Penguin, p. 8.

2 V.I. Lenin 'Economics and Politics in the Era of the Dictatorship of the Proletariat'. *Collected Works*, Volume 30, Lawrence and Wishart and Progress Publishers, 1965.

3 *Op. cit.,* pp. 109-10.

4 *Op. cit.,* p. 113.

5 *Op. cit.,* p. 113.

6 *Op. cit.,* pp. 113-4.

7 Translated by Brian Pearce, Clarendon Press, Oxford, 1965.

8 Although Preobrazhensky's views were already available for a number of years via articles in journals and newspapers, the first edition in Russian of *New Economics* appeared in 1926, and the second, somewhat enlarged, edition was presumably made available in 1927 or 1928. It is interesting to quote in full the statement by the Editorial Board of the Communist Academy Publishing House while releasing the second edition:

> In issuing the second edition of Comrade Preobrazhensky's book, *The New Economics*, the editorial board of the Communist Academy Publishing House considers it necessary to state that this work puts forward views which the editorial board does not share and which are being used as the theoretical foundation for their position by groups of comrades who are at variance with our party. However, the problems of the economy of the transitional period, which are attracting very intense attention in both their practical and their theoretical aspects, call for an all-round analysis. The different tendencies of our Soviet and Party reality naturally find their expression in the field of theoretical analysis, including tendencies of a deviationist nature.
>
> Comrade Preobrazhensky's book has been evaluated in articles written by a number of comrades, including Commrades Bukharin, Goldenberg and others; the problems dealt with in this book have provided the subject of a special discussion in the Communist Academy; and we shall have to return to them again more than once in the pages of the *Vestnik Kommunisticheskoi Akademii*. For these reasons, the editorial board, while not sharing Comrade Preobrazhensky's opinions, nevertheless consider it possible to publish his book, in the interests of ensuring an all-round analysis of the most important problems thrown up by the economy of the transition period.

Such liberalism has not been repeated in the Soviet Union ever since.

9 E. Preobrazhensky, *op. cit.,* pp. 77-146. Also see M. Lewin, *Russian Peasants and Soviet Power*, translated by Irene Nove, George Allen and Unwin, pp. 148-54.

10 '... the concentration of all the large-scale industry of the country in the hands of a single trust, that is, in the hands of the workers' state, increases to an enormous extent the possibility of carrying out on the basis of monopoly a price policy which will be only another form of taxation of private economy'. E. Preobrazhensky, *op. cit.*, p. 111.

11 *Op. cit.,* p. 112.

12 'The more backward economically, petty-bourgeois, peasant, a particular country is which has gone over to the socialist organisation of production, and the smaller the inheritance received by the socialist accumulation fund of the proletariat of this country when the socialist revolution takes place, by so much the more, in proportion, will socialist accumulation be obliged to rely on alienating part of the surplus product of pre-socialist forms of economy and the smaller will be the relative weight of accumulation on its own production basis,

that is, the less will it be nourished by the surplus product of the workers in socialist industry. Conversely, the more developed economically and industrially a country is, in which the social revolution triumphs, and the greater the material inheritance, in the form of highly developed industry and capitalistically organised agriculture, which the proletariat of this country receives from the bourgeoisie on nationalisation, by so much the smaller will be the relative weight of the pre-capitalistic forms in the particular country; and the greater the need for the proletariat of this country to reduce non-equivalent exchange of its products for the products of the former colonies, by so much the more will the centre of gravity of socialist accumulation shift to the production basis of socialist forms, that is, the more will it rely on the surplus product of its own industry and its own agriculture'. *Op. cit.*, p. 124.

13   For an orthodox socialist critique of Preobrazhensky's ideas, see Maurice Dobb, *Soviet Economic Development Since 1917,* Routledge and Kegan Paul, 1942, pp. 185-6.

14   A fact, often slurred over in the writings of anti-socialist authors, is that the so-called 'scissors' crisis which overtook the Soviet economy during 1922-23 was really made up of two separate crises. The first crisis was marked by a violent movement of the terms of trade in favour of farm products and against industrial produce, occurring in the spring and early summer of 1922. This had resulted from the famine of the preceding year, and industry's anxiety to offer attractive terms to procure more foodgrains and raw materials, leading to a 'sales crisis'. 'The fact was that the prevailing high prices for agricultural goods did not spell increased, but rather decreased, incomes for the peasants because they were associated with agricultural shortage; and the income which the urban worker had available to buy manufactured goods had drastically shrunk because of the increased amount he had to spend on food. In other words, the "sales crisis" was an expression of the disproportion between agriculture and industry, under which the marketed surplus of the village was insufficient to supply the requisites of expanded production in the towns.' (Dobb, *op. cit.*, p. 157.) It was in response to this 'sales crisis' that the nationalised industrial units went ahead to form syndicates and trusts so as to avoid cut-throat competition among themselves, as well as to co-ordinate the purchase of inputs. By the late summer of 1923, the pendulum of relative prices has swung violently in the other direction, and the terms of trade became exceedingly favourable to industry compared to what the position was a year ago. This latter phenomenon attracted much greater attention in the outside world, for obvious reasons. That a crisis engendered by an excessive shift in the terms of trade in favour of nationalised industry and against agriculture — as witnessed in 1923 — could be the Achilles' heel of his 'law' is a thought which evidently did not worry Preobrazhensky.

15   For a detailed narration, see Dobb, *op. cit.*, p. 169; E.H. Carr, *A History of Soviet Russia : The Interregnum, 1923-24,* Macmillan and Penguin, Part I, and Alec Nove, *An Economic History of the U.S.S.R.,* Penguin, pp. 93-113.

16   See Isaac Deutscher, *The Prophet Unarmed,* Oxford University Press, 1959, pp. 441-2.

17   Pitted against this position is the view of those others — exemplified by Roy Medvedev's *Let History Judge,* Macmillan, 1971 — who maintain that the wastage, in physical and human terms, implicit in the agrarian policy pursued by Stalin in the 1930s could have been avoided if only a more equitable balance of exchange between town and country had been striven for.

18   Some of these issues will be referred to in the subsequent discussions in Chapter 11.

19   See A. Nove's introduction to the English edition of the *New Economics, op. cit.,*
     p. xv.
20   For a generally unsympathetic and critical discussion of the theoretical and
     practical issues, see David Mitrany, *Marx Against the Peasant,* Weidenfeld and
     Nicolson, 1951.
21   'A New Discovery in Soviet Economics, or How to Ruin the Worker-Peasant
     Bloc', *Bol'shevik,* 10 December 1924 (also published in *Pravda,* 12 December),
     and 'A Critique of the Economic Platform of the Opposition: Lessons of October
     1923', *Bol'shevik,* 15 January 1925; later printed together as a pamphlet, N.
     Bukharin, *Kritika Economicheskoi Platformy Oppozitsii,* Moscow, 1926.
22   See M. Lewin, *op. cit.,* pp. 135-42.
23   For example, '. . . the task of the working class, and the task of urban industry, is
     to develop production in such a way as to satisfy the needs of the population fully
     and cheaply'. N. Bukharin, *op. cit.,* p. 26.
24   N. Bukharin, *op. cit.,* p. 16.
25   No doubt Bukharin could bank on the following passage from Lenin in support
     of his position:
        'Capitalism has created an accounting *apparatus* in the shape of the banks,
        syndicates, postal service, consumers' societies, and office employees'
        unions. *Without big banks socialism would* be impossible'. 'The big banks
        are the 'state apparatus' which we *need* to bring about socialism, and which
        we *take ready-made* from capitalism; our task here is merely to *lop off* what
        capitalistically mutilates this excellent apparatus, to make it *even bigger,*
        even more democratic, even more comprehensive. Quantity will be
        transformed into quality. A single State Bank, the biggest of the big, with
        branches in every rural district, will constitute as much as nine-tenths of the
        socialist apparatus. This will be country-wide *book-keeping,* country-wide
        accounting of the production and distribution of goods, this will be, so to
        speak, something in the nature of the *skeleton* of socialist society'. V.I.
        Lenin, 'Can the Bolsheviks Retain State Power?' *Collected Works,* Volume
        26, Moscow, 1964, p. 106, original italics.
26   For an appraisal of Bukharin's views, see M. Lewin, *Russian Peasants and Soviet
     Power,* Chapter 6, especially pp. 135-42. For a fuller description of the
     controversy between Preobrazhensky and Bukharin on the respective roles of
     industry and the peasant economy in a socialist State, see E. Preobrazhensky,
     The New Economics, op. cit., Appendix, pp. 224-305, and also the author's
     foreword to the second edition, pp. 8-41.
27   The relevant issues were discussed at the Thirteenth Party Congress, Kalinin and
     Krupskaya, among others, particularly dwelling at length on the strengths and
     weaknesses of peasants' committees for mutual aid. See E. H. Carr, *A History of
     Soviet Russia : The Interregnum, 1923-24,* Part I, Macmillan and Penguin,
     Chapter 4.
28   'Lenin speaks of the alliance between the proletariat and the labouring strata of
     the peasantry' as the basis of the dictatorship of the proletariat. Trotsky sees a
     "hostile collision" between "the proletarian vanguard"' and "the broad masses of
     the peasantry". . . . 'Lenin speaks of the *leadership* of the toiling and exploited
     masses by the proletariat. Trotsky sees "contradictions" in the position of a
     workers' government in a backward country with an overwhelming peasant
     population"'. J. Stalin, *Problems of Leninism,* Moscow, 1954, p. 120.
29   J. Stalin, *op. cit.,* p. 391.
30   J. Stalin, *op. cit.,* p. 392.
31   The point not made explicit by Stalin, but which follows from his analysis, is that

with a fully socialised agriculture, the problem of terms of trade between farm and industrial products is automatically resolved in a socialist State, for the straightforward reason that the 'fierce class struggle', which is at the root of the problem, ceases to take place.

CHAPTER 5

Relative Prices, Income Distribution and Growth

It is impossible to over-emphasise the significance of the Soviet debate on the terms of trade between the products of 'town' and 'country'. It concerned what undoubtedly is the single most important issue in economic growth, namely, that of accumulation. Those arrayed on either side of the debate still started from the same postulate: accumulation is basic to growth and, in a closed economy, is largely determined by the terms of trade between the two leading sectors. Once Rosa Luxemburg's schema for accumulation-cum-realisation is internalised, it too, as we have seen, has the same message to convey : the course of capital formation is a function of the mutual price relationship between agriculture and industry. Preobrazhensky's assumptions differ radically from Luxemburg's, but the frame of analysis is not dissimilar : the terms of exchange between town and country decide the rate of accumulation, and class relations decide the terms of exchange. Bukharin disagrees with Preobrazhensky's prescriptions, but does not disown the logical structure set up by the latter. The parameters of class relations keep changing from one author to another; that these are the crucial elements for determining the actual terms of trade between agriculture and industry — and consequently the rates of capital formation and economic growth — however emerges clearly in each case.

Once the Luxemburg-Preobrazhensky lineage was established, the two-sector model for analysing issues relating to the growth of, and the inter-relationship between, agriculture and industry passed into usage. The tradition thus laid down has not been deviated from in any noteworthy manner in later economic writings. Even Ragnar Nurkse's[1] discussion of the problem of capital formation in underdeveloped areas conforms to the tradition.

The lineage is even more prominently traceable in the works of Michael Kalecki, in both his approach to the problem of income distribution in capitalist societies and his prognosis about the feasibility of so-called 'intermediate regimes' in developing

69

countries; his comments on the class character of the State and its impact on growth and distribution too can be considered as adding a footnote to the Preobrazhensky-Bukharin controversy.

The link between Luxemburg's model of accumulation and Kalecki's analysis of income distribution and growth may appear somewhat indirect, that it exists is, however, difficult to deny.[2] Nor should this cause any surprise, since the phenomena of terms of trade and class alignments cannot but affect crucially the pattern of distribution as well as the level of accumulation in an economy. Kalecki's main emphasis in his theorem on the distribution of national income,[3] it will be remembered, is to explain the share of wages in an industrial-capitalist economy in terms of the degree of monopoly and the cost of what he describes as 'basic raw materials'. In the kind of static formulation he has in mind, the wage share is inextricably correlated to the movement in these two variables. Even intuitively it should be possible to suggest that, other things remaining the same, an intensification of the degree of monopoly would lead to a widening of the margin between cost and price or, in other words, to product price rising relatively to the price level of inputs; since the aggregate wage bill is a component of cost, such a rise in the degree of monopoly implies a lowering of its share in national income. Similarly, if other things remain the same, but the outlay on basic raw materials goes up — that is, only the cost of non-labour inputs increases — the wage share once more should be a diminished fraction of aggregate turnover. Kalecki's theory has obviously to be considered along with all its assumptions, namely, that a disturbance in one of the variables, whether short- or long-term, does not affect the other variables and, further, that macro-economic aggregation does not present the same genre of difficulties as are encountered in a whole array of Marxist analysis, beginning with Volume III of *Capital* and ending with Rosa Luxemburg. Once these restrictive conditions are tolerated, the Kalecki model can emerge as an efficient vehicle for exploring the mutual relationship between the agricultural and the industrial sectors, thus immediately confirming its Luxemburg-Preobrazhensky heritage. For instance, in terms of Kalecki's second condition, a rise in the price of farm products — of 'basic raw materials' — leads to a deterioration in the relative economic position of the industrial working class;[4] to express it differently, a shift in the terms of trade in favour of the farm sector lowers the share of wages in industrial income. Given the implicit pre-condition of the Kalecki system, namely, that a shift in the order of magnitude of one variable does not *ipso facto* lead to corresponding shifts in that of others, a further inference is

permissible: a rise in the price level of farm products need not raise
pari passu the wages of farm labour, so much so that the share of
wages in aggregate farm income and, therefore, in aggregate
national income, could actually decline following an increase in farm
prices.[5]

Kalecki invites attention to movements of two sets or relative
prices; between the price level of industrial goods and the money
wage rate, and between farm prices and the money wage rate. It
should, however, be easy to extend the analysis to the consideration
of a third set, namely, that between the prices of agricultural and
industrial products. Besides, in a dualistic structure, monopoly
power is itself capable of diverse manifestations. In addition to the
monopoly power of the industrial bourgeoisie emphasised by
Kalecki, it is possible to conceive a phenomenon of monopoly power
exercised by surplus-raising farmers (and traders) in the countryside;
this possibility is not recognised in Rosa Luxemburg, but looms
large in Preobrazhensky's analysis. The exercise of monopsonistic
power by the industrial bourgeoisie, both in the purchase of raw
materials and in the hiring of workers, is similarly very much a part
of reality : this is implied in Kalecki, though not explicitly discussed.
A parallel category could be the monopsonistic pressure exerted by
the richer peasantry while engaging farm workers. In other words,
instead of the single aspect of monopoly power referred to by
Kalecki, four separate categories are conceivable in the context of a
two-sector economy: (a) the monopolistic role of the industrial
bourgeoisie in the determination of industrial prices; (b) the power
of monopsony exercised by the bourgeoisie in the determination of
industrial wage rates; (c) the monopolistic role of rural oligarchs in
the fixation of farm prices, and, finally, (d) the monopsonistic power
wielded by the rich peasantry in the determination of farm wages.
Even within the limits of a tautological model, it should be possible
to take account of these different facets of monopoly power and their
respective influence on the terms of trade between agriculture and
industry as well as on the pattern of income distribution between the
four relevant classes — industrial capitalists, industrial workers, the
rich peasantry and the agricultural working class.

In Kalecki's income distribution model, the industrial sector holds
the key. Agriculture — which produces 'basic raw materials' — is
external to it; its parameters we are asked to assume as given. This
marks the model out from Luxemburg's peasant economy, which,
though exogenous to the capitalist system, is still greatly influenced
by it. In any extension of the Kalecki-type analysis for studying the
effect of movements in terms of trade on income distribution and

accumulation, it would be realistic to suppose that neither agriculture nor industry is exogenous to the system; as should be obvious, internal developments in either sector — manifesting themselves through shifts in monopoly or monopsony powers — affect the terms of exchange between the two sectors, consequently the processes of growth and income distribution for both and, therefore, for the economy as a whole. In the Kalecki system, the price level of only basic raw materials is introduced as an explanatory variable for analysing income distribution between classes; it would be legitimate for a more general model to take into account the effects of shifts in industrial prices too on the pattern of development in the farm sector and on the structure of income distribution. The distinction between endogenous and exogenous factors is in any case blurred in a situation of dynamics.

The linear relationship between the Luxemburg-Preobrazhensky genre of analysis and Kalecki's theory of income distribution nonetheless stands out. Luxemburg has in mind the image of an underdeveloped pre-capitalist sector engaged in the production of primary goods, including raw materials. Such a sector serves three purposes in her model. First, it is a receptacle for the internally undisposable output of Departments One and Two which together constitute the industrial sector. Second, and this really follows from the first, by resolving satisfactorily the problem of realisation, it sustains the process of capitalist accumulation. Third, it provides the inputs, including raw materials, necessary for efficient and unimpeded production in the two Departments. In Preobrazhensky, the distinction between the two Departments within the industrial sector is obliterated; the essence of the Luxemburg mechanism, however, remains unimpaired: industry must obtain food and raw materials from agriculture, and, in turn, sell its products to the latter at such rates of exchange as would maximise accumulation. Primacy is still given to the cause of capital formation; the rubric of 'non-equivalent exchange' is put together merely to further it. The Kalecki formulation makes no explicit reference to the phenomenon of the raw material-producing sector being compelled to accept, in terms of an unequal exchange, a part of the output of Departments One and Two — which is exploitation according to Luxemburg, and socialist accumulation in Preobrazhensky. In other respects there is, however, a clear convergence of ideas. The pre-capitalist sector in the Luxemburg-Preobrazhensky schematics and the exogenous raw material-producing sector in Kalecki have both a crucial role to play in determining the pattern of endogenous distribution of incomes. In the Luxemburg-Preobrazhensky version, the outlay on account of raw materials — reflecting the terms of trade between the products of industry on the one hand and those of the external sector on the other — determines the level of real income — and consequently, the rate of accumulation — for the economy as a whole. In Kalecki, the cost of raw materials — which once more but reflects the movement in terms of trade — exogenously establishes the pattern of internal distribution between wages and profits of a *given* level of national income. Since the latter in its turn determines the rate and pattern of social accumulation, the echo of Luxemburg-Preobrazhensky is unmistakable.

With just one difference. While Kalecki's theory of income distribution has the context of a capitalist society, the political element is still not explicitly brought in. This is certainly not so in either Rosa Luxemburg or Evgeny Preobrazhensky. Luxemburg talks of 'predatory' capitalism. In the manner it operates, the latter is indistinguishable from State power; it depends on protective tariffs, militarism and imperial exploits to protect and advance the cause of capitalist accumulation. The State, in other words, is the centrepiece in Luxemburg's schema, the principal instrument for enforcing a regime of non-equivalent exchange upon the pre-capitalist economy. Notwithstanding the difference in milieu, in Preobrazhensky's formulation, too, the decision-makers in the industrial sector are in complete control of political power; they define and articulate the will of the State. If the terms of trade need to be manipulated against the kulaks, this task is facilitated by the seizure of State power by the industrial proletariat. In contrast, Kalecki's theory of income distribution, which, by implication, is an analysis of the movement of inter-class terms of trade and its impact on relative income shares, does not directly dwell on the role of the State.

This, one could argue, is a considerable lacuna; for bargaining between classes on relative prices and income shares to take place in a political vacuum is simply inconceivable. That would be a *non sequitur*.[6] The political context can scarcely be dissociated from the analysis of economic phenomena. How aggregate national income is to be divided, at any point of time, between the different social classes is an economic *quaesitum,* but its answer hinges upon political realities, and upon the role which the State decides to play. The nature of the problem remains unchanged even in the context of the long term, that is, where issues of growth and accumulation emerge to the fore. Here, too, the crucial part played by the State in shaping economic decisions cannot simply be wished away. Throughout history, one of the major problems of economic policy has been to decide how accumulation is to be furthered, who among the classes should bear the brunt of the current deprivation which accompanies this process and, conversely, who should benefit the most from national economic growth which accumulation helps to foster. Class antagonisms arise over precisely these grounds. The fact that sometimes, irrespective of whichever classes or combination of classes are in power, considerations of long-run growth are dwarfed by expediences of the short run can also be laid at the door of the same set of causes. The machinery of the State has been used, and will continue to be used till as long as society is riven by class heterogeneities, to advance the interests of those in political power. The challenge posed before ruling groups at any given moment is to evolve an optimising arrangement whereby the promotion of their own class interests is reconciled with the goals of overall economic growth and political stability.

Granted the reality of class antagonism, the problem of growth and accumulation in a pluralist society then reduces itself to a search for conditions which would help in maintaining a reasonable degree of social stability, effect a short-run compromise between the interests of the groups sharing political power, and at the same time ensure the extraction of a satisfactory degree of investible surplus for promoting economic progress. A large number of countries around the globe, particularly those belonging to the so-called Third World, are currently grappling with this issue.

Perhaps to compensate for the somewhat mute role assigned to the State in his theory of income distribution in capitalist society, Kalecki, in a contribution first published in 1964, suggests a framework for analysing the problem of growth in developing economies which offers pride of place to political phenomena. The discussion is in terms of a hypothetical coming together of certain social categories who assume State power and are thus burdened with the responsibility of furthering economic growth in these countries.[7] This political alliance, in Kalecki's view, could be made up of the lower-middle class and the rich and middle peasantry. Kalecki is here evidently floating an idea which goes against Marxist presumptions. The lower-middle classes — whom Rosa Luxemburg, following Struve, had contemptuously referred to as 'third persons' — are not regarded as a viable social category in traditional Marxist analysis. They have been regarded as feeble-minded; in each phase of history, they are expected to lapse into the bland role of hangers-on of the industrial bourgeoisie. In Marx's biting narration of the character of the regime established under Louis Bonaparte, there is a detailed resume of how these elements, in the company of the lumpen proletariat and the civil servants, align themselves with the bourgeoisie and feudal landowners.[8] Surveying the situation obtaining in the underdeveloped countries in the post-World War II period, Kalecki, however, reaches the conclusion that the lower-middle class could, at least on the surface, play a somewhat more positive historical role in the polity of these countries. Expanding the industrial base is the most crucial task facing a hitherto colonised nation now launched on a programme of rapid economic growth. The prime responsibility for the effort initially devolves on the indigenous bourgeoisie. But they are still relatively backward and, more often than not, fail to display dynamism of the right kind.[9] A certain entrepreneurial gap thus develops in the economy, and one which could hold back growth. The bourgeoisie may realise their own limitations and try to save the situation by forming an open alliance with foreign private capital. If the lower-middle class consider such a denouement to be undesirable, they may decide to intervene. They may enter into an alliance with the relatively affluent peasantry, who are to be distinguished from feudal landlords. Such an alliance may enable the lower-middle class and the rich peasantry to capture political power. Once they do so, they could initiate a programme of extensive industrialisation on the basis of State capitalism and effectively quash all attempts on the part of private foreign capital to infiltrate into the economy. In this endeavour, they could also look forward to receiving substantial material assistance from the socialist countries, who would only be too happy to protect them from the onslaught of both predatory capitalism from outside and its 'comprador' counter parts.

A political and institutional arrangement of this nature, Kalecki suggests, is feasible in many developing countries. Rich peasants and the lower-middle class between them form a fairly sizeable part of the population in these countries; provided the economic consequences of the arrangement turn out according to expectations, the alliance should be able to hold its own in the political sphere too. An additional point ensuring its viability is the fact that rich farmers continue to dominate the poorer peasantry and the rural proletariat in the countryside, which is mostly under the control of a local oligarchy consisting of traders, money-lenders and affluent peasants.[10] The coalition could keep on leash the urban proletariat too. Where their number is small, they may be disarmed through the lure of higher wages. In other instances, they may be threatened with loss of work; this should be particularly easy if unionisation is lagging behind.

No political alliance would of course work unless certain direct gains accrue to each of the groups contracting it. The lower-middle class and the rich peasants soon discover that several advantages accrue to them. A rapid growth of the socio-economic infra-structure takes place under State capitalism; the rich peasants and the lower-middle class become its most direct beneficiaries. The expansion of industrial enterprises in the State sector provides executive and technical jobs for young people belonging to the ruling classes. Small-scale industrial and commercial ventures, too, develop as adjuncts of State undertakings; the process is helped through extensive sub-contracting and explicit patronage. Finally, to quote Kalecki, 'land reform, which is not preceded by an agrarian revolution, is conducted in such a way that the middle class which directly exploits the poor peasants — i.e. the money-lenders and merchants — maintains its position, while the rich peasantry achieves considerable gains in the process'.[11]

The adversaries of such an 'intermediate regime', according to Kalecki, belong to contrary ends of the spectrum. At one end is the likely opposition from the upper stratum of the bourgeoisie and the feudal landlords; at the other is the felt alienation of small farmers and landless agricultural workers as well as of the urban working class. The feudal landlords, Kalecki speculates, would in any case be stripped of all political power by the land reforms — howsoever limited — that are likely to be implemented under the arrangements; their hostility could therefore be brushed aside. As far as the bourgeoisie are concerned, with the rapid expansion of State industrial undertakings, they would soon discover that their survival hinges on the extent of support they are able to obtain from the public sector.[12] As realists, they would decide to bury the hatchet, and accept *in toto* the goals and policies set by the State. The only real adversaries of the intermediate regime would therefore be the rural and urban proletariat, who lose all along the line.[13] In the short run, however, their capability for 'mischief-making' is limited, and the regime prospers.

Kalecki's schematics on intermediate regimes is interesting if only because the conglomeration of social forces it depicts has empirical correlates in many underdeveloped lands. In countries such as India, Indonesia or Sri Lanka political power in the post-Independence period, there can be no question, has come to be exercised by coalitions of economic groups who, up to a point, are not altogether dissimilar to categories Kalecki has in mind. Where his framework seems to be somewhat wanting is in the assumption that feudal landlords would be necessarily against such a regime. In the first place, in the context of the countries referred to, it is not always easy to make a precise distinction between feudal landlords and rich peasants. As the extensive literature[14] on the nature of production relationships in Indian agriculture bears out, the actual conditions obtaining in the farm sector are ofter a heterogeneity, and features of feudalism co-exist along with those of nascent capitalism; so much so that it needs quite some daring to separate the class interests of the purely feudal elements from those of the capitalist farmers. In the second place, the land reforms that have been introduced, for example, in India, are even more limited in scope than in Kalecki's conception. In the kind of intermediate regimes which have emerged, feudal landlords are as much a part of the ruling alliance as are the middle and rich peasants and the urban middle class.

There is another area where Kalecki's schema has been overtaken by events. In his analysis, the industrial bourgeoisie, hemmed in from all sides, are supposed to realise the virtues of State capitalism — and thus come to an understanding with the regime — only following a certain interval of time. In several developing countries, the process has been telescoped. In fact, in cementing the political coalition which constitutes the core of the 'intermediate regime', the initiative has been taken out of the hands of the so-called lower-middle class by the bourgeoisie themselves. Political consciousness is actually much weaker among the lower echelons of the middle class than Kalecki has assumed: in this respect, Marx's misgivings seem to be of a solider foundation. Almost by default, therefore, the bourgeoisie have taken the lead to effect economically significant political alliances. They have satisfied themselves that there need be no basic antagonism in the course of economic growth between their own interests and those of State capitalism. Because of historical circumstances and exogenous developments, in quite a number of these countries, any major role for foreign capital is considered to be played out. Such being the case, to ensure survival, as well as accumulation and growth, the bourgeoisie realise the need to align themselves with other indigenous classes. Particularly where the system of parliamentary democracy prevails and heads have to be counted, the conclusion is soon reached that appeasing the lower-middle class and the rich peasantry,[15] and depending upon them rather than upon the chimera of foreign capital, are a preferred alternative. Outside agriculture, it is the bourgeoisie, and not the lower-middle class, who accordingly assume the role of dominant decision-makers.

What Kalecki envisages as a distinct 'intermediate' regime is blurred in no time, in these circumstances: it very nearly becomes indistinguishable from an 'upper' regime. It shades off into a rule by affluent peasantry (including remnants of the feudal class) and the urban bourgeoisie, who emerge as the most powerful social categories in the polity. The lower-middle class reverts to its traditional role as camp-followers of the upper classes and the intermediate regime is divested of one of its supposedly main props.

A few further remarks are called for. In Kalecki's schematics, resources from the socialist nations are to be made available to the intermediate regime, enabling the latter to deepen and extend the public sector industrial base. Such external support from the socialist nations would be crucial to the regime and help it to withstand the pressures applied by the domestic bourgeoisie and private foreign capital. Precisely because of a mistaken notion about the class character of the regimes which have established themselves in these countries,[16] the socialist nations have in effect advanced the bulk of this aid to the industrial bourgeoisie and out-and-out feudal elements. While the object has been the development of the State sector, it has been only imperfectly understood that, under given circumstances, the expansion of the public sector merely leads to a strengthening of the economic base of the bourgeoisie and the landlords, who, in terms of socialist ideology, ought to have been considered as the most retrograde elements in these economies.

Moreover, in Kalecki's formulation, an intermediate regime can sustain itself only if it is able to vindicate its rationale: the political arrangement must succeed in garnering adequate resources from within the system for expanding the capital base and accelerating the process of growth. The reality, however, has been altogether different: it is in meeting this test of surplus mobilisation that the quasi-intermediate regimes have failed in a remarkable way. There is little potential surplus awaiting to be squeezed from the urban and the rural proletariat. The major part of the resources needed for development have therefore been raised from the feudal, bourgeois and petty-bourgeois social groups. But since these are precisely the elements who provide the political support for the regimes, stiff imposts upon them — even of the soft species delineated by Kalecki,[17] mostly via taxation of 'luxuries' — become difficult. At the same time, these very groups keep clamouring for ever-increasing subsidies from the State, or for a larger margin of profit for the products and services they offer for sale in the market. The resulting confusion affects the effectiveness of the administration; in particular, it makes the task of forcing an increase in the rate of domestic savings well nigh impossible, thus eroding heavily the *raison d'etre* itself of these regimes.[18]

When Lord Byron, the poet, passed away, his long-suffering wife was said to have confessed that she could not quite determine whether he was or was not an actor. It is similarly difficult to conclude whether Kalecki himself believed or did not believe in the efficacy of intermediate regimes: he describes the characteristics which feature such regimes, but his attitude toward them is shrouded by a particular reticence.

The analytical frame, however, remains. If one were to consider

Kalecki's later model of intermediate regimes in conjunction with his theory of income distribution in capitalist society, one certainly can discover a continuum of thought. Class issues dominate his theory of distribution of national income in a capitalist State. And even in terms of Kalecki's own postulates, class issues come to the fore in an intermediate regime too; those who come to power in such a regime are interested in furthering their own economic prospects by exploiting the proleteriat classes. It is because the latter are organisationally weak that the regime may prosper in the short period, but its long-range stability depends exclusively upon its ability to speed up the rate of growth. If it fails in the task, class tensions can only increase over time. With capital formation lagging behind, national output would tend to stagnate, and how this more or less static output is distributed between the proletariat and the lower-middle class on the one hand and the ruling feudal and bourgeois groups on the other increasingly emerges as the major social issue. The message implicit in Kalecki's analysis would thus seem to be that, in all societies, income distribution is a determinant of movements in the relative prices — the relative prices of industrial goods and labour, of farm products and labour, and of industrial and farm products — and monopoly and monopsony powers determine these relative prices. We thus return to the theme of terms of trade.

NOTES

1 R. Nurkse, *Problems of Capital Formation in Under-Developed Countries,* Blackwell, 1953.
2 Kalecki himself had recognised this affinity between Rosa Luxemburg's and his own theories. See his Foreword to *Studies in the Theory of Business Cycles,* Basil Blackwell, 1966, p. 1. The fact that both of them hailed from the same part of central Europe may be purely coincidental; but it is an interesting point to note in passing.
3 'The Distribution of the National Income', *Essays in the Theory of Economic Fluctuations,* George Allen and Unwin, 1939, pp. 13-41; later reprinted in *Theory of Economic Dynamics,* George Allen and Unwin, 1954, pp. 28-44, and *Selected Essays on the Dynamics of the Capitalist Economy,* Cambridge University Press, 1971, pp. 62-77.
4 This conclusion of Kalecki's has been subject to fairly wide criticism. For an alternative formulation, see Ashok Mitra, *The Share of Wages in National Income,* The Hague, 1954. Once the interrelation between commodity and factor prices is taken into account, Kalecki's postulates may not necessarily hold good. '... The link between a rise in the price-level of basic raw materials and a fall in the labour share does not seem to be as automatic as Kalecki seems to believe ... if "all prices" are held to be susceptible to a variation in the price of raw materials, it is certainly unreasonable to make an alternative assumption with regard to the reaction of the wage-rate, which is also a price-schedule included within the

structure of an economy. Indeed, the complex interrelationship which exists between raw material price, commodity price and the wage rate is incapable of being handled through Kalecki's mechanistic model . . . . . The static basis of Kalecki's model is further illustrated when the price of basic raw materials is assumed to move in the background of a rigid degree of monopoly. In macro-economic analysis, however, when we are dealing with highly sensitive market variables, it would be unrealistic and hazardous to ignore or assume away the possibility of diverse reactions on the part of each and any of the variables once a disturbance is started somewhere'. Ashok Mitra, op. cit., p. 29.

5   In his theory of income distribution, agriculture is by implication an exogenous factor; Kalecki has therefore no occasion to refer directly to the issue of the share of farm labour in agricultural income; there is, however, a stray sentence suggesting that this share depends on the ratio of farm prices to unit wage costs: 'In agriculture and mining the products are raw materials and the relative share of wages in the value added depends mainly on the ratio of prices of the raw materials produced to their unit wage costs'. M. Kalecki, *Theory of Economic Dynamics, op. cit.,* p. 30.

6   Both of Kalecki's major explanatory variables — the degree of monopoly power and the price level of basic raw materials — are of course derivable from political categories and his famous paper on 'Political Aspects of Full Employment', *Selected Essays on the Dynamics of the Capitalist Economy, op. cit.,* pp. 138-45, discusses at length the extra-economic impulses affecting a capitalist economy. The point here is only to note the absence of any explicit reference to political elements in his formulation of the theory of income distribution.

7   'Social and Economic Aspects of "Intermediate Regimes" ', *Selected Essays on the Economic Growth of the Socialist and the Mixed Economy,* Cambridge, pp. 162-69.

8   Compare, for example, the following passage: '. . . the *extra-parliamentary mass of the bourgeoisie,* . . . by its servility towards the President, by its vilification of parliament, by its brutal maltreatment of its own press, invited Bonaparte to suppress and annihilate its speaking and writing section, its politicians and its *literati,* its platform and its press, in order that it might then be able to pursue its private affairs with full confidence in the protection of a strong and unrestricted government. It declared unequivocally that it longed to get rid of its own political rule in order to get rid of the troubles and dangers of ruling.' *The Eighteenth Brumaire of Louis Bonaparte, Selected Works of K. Marx and F. Engels,* Volume I, Moscow, 1955, pp. 320-1.

9   What Kalecki presumably has in mind must be an inadequacy of both capital funds and an appropriate technological base among the local bourgeoisie.

10 There is a developing trend in these economies for the big peasants to combine the functions of lending, trading and cultivation. See Amit Bhaduri, "Towards a Theory of Pre-capitalistic Exchange", *Economic Theory and Planning,* edited by Ashok Mitra, Oxford, 1974, pp. 134-40.

11 M. Kalecki, *op. cit.,* p. 164.

12 One can trace in this argument an echo of N. Bukharin's prognostication concerning the likely behaviour of the kulaks once State and co-operative ventures spread in the Soviet countryside. See Chapter IV.

13 'Potentially, at least, the urban and rural paupers are antagonistic towards the ruling class since they do not benefit from the change of social systems such as described above, and profit relatively little from economic development. The land reform is conducted in such a way that a major share of the land available goes to the rich and medium-rich peasants while the small land-holders and the rural proletariat receive only very little land. Insufficient effort is made to free the poor peasantry from the clutches of money-lenders and merchants and to raise

the wages of farm labourers. The resulting agrarian situation is one of the factors limiting agricultural output within the general economic development, as under the prevailing agrarian relations the small farms are unable to expand their production. The same is true of larger farms cultivated by tenants. The lagging of agriculture behind general economic growth leads to an inadequate supply of foodstuffs and an increase in their prices, which is again to the disadvantage of the "stepsons" of the system. Even if the aggregate real income of those strata do not decline as a result of the increase in employment, they do not show any appreciable growth'. M. Kalecki, *op. cit.,* pp. 165-6.

14 See in particular Utsa Patnaik, 'Development of Capitalism in Agriculture'. *Social Scientist,* September and October, 1972 and Ashok Rudra, 'In Search of the Capitalist Farmer', *Economic and Political Weekly,* Vol. V., No. 26.

15 The latter specifically because of their ability to influence the small agriculturists and landless farm workers.

16 The compulsions of international *realpolitik* must also have been a major contributory factor towards such assistance.

17 M. Kalecki, 'Problems of Financing Economic Development in a Mixed Economy', *Induction, Growth and Trade : Essays in Honour of Sir Roy Harrod,* Oxford, 1970.

18 For a discussion of this point, see K.N. Raj, 'The Politics and Economics of "Intermediate regimes" ', *Economic and Political Weekly,* 7 July 1973, and Ashok Mitra, 'Inflation and Democracy', *Capital,* Annual Number, 1973.

CHAPTER 6

Immiserisation and Terms of Trade:
A Neo-classical Digression

I

The co-ordinates which define Kalecki's world have a strong classical genesis. Class forces inform his formal structure: the degree of monopoly essentially reflects the reality of relative class strength, prices of basic raw materials too are determined by the alignment of classes, the character of the intermediate regime is shaped by its class constituents, whether an underdeveloped nation will grow rapidly or not depends upon the magnitude of the surplus her ruling classes are able to generate, and this again is a function of the specificity of class alliances. The Ricardo-Marx tradition could not be more strongly entrenched.

This is a milieu way apart from neo-classical economics, which reaches its apotheosis in marginal analysis. The message the latter seeks to transmit is loud and clear: the exploration of economic issues in terms of aggregative categories is neither necessary nor helpful; each economic phenomenon is explainable in terms of marginal principles; one must not therefore get exercised over the theme of class distinctions, which are bound to disappear under a regime of free entry and perfect mobility; class conflicts are economic aberrations.[1] This is debasement of the classical tradition, but succeeding generations of neo-classical economists, presumably taking seriously their role as defenders of the existing order, were observed to play down the possibility of conflicts between classes and the implications of such conflicts for accumulation and growth.

However, as realities of the world kept intruding, even neo-classical analysis was forced to attempt to escape, every now and then, from its own assumptions. The crisis of the world depression, for example, led to a questioning of the nature of economic structures; macro-economics was refurbished, and attained a certain respectability over the years. There were increasingly more frequent references to short-period rigidities which allegedly impair the immaculate working of the market mechanism.

In the circumstances, this was almost inevitable. If neo-classical economics wanted to stay in business, it had to take cognisance of such aggregative categories as oligopolies, trusts and trade unions; tools of micro-analysis were thus pressed into service for explaining both macro-economic phenomena and supposedly short-term anomalies in market behaviour. There was a methodological incongruity here, which in turn has led to a number of other oddities.

One such oddity has a direct relevance to the debate over terms of trade. Neo-classical trade theory lays great stress on an automatic mechanism for the realisation of the gains from trade once untramelled play is given to comparative advantages; the doctrine also implies that economic expansion, propelled by growth in trade, cannot but be wholly beneficial to the developing economies: all that needs to be done is to ensure that prices of the traded goods reflect the appropriate relative factor scarcities. Since tariffs supposedly interfere with prices and artificially affect the terms of trade, a large corpus of literature has sprung into existence over the years which analyses, more or less from the neo-classical standpoint, the relationship between tariffs, external terms of trade, economic growth and the distribution of domestic product. The major thrust in these studies is on enquiring how the endogenous factors which contribute to economic expansion are stimulated or retarded by the movement in the prices of the products of an economy relative to the international price level. While the urge to trace the effect of tariffs on growth, via their effects on terms of trade, has provided the original impulse for these investigations, the focus has soon shifted. The issue of tariffs has tended to slide into the background, and in many instances the enquiry has widened into an attempt to explore the relationship between external terms of trade and internal growth and distribution.[2] The neo-classical assumptions have been retained, but the neo-classical *quaesitum* has been somewhat altered.

Once the issue of tariffs is pushed off the centre, the problem re-emerges in a slightly different form. If, as a consequence of expansion in output and trade, the price level of the commodities which a country produces, and offers for sale to the rest of the world, is influenced in a particular manner, this would naturally have an impact on the relative movement of domestic and international price levels — that is, on the terms of trade — and thus on the level of real income accruing to the country. For instance, if, as a consequence of unbridled growth, the output of traditional exports increases in a manner such that their unit price declines steeply, the rationale of growth would itself come under scrutiny. This cannot by any stretch be a comfortable conclusion to arrive at for practitioners of neo-classical analysis, but it has still emerged as a major by-product of studies concerning possible barriers to trade. To the so-called 'structuralist' school amongst Latin American economists in particular, the problem is germane to the conditions obtaining in their countries. The adverse consequences of shifts in terms of trade on the process of domestic growth have been at the root of many of the outstanding political issues between the United States of America and a number of countries in Latin America. Structures and institutions are anathema to neo-classical logic: yet, by a quirk of circumstance, in this instance the neo-classicals, it would seem, are hoist with their own petard.

From here, it is only a short step forward to the recognition that movements in the internal terms of trade — in other words, in the relative movements as between the prices of the products of the different sectors of an economy — should have an equal significance for growth. As with international price movements, shifts in the price level of the products of one sector of the economy in relation to that of another sector are also bound to affect the pattern and rate of expansion of either sector, and therefore overall domestic growth. Such terms of trade, after all, determine, to some extent or other, the structure of income distribution between the sectors, which has obvious implications for national savings and capital formation.[3] At the same time, the rate and pattern of sector-wise growth should in turn influence the inter-sectoral terms of trade, too, thereby establishing a two-way relationship between domestic terms of trade and economic development. Thus, even on the basis of neo-classical premises, it appears impossible to hide the reality either of inter-sector terms of trade affecting growth or of these terms of trade being affected as much by structures and institutions as by factor endowments.

II

This opens up an area of analytical possibilities. In a note[4] on the problem of terms of trade and growth, Jagdish N. Bhagwati — basing himself entirely on neo-classical assumptions — spells out a set of conditions under which an economy could, in the course of economic growth, arrive at a position where it finds itself poorer in real terms compared to where it was at the beginning of the development process. The possibilities of immiserising growth, according to Bhagwati, are fairly strong if the following conditions obtain simultaneously:

(a)   the ratio of domestic production to imports is small; in other words, imports constitute a relatively large proportion of domestic output;

(b) the price elasticity of demand for imports is low, that is to say, domestic demand is relatively inflexible to shifts in import prices; and

(c) the price elasticity of domestic supplies too is low in the case of importables, in other words, the domestic output of the commodities in question is unlikely to rise to any large extent even if import prices were to increase appreciably.

These conditions are self-evident. It stands to reason that if the proportion of imports to domestic output is high, a rise in national income will, other things remaining the same, lead to an intensification in the country's demand for imports; under assumptions of comparative statics, a higher level of domestic income will, on the other hand, reduce the degree of relative scarcity of the country's products in the world market. The country's external bargaining position will therefore be adversely affected by economic growth; that is to say, the terms of trade will move against it.

The second condition, namely, that the country's demand for imports remains more or less invariant even when import prices rise sharply, implies that, across the bargaining counter, the rest of the world happens to be in a stronger position. What the final condition says is that there are but limited technological possibilities for import substitution; rising import prices cannot hence lead to a spurt in new domestic ventures. Where all the three conditions happen to be present together, growth — Bhagwati seems to suggest — could only connote misery for a country.[5]

For neo-classicals who swear by the infinite welfare possibilities of economic and trade expansion, this spectre of immiserising growth has turned out to be a matter of some embarrassment. The Bhagwati case, Harry G. Johnson had to rush to judgment, was 'a curiosum',[6] implying that the three underlying conditions obtain but rarely in the real world. The 'structuralist' school holds a contrary view, and certainly are able to adduce considerable empirical evidence in support of their position.

The Bhagwati conditions are, of course, admissible only if the underlying neo-classical assumptions, such as a consistent preference map for groups of consumers and its immutability over time, are taken for granted. One is under no compulsion to take them for granted. Yet it may be instructive to study the implications if these conditions are supposed to affect the relationship between inter-sector terms of trade and domestic economic growth. For appraising the consequences of a relatively high rate of expansion in the farm sector in a closed economy, the effect of this expansion on the terms of trade between agriculture and the rest of the economy will then have to be taken into account. The policy issues, too, will then become obvious. Provided it is assumed that each of the conditions of immiserising growth is present in a given situation, the principal decision-makers in agriculture — feudal landlords, rich farmers, or whoever they may be — faced by the prospect of a loss of real income, could, between themselves, reluctantly agree to cut back on their production plans.[7] And to form a judgment on the likely trend in the terms of trade between agriculture and industry at any point of time, it would be necessary to have information on: (a) the proportion of non-farm products absorbed by the farm sector; (b) the scope of reducing the farm demand for industrial products in case of a rise in their prices, and (c) the technological possibilities of substituting non-farm products, again in case their prices rise, by products originating within the farm sector itself. Provided it could be shown that, as a result of farm growth, the Bhagwati conditions begin to manifest themselves in an economy, the neo-classical message would be that the dominant groups in agriculture would then prefer to place a moratorium on further expansion.

The point can be pursued by considering the instance of Indian agriculture. The demand for non-farm products emanating from the Indian farm sector is currently not altogether insignificant. From certain data analysed for the period 1952-53 to 1964-65, it seems that, in terms of size, the rural market for non-farm products — for industrial inputs, consumer articles as well as capital goods — was nearly twice as large as the urban market;[8] the position may not have altered in any substantial manner since then. Besides, the demand for industrial products on the part of the non-subsistence segments of agriculture is likely to have risen over the years as a consequence of the gradual spread of the so-called New Technology in the farm sector. The possibility of the combination of rising farm incomes and a skewed structure of income distribution contributing further to the demand for industrial goods must not be ruled out either. The first Bhagwati condition may therefore be expected to make its presence felt in the circumstances obtaining in India.

Whether a rise in the price level of non-farm products would lead to a relative tapering off in their demand on the part of the Indian agricultural community would largely hinge upon a set of behavioural issues. If, as a consequence of rising farm production and incomes, there is an increasing urge for modernising both agriculture and the conditions of living of those who subsist on agriculture, the demand for non-farm products could then be marked by a relatively high degree of price inelasticity.[9] This would then reinforce the trend towards an emerging adverse terms of trade, and accelerate the process of immiserising farm growth. However, were the pattern of agricultural organisation such that farm inputs are mostly derived from within the sector and the demand for sophisticated technology — for example, tractors and power tillers, chemical fertilisers, pesticides, insecticides, etc. — is kept to a minimum, and, further, rising levels of farm income do not lead to a rise in the demand for industrial consumer goods either, the denouement might be somewhat different. A rise in the prices of non-farm products could then lead to a reduction in the purchase of industrial products on the part of the farming community; to that extent, there could be an escape from the immiserisation trap.

It remains to consider the final aspect of the matter, namely, whether, with rising farm output, the technological possibilities for doing without industrial inputs increase or decline. Here too, a categorical answer is difficult. If the bias of the existing farm technology is towards the progressive utilisation of more sophisticated methods and there is an increasing turning back on relatively simple techniques, the demand for industrial products should then expand with rising levels of output. On the other hand, if the institutional predilection is for encouraging innovations on the basis of small-scale production and mutual self-aid programmes, with a minimum of dependence on outside purchases, the improvement in agricultural output and productivity could then well be technologically neutral in relation to the use of non-farm products: growth need not therefore bring about a worsening of the terms of trade.

These speculations can be summarised. Even within the boundaries of the Bhagwati conditions, whether agricultural progress would be immiserising or otherwise evidently depends to a large extent upon social and institutional arrangements. Under given assumptions, a pattern of growth, characterised by a skewed structure of internal income distribution and a pronounced bias toward modern technology, runs the risk of bogging down to quasi-stagnation. For beyond a point, given the institutional and technological conditions, as growth occurs, the terms of trade could begin to tilt rapidly against farm products, so much so that a steep fall in the real level of farm incomes becomes unavoidable, and acts as a damper to plans for further expansion of output. In contrast, again under given assumptions, an agriculture, based on a relatively equitable social system and a mode of technology which pays greater obeisance to the traditional modes of production, should have much less to worry over the prospects of a worsening terms of trade; it could continue to grow, unshackled by considerations of a possible erosion of real income caused by adverse shifts in inter-sector terms of exchange.[10]

If economists are expected to offer prescriptions on issues of policy, and the overriding norm they should set for themselves is to strive for a policy mix which provides an optimum combination of growth and income equalisation, it would then indeed be satisfying to discover that a modality of farm growth, which presupposes an equitable social structure and does not entirely throw out of the window traditional techniques of production, is also the one which does not contain within itself the seeds of its own destruction. Astonishingly or otherwise, this conclusion is in total consonance with, and directly follows from, the Bhagwati conditions. In contrast, if rural institutions are marked by blatant inequalities and there is a mad rush to embrace indiscriminately the newest technologies, the process of agricultural growth could — again it is implied in the Bhagwati conditions — come to a halt in no time, since, under these circumstances, an indefinite expansion of farm output is likely to tilt the terms of trade sharply against agriculture and thus turn the process of development into a futile, frustrating exercise. And, given the organic link between agriculture and the other sectors, stagnating farm output would dim the prospects of growth for the economy as a whole.

What inferences does the Bhagwati model, with all its underlying assumptions, permit one to make in case its implications are studied in the context of the industrial sector of an economy and agriculture is considered as exogenous to it?[11] Again, for a closed system, particularly in the case of a developing economy, the first condition of immiserising growth would seem to hold good for the industrial sector: the proportion of importables — in this instance, of farm products — is likely to be substantial. The second condition, namely, a relatively low price elasticity of demand for imported goods — in this instance, farm products — may not, however, always be satisfied. There can be, it is true, no obvious substitutes for foodgrains; nonetheless, industry may, under assumptions of a Cobb-Douglas kind of production function, substitute labour by other factors, and to that extent obviate the need for foodgrains for feeding industrial labour. Similarly, a rise in the price of raw materials may intensify the search for industrial substitutes, which would be akin to supplanting farm purchases by purchases from within the manufacturing sector itself. But, then, either of these two types of substitution would depend upon a minimum order of advance in industrial technology; the specific Bhagwati condition could thus still apply toward the beginning of the process of development, and hold back industrial advance. As far as the third condition, namely, the technological possibilities of, in this instance, substituting farm products by industrial goods, is concerned, there is once more no question that such possibilities increase enormously with industrial progress, which is generally characterised by a widening as well as a deepening of the technological base. Since the frontiers of technological knowledge expand all the while with industrial growth, new processes, which facilitate the progressive substitution of primary products by products of industry itself, are likely to make their appearance at an increasing rate. Even so, here again, much could hinge upon the ability of the industrial sector to attain a certain 'threshold' of progress. Where this eludes it, as in agriculture, the spectre of stagnation — the neo-classical assumptions suggest — would stalk across the industrial sector too.

III

This digression has, it is hoped, served one specific objective. Its purpose has been to show that, even under remote neo-classical assumptions, economic growth cannot escape being heavily influenced by the social and institutional infra-structure; the latter casts its shadow on the inter-sectoral terms of trade, and movements in the latter affect the real level of output and the distribution of income. For those holding the neo-classical faith, the conclusion that, under certain circumstances, growth could only lead to the immiserisation of specific sectors or groups must be jolting to confidence; for this anathema of a conclusion follows directly from their own postulates.

This fact not withstanding, it is obvious that the neo-classical framework is ill-suited to cope with the issues germane to terms of trade and economic growth. One of course has merely to point out its inherent absurdities such as the assumptions of the competitive mechanism, the absence of tariffs and other forms of market intervention, the existence of full employment in all sectors of the economy, unchanging preference pattern for all groups, and so on. The moment it is argued that terms of trade and, consequently, growth would to an extent be determined by the elasticities of supply and demand, the incongruity of the framework is even more starkly revealed. What gives rise to a high or a low price elasticity of demand — or of supply, what shapes the institutional structure which even otherwise affects the terms of trade, what determines and regulates the speed of accumulation in the economy as a whole or in the farm and the non-farm sectors respectively: none of these queries can be answered without bringing in the explicit factor of classes and class relations. There is, it seems, no way of disowning the classical heritage.

NOTES

1 That dyed-in-the-wool neo-classical, Lionel Robbins, went to the length of authoring a tract, *The Economic Basis of Class Conflict* (Macmillan, 1939), whose object was to establish the point that, from the economic point of view, no basis exists for class conflicts: the apparent tensions that arise are all on account of factor immobilities and specificities, which are capable of resolution at the market place: 'The objective clashes of interests which can be actually demonstrated to operate in the world of reality suggest a classification of social groups more related to the phenomenon of market and to possible limitations on industrial or international mobilities than on any which rest on a general division between the property and the property-less'. L. Robbins, *op. cit.*, p. 23.

2 See, for example, H.W. Singer, 'The Distribution of Gains Between Investing and Borrowing Countries', *American Economic Review*, May 1950, pp. 473-85; Lloyd A. Metzler, 'Tariffs, the Terms of Trade, and the Distribution of National Income', *Journal of Political Economy*, February 1949, pp. 1-29; Harry G. Johnson, 'Economic Development and International Trade', *National-okonomisk Tidsskrift*, 1959, pp. 253-72.

3 The classical prescription of economic growth postulates a transfer of surplus from the primary sector, agriculture, to other sectors. Where, as in neo-classical analysis, the role of the State, and therefore of compulsory devices such as taxation, is de-emphasised, the mechanism of such transfers becomes less obvious, particularly if prices are claimed to represent equivalent exchange which rules out the phenomenon of exploitation. That these transfers can occur through shifts in the terms of trade is now increasingly being acknowledged, however grudgingly, in neo-classical writings. Compare the following passage:

Compulsory deliveries of food under the Marx-Leninist approach clearly represent a direct tax on the farm sector on behalf of the nonfarm sector. It is not so obvious that a market-oriented family farming system also provides an extremely efficient means to such inter-sectoral taxation. The form of the tax and its method of collection are quite different than under the Marx-Leninist model, but that it exists cannot be denied ... its existence constitutes a development imperative.

Simply stated, the gain to the nonfarm sector, under the Mill-Marshallian model, takes the form of an intersectoral profit on technological progress. It represents a residual surplus accruing to the nonfarm sector on the rewards of economic development in the farm sector, over and above any equivalent sharing by the farm sector in the corresponding gains from technological progress generated in the rest of the economy. In place of the delivery of a quota of farm production to the "people's government" under the political compulsions of communism, the market-oriented, family farming system delivers to the nonfarm sector, under the compulsion of the competitive market, progressively increasing supplies of food at progressively lower costs. This is to say that, under these circumstances, the benefits of technological progress in agriculture are automatically and rapidly passed on to nonfarm processors and consumers as the cumulative impact of innovating farmers increases the total market supply of the farm commodities in question and produces a corresponding fall in the average market price. (Wyn F. Owen, 'The Double Developmental Squeeze on Agriculture', *American Economic Review*, March 1966, p. 54.)

This essentially implies that, according to neo-classical theory, with agricultural development, the terms of trade move against the farm sector 'under the compulsion of the competitive market' and thus act as a surrogate for extracting the surplus!

4   Jagdish N. Bhagwati, 'Immiserising Growth: A Geometrical Note', *Review of Economic Studies,* June 1958, pp. 201-5.

5   The conclusions here are echoed in the analysis of Linder : '. . . the per capita income gap as between u[nderdeveloped] countries and growth countries will grow faster under trade than under autarchy'. S. B. Linden, *An Essay on Trade and Transformation,* John Wiley, p. 135.

6   Harry G. Johnson, *op. cit.,* p. 260.

7   It may seem unrealistic to assume that production decisions in agriculture could be centralised in this manner; decisions affecting the size of market arrivals may certainly, however, be influenced to a considerable extent by a limited number of individuals or groups.

8   Ranjit Sau, 'Some Aspects of Inter-Sectoral Resource Flow', *Economic and Political Weekly,* Special Number, August 1974.

9   In a class-differentiated society, rising incomes are likely to be accompanied by a large-scale substitution of so-called Giffen goods.

10   This discussion immediately brings to the fore some of the merits of the agricultural system the People's Republic of China and, to some extent, Vietnam are experimenting with. The stress on traditional technology and organic fertilisers in these countries has ensured that agriculture continues to make advances without leaning too heavily on the industrial sector; frugal living standards, combined with an equitable structure of income distribution, has also prevented an inordinate rise in the demand for industrial consumer goods; systematic encouragement is also being accorded to efforts at raising the levels of local skills and local technology. In other words, in both these countries, conditions exist which forestall the danger of farm growth being vitiated by deteriorating terms of trade. (This is quite apart from the fact that developments *at the political level* have independently taken care of the problem of inter-sector terms of trade.)

11   Such a procedure of applying the conditions separately for agriculture and industry may not be considered as analytically impeccable, for neither sector exists in isolation of the other. It is still useful for drawing attention to a few asymmetries which mark the two sectors.

CHAPTER 7

A Schematics of Class Relations

I

The rest of this volume concerns itself with a construct of how class forces, operating through terms of trade, affect the prospects and modality of growth in a poor country. While the discussion will be along fairly general lines, the focus is on drawing inferences from recent developments in India. As will be seen, the analysis takes off broadly from Kalecki's formulations relating to the degree of monopoly power and the viability of an intermediate regime. Unlike in Kalecki, however, the issue of the terms of trade is explicitly brought to the fore.

The explanation of economic phenomena in terms of the operation of class forces presents one particular problem in the case of a developing country. Such a country is by definition characterised by unstable correlates; social categories are yet to crystallise; flux and change dominate the milieu. All this could make it difficult to identify a class in terms of pre-determined co-ordinates. The different sectors of the economy may be marked by disparate levels of growth, and the formation of classes may be yet inchoate. Going by one set of indicators, a crystallisation of classes could seem to have already taken place. Another set of considerations may provide an altogether different impression, and a wide divergence in attitudes and patterns of behaviour could be discerned among the presumed constituents of a particular class. To formulate economic — or, for that matter, sociological or political — hypotheses on the assumption of sharply delineated class divisions may then turn out to be a premature exercise. In any scientific analysis, the relevant categories, it could be argued, must be capable of being adequately defined before premises are formulated about their operational attributes; where an analysis is predicated on relationships between classes, if the classes themselves are not fully formed, the whole exercise may appear fragile.

The problem need not be that intractable. Under all circumstances, it is possible to draw a distinction between *class consciousness* which is fully developed and articulated and *class interest* even when the latter is not explicitly formulated. In given situations, the interests of the various classes in society can of course be clearly demarcated and poised against each other; it may thus be possible to develop clear-cut economic hypotheses on the assumption of a clash of class forces, and which tend towards clear-cut economic conclusions. But it should be equally possible to conceive of other situations where the interests of specific economic classes await a fuller formulation and articulation, for the altogether straightforward reason that class consciousness is still lagging behind. Should all economic hypothesis-building postulated on the clash of classes be held over in such circumstances? Despite a lack of maturity in the state of consciousness, could not a homogeneity of economic and social interests still bind a cross-section of individuals? After all, the dialectics of classes do not cease functioning merely because consciousness about class interests is not perfect. The consciousness itself is an aspect of maturing experience. Viewed in purely concrete terms, sections and groups find themselves in quasi-proximity on some economic and social issues and begin to come together, notwithstanding the fact that they may have significant differences on some other issues. There could be sharp divergences of attitudes in the matter of even some short-term socio-economic goals among individuals who nonetheless find themselves willing to unite in a common political battle against another group of individuals, from whom their distance is even greater. Alternatively, while such individuals may converge towards one other on account of some purely coincidental short-term interests, their long-range interests may seemingly be in conflict. Even in such cases, a harmonious class interest may yet emerge, even though the consciousness of it remains somewhat remote. This can happen provided, for instance, in the wake of the temporary alliance, a process of mutation of.interests sets in motion. The angularities and egocentricities of individual positions may then gradually tend to wear off, the realisation could begin to dawn either that the short-term contradictions were of a trivial nature or that, despite the initial disharmony in long-range goals, the common struggles and endeavours should lead to a re-ordering of interests on both sides. In this manner, through successive approximations, convergence could establish itself as the overwhelming trend, and disparate groups merge into a class.

This is certainly perilous ground. Whether an emerging — but as yet passive — unity of class interests can be a surrogate for an articulated class consciousness can be debated interminably. For analysing socio-economic developments over time, one need not, however, await a complete and uniform unfolding of certain common characteristics in specific groups or sections. To insist on such a prior condition may render impracticable any meaningful prognoses of social and economic processes in class terms. While some of the analytical categories, otherwise considered crucial, may be without well-defined empirical correlates, it should still be possible to determine, through a series of inferences, a range of behaviour which fits them.

In forming a judgment about what constitutes a class in a particular situation, it should therefore be a defensible procedure to take some liberty with the given corpus of data. In the species of polity which many developing countries illustrate, given the fact of regional variations and disparities in economic and social developments, it would be pointless to look for a uniform set of characteristics in a particular class. Even among individuals or groups supposedly belonging to the same class, significant disparities in attitudes and patterns of behaviour are only natural at any point in time. Notwithstanding the heterogeneities which hit the eye, it is the presence or otherwise of a common set of interests which ought to be considered to be of greater relevance. It should be enough if there were a convergence of the basic interests of the constituents of a class even when its actual formation is still a prospective event. This convergence of class interests may in some cases be overt, in other cases tentative and subterraneous. Where the formation of the class is not complete, elements from within the partly-formed mass — either on their own, or assisted by elements from outside — may nonetheless try to spark off a prior consciousness of interests for the yet-to-be class. Provided such a consciousness is fostered at different levels, and on a sustained basis, the actual formation of the class may turn out to be a direct function of this endeavour itself: the attempts to engender a commonness of interest among groups of people could become the precursor, so much so that even were the class not yet fully formed, the strivings towards creating this common bond might emerge as an effective surrogate for articulated class consciousness. If a particular development in the socio-historical process can be projected on the basis of an assumed confrontation between different classes, it can also be anticipated with equal felicity on the basis of the existence, in lieu of the actual class consciousness, of categories of endeavour representing the interests of the respective classes.[1]

That this has to be so is borne out by the cliche that revolutionaries precede revolutionary classes. And it is in this context that the role of the early organisers of class-based movements is acknowledged in tradition. These organisers do not necessarily belong to the class whose cause they choose to defend and expound. They may spring from alien territory, and have genealogical roots in a class which is historically hostile to the class whose interests they propound. The history of class struggles is replete with such examples of individuals who have marched across the barricade and articulated the interests of classes whose state of consciousness had till then failed to keep pace with objective reality.

In a schematics involving class relations, it need not therefore be considered fatal if the identification between conceptual categories and the corresponding operational correlates is less than perfect. This identification is a function of developing class consciousness, and hence itself a process. Particularly in the case of an economy which is marked by uneven developments, the principal economic phenomena are conditioned by a medley of class interests interacting with — or against — each other. This can present a nightmare for analysis. To understand the nature of the processes at work, it may on occasion thus be useful to separate the principal influences at work from the subsidiary ones, just as it may be useful to define a class in terms of its dominant characteristics while for the present ignoring the rest.[2] Such a procedure also makes the use of theoretical constructs somewhat more meaningful. If analytical tools are to serve any worthwhile purpose, axiomatic hypotheses must obviously give ground to scientific ones. This transition can, however, be hastened if we are able to hack through an indiscriminately large number of variables and present our formulations in terms of only a few. This would not only minimise the risk of missing the forest for the trees, but would also facilitate the construction of models of socio-economic processes which could be used to predict, within reasonable margins of error, the course of future events in response to shifts in the parameters of the determining variables.

The emphasis should therefore be on identifying the dominant elements. It is pointless to argue, for instance, that the analysis of socio-economic processes in terms of class structures will be replete with inconsistencies since the social categories described as classes are themselves marked by contradictions. This is a commonplace, and does not advance the frontiers of knowledge. To assess the nature of the contradictions and to find out whether the major contradictions cannot be distinguished from the minor ones is a task which social scientists would be ill-advised to delegate to others. For to place an equal emphasis on the roles of the major and minor protagonists of a class struggle, as well as the major and the minor contradictions vitiating a class, would be tantamount to getting lost in an analytical *cul de sac*. If it is the interpretation of social processes that is expected of a social scientist, his obligation should be to concentrate on the major forces that are at work. The minor characters and episodes in history are usually forgotten; it would be an intolerable burden if they were not.[3]

II

The relevance of this discussion should be immediately obvious. By convention, the concept of class is a bounded one: it is the presence or absence of a homogeneity of characteristics which defines it. The essence of the debate concerns whether too rigid a view needs to be taken about the incidence of these characteristics, or its intensity, among any particular category of individuals or groups of individuals before they could be described as belonging to a specific economic or social class.

For instance, in view of the uneven evolution of the Indian economy, dissimilar modes of production exist simultaneously in nearly each sector of productive activity. As the modes vary, so do the production relations among groups associated with each activity. In agriculture, for example, we come across an entire spectrum beginning with a near-pastoral system and ending with full-fledged capitalist cultivation, encompassing within these limits pre-feudalism, feudalism, semi-feudalism, and the subsequent other intermediate stages.[4] In industry, similarly, a universe, which consists of cottage output, small-scale crafts, medium-scale modes of production, assembly-line manufactures and highly automatised processes, represents an unusually broad vista of heterogeneity. Similar diversities mark the tertiary sector too. It is easy to multiply such instances. Specific technologies have developed in response to the demands of these production relationships. At each point of the technological scale, production arrangements reflect — and, in turn, have been reflected in — the mutual relations obtaining between the classes — or groups — involved in the activity of production. Capital accumulation has varying degrees of significance for the different modes of output; the extent of alienation of labour from the process of accumulation too finds its reflection in the phenomenon of production arrangements.

In these circumstances, it would be stretching the laws of dogma to express one's preference for constricted definitions for social and economic categories; the concept of a dominant reality, as suggested above, would seem to be operationally more useful. For otherwise whatever observations are made about aspects of economic or social behaviour for any class in India would run the danger of being contradicted by other observations. This would relegate socio-economic analysis into a near-impossibility.

One can illustrate the point once more with reference to conditions prevailing in Indian agriculture, where it is easy to discover literally scores of production relations co-existing next to one another. / Tenurial problems have varied in the past, and continue to vary today, from region to region and State to State. Within a State, too, because of historical factors, tenurial forms may change from district to district and area to area. Again, depending upon whether the land is relatively fertile or arid, or whether facilities for irrigation are available or not, production relations in different farming tracts have evolved in a disparate manner. Fertile lands have usually attracted a higher concentration of population, which in its train has brought about kinds of production relationship not seen elsewhere. Obviously, without recourse to the convenience of a dominant reality, generic formulations will have to be ruled out, and it would be impossible to describe the general structural attributes of Indian agriculture in terms of a common set of postulates. This is a situation which a social scientist will find difficult to accept; he would prefer to sacrifice the details in order to be able to construct certain general hypotheses. Such hypotheses may not altogether faithfully subsume the individual nuances of each developing situation; still, the sacrifice involved need not be considered incalculable. To put it even more explicitly, while it is always possible to formulate a whole range of premises, which would compete among themselves for claiming the distinction of providing the most accurate description of the production relations obtaining in Indian agriculture, not much is likely to be lost if we decide to opt for just one, as long as it does not violate the principal realities of the situation. If, for instance, the farming community in the country is divided into two broad strata, namely, small peasants, inclusive of landless labour, on the one hand and surplus-raising farmers on the other, while several specific aspects of the current hierarchical arrangements would no doubt be blurred, no great harm is likely to be done in so far as the essence of the dominant reality is concerned. It is ultimately a question of integrating the frame of analysis with the objective of analysis. A bland division of agriculture between subsistence and non-subsistence farming may appear somewhat disrespectful of other, subsidiary realities, but — as will be shown — for tracing the relationship between terms of trade, agricultural growth and accumulation and growth elsewhere in the economy, this schematics of class forces may indeed prove adequate.

In the subsequent parts of this book, we shall accordingly proceed with this two-way division of the agricultural community. Small farmers, in our context, are those who either have no land and therefore work for others, or lease land from others, or, if they own some land, the realisation from the latter is barely able to meet the expenses of production and the needs of subsistence. Such subsistence (or below-subsistence) operations may not be confined to the cultivation of food crops alone. A small farmer, in possession of some land, can raise cash crops as well, but the total realisation may still be such that, in the overall, he is left with no surplus above his cost of production and expenses of living: although he may be coming to the market to dispose of his non-food output, in effect he is no different from a subsistence farmer specialising in foodgrains, who too may on occasion come to the market but only to exchange a portion of his food crop against textiles and other non-food necessities. In either case, the farmer comes into contact with the market, but remains a subsistence cultivator.[5]

Data vary from State to State and region to region, but landless workers and subsistence farmers would together perhaps constitute as much as four-fifths of the Indian farming community. The rest constitutes the class of surplus farmers; in this case, the producers not only come to the market, but their gross realisation provides scope for savings net of deductions for the cost of production and the needs of subsistence. Such farmers belong to the categories usually described as rich and middle peasants.

In any dichotomy,[6] the border-line cases present a problem. A farmer producing for the market and earning a surplus at a particular point of time may lapse into subsistence in a subsequent period; similarly a subsistence farmer can, following an increase in the productivity of the land he owns or has leased in, find himself in the role of a surplus producer; periodic reversals of positions can also take place. None of these, however, detract from the central reality, namely, that two broad sets of characteristics inhere respectively in the two economic categories into which we have classified the Indian farming community.

A similar two-way classification should be possible for the categories outside agriculture. Again, in view of the heterogenous growth in non-farm activities, a large number of production relations are observable. To try to place these different relations within the straightjacket of a dichotomy of classes is a difficult exercise. It is nonetheless useful to reiterate the principle of dominant reality and principal contradiction, and to describe the community outside agriculture as belonging to two broad classes, namely, the bourgeoisie — including their mercantile components — and the working class, including the fixed-income earning professional groups. There are of course countless instances of internal contradiction in the economic and social behaviour of groups brought under the umbrella of either of these categories. The industrial and mercantile bourgeoisie may, and do, often work at cross purposes. The industrial bourgeoisie in one part of the country may not always see eye-to-eye with their counterparts in some other part or parts. Similarly, the working class and fixed income groups may be — and indeed often are — riven by internal dissensions of varying degrees of intensity: these can also sometimes assume the form of regional, linguistic, or craft animosities. Even so, to attempt to develop separate analytical constructs for explaining the norms of economic and social behaviour of each such group may be counter-productive at this stage, particularly since many of these groups are still groping for coherence, and class consciousness of the kind discussed above is in most cases only imperfectly developed. It is possible that in some cases a pattern of class behaviour has begun to emerge, but to concentrate excessively upon such instances could impair an objective analysis of the broader and more basic historical developments. Once a model is there which explains more or less satisfactorily the principal movements taking place on the base of an economy, individual departures from it can be taken care of and separately examined. On the other hand, an attempt to develop a model of socio-economic processes purely on the basis of a set of random and stochastic influences, while it could contribute to satisfying the ego of skill-fetishists, may be of little assistance towards interpreting either the sweep of history or contemporary economic and social reality. To repeat, in what follows, we shall, accordingly, express the class forces operating in the Indian economy in terms of two simple inter-acting production relationships, one for the farm sector and the other for the universe outside agriculture. In the farm sector, the two classes exhausting the genus are the surplus-raising rich (and middle) peasants and the small and landless ones. Outside agriculture, the two major economic categories are the bourgeoisie and the working class. For those who may view this taxonomy as being marked by a certain arbitrariness, one can do worse than invite their attention to Mao Tse-Tung's comment on the content of principal contradiction: '. . . in capitalist society, the two forces in contradiction, the proletariat and the bourgeoisie, form the principal contradiction. The other contradictions, such as those between the remnant feudal class and the bourgeoisie, between the proletariat and the peasant petty bourgeoisie, between the non-monopoly capitalists and the monopoly capitalists, between bourgeois democracy and bourgeois fascism, among the capitalist countries and between imperialism and the colonies, are all determined or influenced by this principal contradiction'.[7]

III

Once we admit the role of class forces in regulating the growth and distribution of national and sector incomes, a transmutation takes place in economic realities and we enter a world of tension. In this world, three sets of terms of trade are constantly engaged in trying to affect the pattern of income distribution, and, therefore, the process of accumulation and growth: the terms of trade between agriculture and industry, between the rich peasantry on the one hand and small peasants and farm workers on the other and, finally, between the industrial bourgeoisie and industrial labour. As between the affluent farmers and the poorer peasantry, the terms of trade find concrete expression through the fixation of rent and farm wages, the conditions of tenancy and share-cropping, as well as the conditions of usury, and reflect the degree of monopoly power enjoyed by the rich peasantry; similarly, the terms of trade between the bourgeois capitalists and the industrial working class are reflected in the movement of industrial wages and thus in turn reflect the degree of monopsony power commanded by the bourgeoisie at any point.[8]

How the national income is distributed between the four broad economic classes in our universe, namely, the surplus-raising farmers, the industrial bourgeoisie, industrial labour and the poor peasantry, is largely the consequence of how the three terms of trade referred to above move over time. A series of struggles continuously engages the classes: each class strives to tilt the terms of trade *vis-à-vis* the other classes in its own favour; in the process, the economy is rendered into a battleground; skirmishes, big and small, occur all the while; the outcome of each skirmish is reflected in shifts in terms of trade; these shifts in turn determine the pattern of shift in the distribution of national income. A strong element of autocorrelation inevitably affects the process. The distribution of income at any given moment influences the distribution of assets and, as we have seen, the structure of asset distribution in its turn heavily influences relative prices and thus the distribution of income in the subsequent period. Class interests reveal themselves, overtly or otherwise, in the marketplace, the terms of trade become the instrumentality for articulating these class interests, and the outcome of the tussle over terms of trade signals changes in relative economic positions. On the assumption of a two-sector economy, other things remaining the same, it is these movements in the terms of trade which determine the distribution of aggregate national income between agriculture and industry. In addition, they determine the distribution of farm income between landless labourers and small farmers on the one hand and the rural oligarchs on the other. Between them they also allocate in the first instance the distribution of aggregate industrial income between the bourgeoisie and the working class.[9]

In these unceasing rounds of warfare and continuous adjustments of the terms of trade in response to oscillations in the relative bargaining power of the different classes, the State could hardly remain passive. Our earlier discussion, spanning from the views of classical economists to Michal Kalecki's observations on the attributes of intermediate regimes, has illuminated one important historical truth, namely, that the State is hardly a neutral entity. It reflects the concentration of power and authority. This authority can be directly deployed for affecting the terms of trade between classes, and thus for re-ordering the structure of relative prices. The objective can be achieved through an authoritarian setting of prices, but it can also in part be accomplished through the intermediary of other instruments, such as monetary and fiscal measures, policy on trade and tariffs, investment decisions, licensing and controls, etc. Those who have come to power represent certain class interests.[10] They have seized power not for its own sake; the seizure of power has a purpose, which is to affect the structure of asset and income distribution in society along particular directions. The processes of an economy can thus scarcely be viewed as analogous to the proceedings of a soccer match, nor can the State be promoted to the position of a referee, who is a detached, non-involved entity exclusively interested in ensuring that the partisans on either side conform to the rules of the game. In a class war, no holds are barred, there are no classical 'rules of the game', and therefore no scope for a 'neutral' referee shuffling across the field. It is, on the other hand, both the obligation as well as the intent of those in authority, that is, those who control the apparatus of the State, to ensure that such authority is exercised in favour of that class, or those classes, from whom they draw support. Other things remaining the same, therefore, it is the objective of State policy to influence continuously the terms of trade in the interests of the favoured classes and against the interests of those who are antagonistic towards them.

There are, of course, constraints at work. Even were a particular class in total control of the State apparatus, objective circumstances might not permit it to pursue an out-and-out discriminatory terms of trade policy favouring its own products; to do so could lead to a breach in a number of limiting conditions. As discussed earlier, in the Preobrazhensky-Luxemburg type of model, such limits could be reached if, for instance, the terms of trade are forced against agriculture to an extent where the value received for a standard unit of farm output does not cover the socially necessary labour for its production. Similarly, whether in agriculture or in industry, the

UNIVERSITY COLLEGE LIBRARY SWANSEA

terms of trade cannot obviously be pushed against labour beyond the point where wages fall below the minimum needed for survival.

A number of political restraints too are likely to condition the battle of the terms of trade taking place on the base of a class-ridden economy. Although they vary from polity to polity, these constraints in fact come close to defining the rules of the game. For example, in our four-class model, it may not be prudent for any single class — whether the rural oligarchy, the industrial bourgeoisie, the poor peasants or the urban working class — to develop antagonistic relationships with each of the other three classes at the same time. The strategy for winning the war of terms of trade may then involve tactics of isolating this or that class in the short run, and allying with this or that other class.

The point can be elaborated with reference to the conditions currently obtaining in India. India is formally a parliamentary democracy; it has a federal constitution where legislative and executive authority is distributed between the Union government and the federating States. At the Centre and the States, elections are periodically organised on the basis of adult suffrage; those who succeed in the elections come to political authority in the respective spheres. These circumstances immediately suggest several possibilities in regard to class alliances for waging the battle over terms of trade.

A considerable debate has ensued over the identification of the leading economic class in the country; the criterion for this identification is usually the degree of influence exerted by a class on the political processes both at the Centre and in the States.[11] However, in the present situation it would obviously be difficult for a single economic class to exercise exclusive political authority over the entire country. Given the dominance of rural voters in the total electorate and the preponderance of illiterate, economically weak and poorly organised elements among the former, other things remaining the same, that class which succeeds in enforcing the loyalty of this part of the rural electorate is likely to exercise a strong influence upon the process of government. The rural oligarchy currently would seem to occupy this position. But for historical reasons, it may not have an adequate base of expertise, skills and technology within its fold to conduct the affairs of administration, including external relations and the management of the army and law and order. It may therefore decide to seek alliances elsewhere in society.

It is the contention in the rest of this work that political authority as it is at present exercised in India reflects a duopolistic arrangement between the rural oligarchy and the industrial bourgeoisie. The bourgeoisie control the levers of power in the industrial sector and exercise a dominance over the organised working class. It too, however, cannot survive without support from outside. An alliance of convenience is thus struck with the rural oligarchy. Given the lack of political and economic organisation among agricultural workers and the poorer peasants, and their heavy economic dependence on the rural oligarchs, the latter are in a position to keep under their complete sway major sections of the electorate in the countryside. By entering into a coalition with them, the urban bourgeoisie ensure a parliamentary majority for themselves. Such a coalition is also facilitated by the fact that, while their economic interests are not necessarily in complete harmony and contradictions do abound, the bourgeoisie themselves have sprung from rural feudal and quasi-feudal elements, and there is a lingering trace of what sociologists describe as 'kinship' relations.

This alliance of the industrial bourgeoisie and the peasant oligarchy can survive only on the basis of mutual trade-offs. The sharing of political power assists the planning and execution of these trade-offs. To either class, the machinery of the government appears as a vast spoils system: through operating via the terms of trade and through its activities of buying and selling, taxation and subsidies, lending and borrowing, the administration can heavily influence the distribution of income in society. The bourgeoisie depend on the rural oligarchy not just for the supply of food and raw materials but, much more importantly, for the supply of votes, they also recognise that certain payments are due to the affluent farmers in lieu of the crucial service they render; the apparatus of State power is used to organise these.

The mutual trade-offs take various forms, but the instrumentality of terms of trade policy cannot but fill a large part of the picture. The rules of the game which the industrial bourgeoisie and the rural oligarchy have established in relation to terms of trade for furthering their coalition, this book maintains, is corrosive of growth, apart from being wholly detrimental to the interests of the working classes both in the countryside and in urban areas. In the chapters that follow, we propose to review at some length developments which have affected both agriculture and industry as a consequence of State power being exercised exclusively in the interests of the coalition of classes which is in power, as well as their impact on capital formation and general economic growth.

NOTES

1   See Georg Lukacs, *History and Class Consciousness,* Merlin Press, pp. 46-81, and E. J. Hobsbawm, 'Class Consciousness in History', *Aspects of History and*

Class Consciousness, edited by Istvan Meszaros, Routledge and Kegan Paul, pp. 5-21.

2 Mao Tse-Tung's dictum about principal and secondary contradictions has an echo here: '. . . there is no doubt at all that at every stage in the development of a process, there is only one principal contradiction which plays the leading role. Hence, if in any process there are a number of contradictions, one of them must be the principal contradiction playing the leading and decisive role, while the rest occupy a secondary and subordinate position. Therefore, in studying any complex process in which there are two or more contradictions, we must devote every effort to finding the principal contradiction. Once this principal contradiction is grasped, all problems can be readily solved. . . There are thousands of scholars and men of action who do not understand it, and the result is that, lost in a fog, they are unable to get to the heart of a problem and naturally cannot find a way to resolve its contradictions'. Mao Tse-Tung, *Four Essays on Philosophy,* Peking 1966, pp. 53-4.

3 Again, it may be worthwhile to refer to a passage from Mao Tse-Tung: 'In studying the particularity of contradictions, unless we examine these two facets — the principal and non-principal contradictions in a process, and the principal and the non-principal aspects of a contradiction — that is, unless we examine the distinctive character of these two facets of contradiction, we shall get dragged down in abstractions, be unable to understand contradiction concretely and consequently be unable to find the correct method of resolving it. The distinctive character or particularity of these two facets of contradiction represents the unevenness of the forces that are in contradiction. Nothing in this world develops absolutely evenly; we must oppose the theory of even development or the theory of equilibrium. Moreover, it is these concrete features of a contradiction and the changes in the principal and non-principal aspects of a contradiction in the course of its development that manifest the force of the new superseding the old. The study of the various states of unevenness in contradictions, of the principal and non-principal contradictions and of the principal aspects of a contradiction constitutes an essential method . . .' *op. cit.,* p. 59.

4 There is a fairly extensive literature which deals with production relationships in Indian agriculture. See, in particular, Utsa Patnaik, 'Capitalist Development in Agriculture', *Economic and Political Weekly,* 23 September 1971; Paresh Chattopadhyay, 'On the Question of the Mode of Production in Agriculture: A Preliminary Note', *Economic and Political Weekly,* 25 March 1972; Utsa Patnaik, 'On the Mode of Production in Indian Agriculture: A Reply', *Economic and Political Weekly,* 30 September 1972; and also Utsa Patnaik, 'Development of Capitalism in Agriculture', *Social Scientist,* Numbers 2 and 3, 1972.

5 See Ashok Mitra, 'The Concept of Subsistence', *Economic Weekly,* 25 May 1957, pp. 659-61.

6 The taxonomy adopted may give the impression that the two agrarian classes between themselves form an all-exhaustive classification. At any given moment, this may not of course be true. The classes we have picked up for analysis — namely, the small farmers and landless labourers on the one hand and surplus-raising farmers on the other — need not between them always exhaust the total universe, they are merely the leading actors in the drama we are interested in; the other 'intermediate' classes, for reasons made obvious in the text, could be expected eventually to line up behind the two main rural classes.

7 Mao Tse-Tung, *op. cit.,* p. 51.

8 The terms of trade between agriculture and industry is closest to the Kalecki variable movements in the 'price of basic raw materials', while the terms of trade

between the bourgeoisie and the working class would be a rough surrogate of what he calls the degree of monopoly.

9   As discussed earlier, within the rural oligarchy or the small farmers or the industrial working class, it is indeed possible to discover inner contradictions that are either antagonistic or non-antagonistic. But these specificities do not affect the nature of the broad economic realities as described here.

10   See Chapter I for a discussion on this point.

11   See, for instance, S. Naqvi, 'Class Character of State Power in India', *Social Scientist*, August 1973, pp. 83-90.

CHAPTER 8

Class Bias in Indian Farm Price Policy

I

This chapter and the ones that follow take off from the preceding one. They are intended to provide, from the annals of recent Indian economic history, certain empirical foundations for the hypothesis on terms of trade and class relations suggested in Chapter 7. It is, however, necessary to enter a few caveats right at the outset. The quarter of a century since Indian independence can scarcely be considered as having been marked by homogeneous economic developments. Notwithstanding structural changes in many directions, uneven rates of growth between regions and sectors have been the dominant phenomenon, and diverse impulses have been at work. Official policy — even in specific economic matters — has itself not followed a uniform pattern. Shifts in policy have occurred in response to exogenous as well as endogenous developments, or even as the composition of the Union government has slightly altered, or the relationship between it and the individual State governments has undergone mutations. The significance of the so-called 'learning process' is not to be discounted either. Even were a particular policy accepted in principle by the authorities, the *modus operandi* of translating the policy into practice might not be perfect at any moment. Often, the ramifications of a policy too are appreciated only with a time-lag; a series of trials and errors could mark the operational phase. A distinction thus needs to be drawn between *consciousness of class interests* and *awareness of the most efficient mechanism for furthering those interests.*

The key problem is to identify the principal class interests on a given social base, and has two separate facets. The first concerns the task of isolating the influences which reinforce the major contradictions in society and push them towards a situation of nodality; the second is related to the sheer operational aspects. The historicity of circumstances may appear to be altogether clear-cut if one were discussing the question of class relations at a level of abstraction; confusions and doubts may, however, persist when it is a question of dealing with facts. The heterogeneities afflicting a developing society are well known. In the Indian case, these could be linked to, for example, linguistic fissures, regional variations, disparate levels of education and literacy, the juxtaposition of dissimilar production relations within a given milieu, and so on. The existence of second- and subsequent-order contradictions underlying the principal ones is inevitable in the circumstances.

The anomalies which ensue have their impact on policy-making at all levels, including at the level of the determination of farm price policy — the theme of discussion in the present chapter. If class alignments had attained an approximate order of uniformity over the entire country, one could have expected prosperous agricultural producers in the different parts to combine in order to try to bring about a common set of policies affecting the terms of trade between different farm products and between the products of agriculture as a whole and those of the other sectors of the economy. This has not come about, and for fairly cogent reasons. The most obvious one is locational imperfection, that is, the geographical distance separating farm groups in far-flung parts of the country. Agro-climatic conditions have also played their part, besides varying pressures of population and consequential regional differences in the average size of holdings. Even the definition of big or middle-sized farmers varies from region to region, depending as it often does upon the productivity of holdings in the different areas. The pattern of growth of irrigated area has also to be considered. In the so-called *kharif* belt, for instance, in such States as Gujarat, Karnataka, Madhya Pradesh and Maharashtra the net area under irrigation is barely 10 per cent of the net sown area: in contrast, irrigation covers close to two-thirds of the net sown acreage in the traditional *rabi* States:[1] views and attitudes of groups of farmers towards price policy cannot but be substantially conditioned by the extent of availability of irrigation, since it is the latter which in many instances determines whether a farmer has begun to produce for the market, and has thus developed a stake in market prices.

For the present, the impact of the operation of class forces is therefore unlikely to be either uniform or predictable in different parts of the country. The nature of the principal contradictions will vary from region to region, from tract to tract, and, in a few cases, from cropping pattern to cropping pattern. Generalisations will be full of pitfalls. One or two micro-studies may support conclusions which follow from a model based more or less exclusively on the dialectics of the principal contradictions; other micro-studies may have a different message to transmit. Confronted with such a situation, one may be tempted to have recourse to more elaborate models. Even that could be counter-productive.[2] A model which pretends to take into account each and every minor element influencing the operation of class forces could indeed turn out to be unmanageable: given the complexities which Indian society currently mirrors, the variables that might need to be taken into account could be legion, and their influences over the short run indeterminable. In many instances, the basic data too could be lacking.

In this chapter, the assumptions have accordingly been stripped to the barest essentials. They deal with only those factors which are considered to be the principal constituents of the drama of class relations in the Indian situation. Because of its deliberate neglect of a number of the subsidiary aspects, the drama as presented here might seem somewhat smaller than life, but to compensate for that, there has been — or so it is hoped — a gain in clarity.

II

A remarkable shift has taken place in the course of the past decade in the terms of trade between agriculture and industry in India. With 1961-62 = 100 in each case, in 1973-74, the official price index of food articles was 363.6, of foodgrains, 400.7, and of industrial raw materials, 327.4; for manufactures as a group, the price index was 254.5, for machinery and transport equipment, 254.5, and for finished products, 238.6.[3] The weighted terms of trade between agriculture and industry have over the period thus moved by close to 50 per cent in favour of the former. This shift in the terms of trade towards the direction of agriculture reflects the extent of decline in the relative unit value of non-farm output and, correspondingly, the rise in the relative unit value of farm products.[4]

The movement in the terms of trade, we may maintain, does not represent any particular bias in policy, but is the consequence of divergent rates of growth in the two sectors. Is this hypothesis borne out by facts? During the quinquennium 1965-66 to 1970-71, for example, the index of farm production (base: triennium ending 1961-62 = 100) rose by roughly 25 per cent;[5] the rise in the index of industrial output (base 1960 = 100) over these years was actually less, namely, around 20 per cent:[6] even so, the terms of trade moved in favour not of industry, but of agriculture, and to the extent of around 25 per cent. For the entire period from the early 1960s till 1974-75, the rate of growth in the organised industrial sector turns out to be greater than in agriculture since, in more recent years, there has been a perceptible falling off in the rate of increase in farm output. But, as will be argued below, this development itself can be causally related — at least in part — to the shift in terms of trade: differential price incentives, fiscal and monetary policies, and the political-institutional setting in general have significantly affected the elasticity of expectations in both sectors. One should perhaps also mention a further factor: through a series of historical accidents, a paraphernalia of administrative prices obtains over a large segment of organised industry and tends to exert a dampening influence on industrial prices during inflationary periods. No such administrative road blocks have stood in the way of farm prices: on the contrary, as is being argued here, administered prices have been deployed in recent years entirely for the purpose of pushing up prices.

Whatever the contributory factors, the general inflationary trend has been overshadowed, in the course of the past decade, by the phenomenon of agricultural prices gaining perceptibly over industrial prices.[7] The implications of this development for income distribution and growth apart, it has brought into focus a range of issues which have emerged in other lands in other forms but which, in the Indian context, has a specificity of its own.

The precise mechanism through which the inter-sectoral shift in terms of trade has been brought about is discussed below. The State has played a crucial role here, and pressures have been applied at various levels to influence official decision-making. At the purely populist level, the sentiment built round the fact that agriculture constitutes the principal economic activity in the country and provides the means of livelihood for the majority of the population has been exploited *in passim* over the past quarter of a century. The farm sector, it has been continuously harped upon, was neglected in the past; a number of special incentives must therefore be offered to it to make up for lost ground, more so since the nation has adopted the objective of self-sufficiency in agriculture. Scarcely any opportunity has been missed to stress the point that farm growth is equally vital for industrial progress, since it provides, on the supply side, the wage-goods and the necessary raw materials for processing and, on the demand side, a major part of the potential market for finished manufactures. Little attempt has been made in such arguments to distinguish between the different economic categories which exist within the farm sector, or to analyse separately the impact of shifting terms of trade on the different sections of the agricultural community.

The trend towards shifting the relative prices in favour of agriculture and against industry was reinforced by the ideological ferment engendered by the so-called New Agricultural Strategy. A major adjunct of the Strategy is across-the-board subsidies — direct as well as indirect, and including so-called incentive prices — for the entire range of farm output. The emphasis in research and analysis which accompanied the induction of the Strategy is on demonstrating that price incentives are an essential ingredient of the total package of measures — consisting of high-yielding seeds, controlled water management, adequate dosage of fertilisers and induction of pesticides — for raising farm productivity. While propagating the strategy, enthusiasts have freely borrowed ideas from the experience of the United States, where agricultural operations continue to be subsidised till this day.[8]

We must, however, explicitly discuss the modalities of official intervention for raising farm prices and tilting the terms of trade against non-farm goods. Apart from fiscal and monetary measures, the instrument which has been most effectively deployed for the purpose during the past decade is the network of administered prices policy for the farm sector.[9] Both minimum support prices — intended to ensure the producers a minimum price covering cost of production in the eventuality of a crash in market prices — and procurement prices — which are prices at which official agencies are expected to purchase either a gain or a cash crop for serving the objective of either public distribution or building buffer stocks — have been repeatedly pushed upwards during the period since 1964-65, irrespective of the size of the crop and of other considerations.[10] This has had two effects. First, official agencies, as the leading price-setters in the case of each crop, have immediately succeded in imparting a bullishness to the state of market expectations. While at the operational level the policy of minimum support prices has not played a significant role, the same can hardly be said in regard to procurement prices: in quite a number of years, and in the case of quite a number of foodgrains, the increase in the level of official procurement prices by a certain proportion has acted as a signal for a spurt in open market prices by a similar proportion. Second, as the pitch of market prices in the case of a particular crop has been queered by the rise in its procurement price, the prices of other crops too have risen in sympathy, and the increase in farm prices has emerged as a general phenomenon.

Other things remaining the same, each shift in the terms of trade in favour of farm products contributes to the holding power of surplus farmers and traders, enabling them to bid for still higher prices in the subsequent season. The fact that the tax burden, in particular the burden of direct taxes, is as good as negligible for the relatively affluent agriculturists,[11] has further contributed to the progressive strengthening of their capablity to hold back stocks; the policy of liberal monetary advances made to this section of the farming community under the New Agricultural Strategy has imparted an additional bullishness, year after year, to market prices for farm products, so that even a larger-sized crop has not led to a decline in prices, but its opposite.[12]

Doubts can still persist regarding the extent to which either Government price-setting operations or the activities of surplus farmers and traders can affect market prices for the entire range of agricultural commodities. Farming activity, it may be suggested, is carried out in hundreds and thousands of units dispersed over hundreds and thousands of villages. Agronomic practices vary from State to State and region to region; the socio-economic conditions of farmers differ in the different regions and often within the same region; the adopted technology too shows wide variations. Against this background, it may become difficult to visualise a situation where prices are determined by a restricted number of affluent peasants and their trading partners. Attention can of course be drawn to the fact that more than 60 per cent of the total arable land in the country is either owned or operated by barely 10 per cent of the farming community. The *prima facie* improbability of oligopolistic price-setting is not reduced thereby. Even 10 per cent of the total farming population represents close to 40 million individuals, or roughly 8 million households; that so many households can come to a mutual understanding as to how farm prices are to be determined in the market would be considered as most far-fetched. On the assumption that there are only twenty major crops — which of course is not the case — there would still be on the average as many as 200,000 households associated with activities concerning each crop. Collusive price-setting by such a large number of decision-making units may appear to be inconceivable.

Analogous arguments could be put forward questioning the importance accorded above to the role of, for instance, procurement prices, in influencing market trends. Aggregate procurement in the country, it could be pointed out, has never exceeded 8 per cent of the annual output of foodgrains. Major strides were made with the procurement of wheat during the years 1968-69 to 1970-71; even so, procurement hardly exceeded 15 per cent of the output of the grain in these years. In the case of rice, the authorities have been unable to procure even 10 per cent of total production in any year. The record is significantly worse in the case of coarser grains. For the cash crops, the history of procurement is generally scrappy, and has not gone beyond 1 to 2 per cent of production. Such marginal involvement in the market on the part of the Government, it may be said, could not possibly sway market prices in any appreciable manner.

In the final analysis, prices, it could be further remarked, are determined by the objective conditions obtaining in the market: if the crop is good, prices will decline; if it is disappointing, prices will firm up. Similarly, if effective demand is strong, prices will rise, while a levelling off of this demand will lead to a downward drift in the price level.

Such a point of view misses out one of the most crucial elements in market structure. In an open market, it is operations at the margin which determine the basic trends. Admittedly, for each crop, the number of households involved in actual cultivation is legion: even were the rich farmers in each region or State considered together, their share in the total output of any particular agricultural commodity is still likely to be negligible. The quality of influence they bring to bear upon the state of expectations in the market is nonetheless crucial. The big farmers, and the traders associated with them, may control at any moment only a minor proportion of the marketed part of a crop; even so, they are in a position to decide the location and timing for the release — or withholding — of stocks. There are a number of focal points in the marketing of farm products: developments at these points on particular days and hours have a chain effect on prices on a wide front. What takes place is a replica of brokerage operations in the stock market where a speculator, by merely making full use of the instrument of 'margin' operations, can influence the entire market.

Similar is the role of administered prices set by the Government. Here too expectations play a significant part in moulding the psychology of the market. It is as if what the Government does or does not do is in the nature of an early-warning signal for others. If the Government raises administered prices, it stimulates prices over the entire range of market operations; if it marks down administered prices, its decision acts as a depressant which again casts its spell over the rest of the market. As long as the belief is promoted that the Government is the price-setter, whatever the objective reality in the initial stages, the administered price becomes, after an interval of time, the actual price-setter for all effective purposes.

III

All this brings us back to the central issue. The shift in terms of trade in favour of agriculture has been consistently advocated on the purported ground that it would spark off a spurt in farm output. Has this objective been realised, are any positive results discernible in terms of a major increase in either agricultural production or the marketed surplus? The relevant data are in a number of instances subject to multiple-interpretations, and results from micro-level analysis have tended to be mutually inconsistent. Even so, a study of the trend of agricultural production in the country over the past decade, that is, since the initiation of the New Agricultural Strategy, belies the claim of a breakthrough: the overall rate of growth of both farm output as a whole as well as foodgrain production in this phase has not been superior to what obtained in the preceding fifteen-year period; in fact, it has been worse.[13] What is more — as Table 8:1 brings out — with the exception of the preponderately wheat-growing ones, in no other State is there any sustained evidence of a rising trend of production during the past decade. While in individual years a certain peak in output is noticeable for each State, it stands in splendid isolation, and is not necessarily reached in the same year or years in the different States. Once the peak is blotted out, and the influence of wheat excluded, the rest of the story is one of quasi-stagnation; climatic factors by themselves can scarcely be held responsible for this denouement. Between 1964-65 and 1974-75, the compound rate of growth of agricultural production appears to have been only around 1.7 per cent per annum. Inclusive of wheat, the compound annual rate of growth of foodgrain output in the country during this decade is of the order of 1.4 per cent; excluding wheat, it is as low as 0.6 per cent.[14] While the trend is certainly different if one concentrates on Punjab and Haryana, or exclusively on the production of wheat, it is open to question to what extent this difference is to be attributed to the stimulus of price incentives, as distinct from the impact of other, more basic factors, such as the availability of high-yielding varieties of seeds and facilities of irrigation.[5]

        It could nonetheless be maintained that to compare the crude rates of growth of output in the pre- and post-1964-65 periods is not altogether appropriate; during the 1950s, growth was propelled by the expansion of acreage, whereas, in the past decade, the impact of price incentives has led to the induction of new technology, which in turn has resulted in a breakthrough in productivity, so much so that the consequences of the shift in terms of trade should be traced in the marked rise in per hectare productivity in the recent period. How much is this assertion in harmony with the realities of the situation? Table 8:2 presents the State-wise details of productivity for the principal crops in the country for the years 1949-50 to 1971-72. It reveals several significant facts. During the period 1949-50 to 1963-64, the rise in per hectare productivity was not exactly trivial: it was as much as 50 per cent or more for most of the crops under review. For example, in the case of rice, productivity per hectare advanced

TABLE 8:1

PRODUCTION OF FOODGRAINS IN INDIA, 1964–65 TO 1973–74

('000 tonnes)

State	1964–65	1965–66	1966–67	1967–68	1968–69	1969–70	1970–71	1971–72	1972–73	1973–74
Andhra Pradesh	7,704	6,098	7,718	7,186	6,847	7,400	7,406	7,291	6,708	8,331
Assam	1,975	1,910	1,811	2,037	2,304	2,119	2,034	1,996	2,396	2,171
Bihar	7,531	7,190	4,133	8,627	8,870	7,546	7,881	9,067	9,320	7,661
Gujarat	2,880	2,416	2,186	3,330	2,346	3,221	4,406	4,222	2,215	3,629
Haryana	2,704	2,077	2,573	3,992	3,066	4,567	4,751	4,545	4,835	3,839
Himachal Pradesh	847	617	772	898	961	982	950	945	914	938
Jammu & Kashmir	566	499	652	682	1,099	1,152	944	959	960	1,010
Kerala	1,150	1,025	1,112	1,151	1,427	1,243	1,321	1,373	1,397	1,376
Madhya Pradesh	10,233	6,823	6,311	10,232	9,460	9,769	10,922	11,634	10,632	10,410
Maharashtra	6,745	4,695	6,050	6,825	7,157	6,914	5,390	4,953	3,052	7,237
Mysore	4,839	3,545	4,173	4,665	5,049	5,891	5,962	6,065	4,600	6,151
Orissa	4,945	3,731	4,355	4,335	5,429	5,033	5,104	4,354	5,360	5,310
Punjab	4,039	3,391	4,217	5,407	6,252	6,937	7,306	7,928	7,694	7,720
Rajasthan	5,308	3,839	4,351	6,602	4,007	4,750	8,838	6,335	5,158	6,717
Tamil Nadu	5,693	5,032	5,790	5,761	5,415	6,239	6,974	6,943	7,167	7,258
Uttar Pradesh	15,272	13,311	11,874	16,779	16,296	17,547	19,585	17,698	18,154	15,780
West Bengal	6,259	5,448	5,377	5,741	7,162	7,364	7,491	7,856	6,772	6,865
All-India	89,356	72,347	74,231	95,052	94,013	99,501	108,422	105,168	97,026	103,611

Source: Directorate of Economics and Statistics, Ministry of Agriculture, Government of India.

TABLE 8:2 AVERAGE YIELD OF PRINCIPAL CROPS IN INDIA (Quintals/Hectare)

Year	Rice	Jowar	Bajra	Maize	Ragi	Small Millets	Wheat	Barley	Gram	Tur	Other Pulses	Ground nuts	Sesamum	Rape & Mustard	Linseed	Castor Seed	Cotton Lint	Jute	Sugarcane
1949–50	7.7	3.8	3.1	6.3	7.0	4.2	6.5	7.1	4.6	4.6	3.6	3.6	2.1	5.1	2.7	2.2	1.0	11.9	34.2
1950–51	6.7	3.5	2.9	5.5	6.5	3.8	6.6	7.6	4.8	7.9	3.3	7.8	2.0	3.7	2.6	1.9	0.9	10.4	33.4
1951–52	7.1	3.8	2.5	6.3	6.0	4.0	6.5	7.5	5.0	9.0	3.4	6.4	1.9	3.9	2.4	1.9	0.9	10.7	31.8
1952–53	7.6	4.2	3.0	8.0	6.0	3.8	7.6	9.0	5.8	7.1	2.2	6.1	2.0	4.1	2.7	1.9	0.9	11.3	29.5
1953–54	9.0	4.6	3.7	7.9	8.0	4.4	7.5	8.4	6.1	7.7	3.4	8.1	2.2	3.9	2.8	1.9	1.0	11.3	31.5
1954–55	8.2	5.3	3.1	7.9	7.2	4.4	8.0	8.7	6.1	7.2	3.5	7.7	2.3	4.2	2.9	2.2	1.0	10.6	36.3
1955–56	8.7	3.9	3.0	7.0	8.3	3.9	7.1	8.2	5.5	8.1	3.4	7.5	2.0	4.1	2.8	2.2	0.9	10.8	32.9
1956–57	9.0	4.5	2.6	8.2	7.9	3.9	7.0	8.1	6.4	8.7	2.9	7.9	2.0	3.9	2.0	2.0	1.1	10.1	33.9
1957–58	7.9	5.0	3.2	7.7	7.4	3.6	6.8	7.5	5.4	6.2	2.9	7.3	1.7	4.3	2.9	2.4	1.0	10.3	34.5
1958–59	9.1	5.1	3.4	8.1	7.7	4.2	7.9	8.1	7.0	6.9	3.8	8.3	2.3	3.7	2.3	2.0	1.1	12.8	37.7
1959–60	9.4	4.8	3.3	9.4	7.9	3.9	7.7	8.0	5.4	7.0	3.7	7.1	1.7	4.7	2.2	2.3	0.9	12.0	37.0
1960–61	10.1	5.3	2.9	9.3	7.3	3.9	8.5	8.8	6.7	8.5	3.7	7.5	1.5	4.3	2.3	2.3	1.3	11.8	46.1
1961–62	10.3	4.4	3.2	9.6	8.1	4.2	8.9	9.5	6.1	5.6	3.8	7.3	1.7	4.2	2.3	2.3	1.0	12.5	43.0
1962–63	9.1	5.3	3.6	9.9	8.2	4.0	7.9	8.0	5.8	6.6	3.6	7.0	1.9	4.2	2.3	2.3	1.2	11.5	41.9
1963–64	10.4	5.1	3.6	9.9	7.9	4.4	7.3	7.3	4.8	5.6	3.4	7.7	1.8	3.0	1.9	2.1	1.2	12.8	47.0
1964–65	10.7	5.5	3.8	9.9	8.2	4.3	9.0	9.3	6.4	7.7	3.8	8.7	1.9	4.9	2.3	2.3	1.2	13.0	48.4
1965–66	8.7	4.3	3.2	10.0	5.2	3.7	8.2	9.0	5.3	7.0	3.3	5.7	1.7	4.4	1.9	2.0	1.1	10.6	43.5
1966–67	8.6	5.1	3.7	9.6	7.0	3.3	8.9	8.3	4.5	4.5	3.1	6.0	1.5	4.1	1.7	2.7	1.1	12.1	41.3
1967–68	10.3	5.5	4.1	11.2	8.2	3.9	11.0	10.4	7.2	6.5	3.7	7.6	1.7	4.8	2.5	2.8	1.2	12.9	47.8
1968–69	10.8	5.2	3.2	10.0	7.4	3.8	11.7	8.8	6.1	7.2	3.7	6.5	1.7	4.7	1.9	2.9	1.2	10.0	50.7
1969–70	10.7	5.2	4.3	9.9	7.6	3.7	12.1	9.8	7.2	6.9	3.7	6.2	1.9	4.9	2.6	3.1	1.2	13.3	50.1
1970–71	11.2	4.7	6.2	12.8	8.7	4.2	13.1	10.9	6.6	7.1	3.9	8.3	2.3	5.9	2.5	3.1	1.1	11.9	49.6
1971–72	11.5	4.6	4.6	8.9	9.0	3.5	13.8	10.3	6.4	6.8	3.7	7.9	1.9	4.0	2.6	3.5	1.5	12.6	48.5

Source: *Statistical Abstracts*, Government of India.

from 7.7 quintals in 1949-50 to 10.4 quintals in 1963-64; for jowar, it rose from 3.8 quintals to 5.1 quintals. In the case of bajra, the improvement in productivity was of a lower order; it was nonetheless at least around 10 to 12 per cent. Per hectare productivity of maize increased by more than one-half during the period; in the case of ragi, the improvement was around 15 per cent. For the major commercial crops, the improvement in productivity was much less significant. Sugarcane, however, was an exception: the productivity of cane cultivation went up by as much as 20 per cent during the 1950s.

What has been the experience since 1964-65? We now have the records of nearly one full decade for studying the influence of price incentives on the productivity of the principal crops. Contrary to general expectations, Table 8:2 indicates that productivity per hectare in the case of rice, jowar, bajra, maize, ragi, small millets, gram, groundnut, linseed, other oilseeds, cotton, jute and sugarcane has not gone up at all in the past decade. With the solitary exception of wheat, productivity in fact has during these years stagnated in Indian agriculture.

Certainly wheat appears to be a special case. While between 1949-50 and 1964-65, the rise in per hectare productivity for the crop was around 30 per cent, it has increased by as much as 80 per cent over the past decade. How much of this improvement in wheat productivity can however, be exclusively ascribed to price incentive? Much the larger contribution to this rise in productivity, there can hardly be any question, was on account of the induction of high-yielding varieties of seeds and the pre-emption of the acreage under irrigation. Developments since 1971-72 would seem to confirm this proposition. Some recent attempts to expand the acreage under wheat further by extending the cultivation of the grain to areas not yet served by irrigation have proved infructuous; the increase in acreage has not led to any corresponding rise in total production. The average productivity per hectare has reportedly declined in the case of wheat because of, among other factors, this expansion of cultivation to inferior land not served by irrigation. Other things remaining the same, the high level of market prices for wheat since 1972-73 should have had a positive impact on productivity. That it has not been so suggests that price by itself is not an adequate factor for improved productivity.[16]

To sum up, rising levels of prices as such have certainly made little impression on the trend of output — or productivity — of major foodgrains. The rates of growth for the majority of the commercial crops have been no better either. How far, notwithstanding the absence of basic institutional reforms, output could expand merely through the instrumentality of price incentives, is thus an issue which remains open. Indeed, under certain assumptions, it is possible to argue to the contrary: till as long as dependable varieties of high-yielding seeds remain undiscovered, irrigation facilities remain unexpanded, fertiliser supplies continue to be uneven and the structural reforms necessary to ensure the flow of credit to the small-holdings are unaccomplished, attempts to force the terms of trade excessively in favour of farm products might even lead to the emergence of a supply curve which turns upon itself.

This last point can be pursued. Earlier in this chapter, attention has been drawn to the phenomenon of a progressive strengthening of the holding power of surplus farmers and traders because of the increase in prices. A pattern which is fairly familiar in the Indian countryside is the combining of farming activity, money-lending and trading on the part of many individuals.[17] If maximisation of profits is the overriding objective, the expansion of farming activity may then beyond a point come into conflict with the predilection towards extending trading and lending operations. A rise in output, which farm expansion brings about, cannot but eat into the potential profits from speculative trade and money-lending. It is thus entirely possible that funds advanced to sections of the agricultural community for stimulating farm output could be diverted to finance lending and speculative operations.[18] Conventional price incentives too would in these circumstances have little positive impact on production, and the mechanism of terms of trade might actually contribute towards a developing stagnation.

Nor can it be maintained that what has been suggested in the paragraph above is pure speculation. In 1972-73, following the failure of the *kharif* crop, the Government of India announced an emergency production programme for the *rabi* season. Nearly Rs.250 crores of public funds were distributed in the form of short- and medium-term loans with a view to raising an additional output of 15 million tons of foodgrains over the level attained in the preceding year. The funds were intended to facilitate quick execution of minor irrigation works which could bring in new areas for cultivation and to provide assistance to farmers by increasing the supplies of fertilisers, seeds, insecticides, pesticides, drilling rigs, pump-sets, cement and steel. Despite this massive expenditure, actual output, instead of rising, actually fell by almost 4 million tons. There was a decline in production in the case of each crop, and in nearly every State. Established norms of financial control were by-passed to rush through the outlays; as a consequence, a major part of the funds, it is now generally acknowledged, were diverted by the big farmers for non-productive purposes.[19] It is thus most plausible that, under certain specified conditions, the rising level of farm prices too would itself be the greatest deterrent, even if not to increased output, at least to increasing supplies for the market.

IV

The implications of pushing farm prices interminably can be illustrated with the help of the diagram below. The initial equilibrium is attained with output at OA, and the equilibrium price PA is determined by the usual point of intersection of the demand and supply curves. Assume that it is now decided to attempt to expand output by offering an incentive price. The policy-makers could then extend production to OB at the cost of a subsidy to the producers amounting to HS′GK. No *a priori* ground exists for either supporting or opposing this order of subsidy for gaining the additional output AB.

Suppose however that, in view of the impact of the subsidy on production, pressure is generated to raise further the producer's price. Let this new producer's price be fixed at OE. Three alternative possibilities remain open at this stage: (a) the supply curve

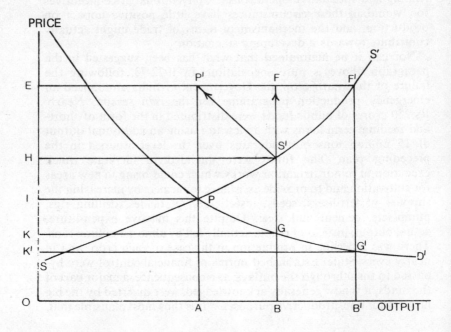

develops — because of reasons discussed above — a tendency towards sloping backwards, so that, instead of rising, output shrinks;[20] (b) output, while not declining, merely remains the same, and (e) the supply curve is normal, and output expands, as in the earlier instance. In the case of (a), since output recedes to OA, the State is offering a producer subsidy of EP'PI for attaining a level of output which previously did not call for any subsidy. In the second case, too, while there is no fall of production which stays put at OB, the additional subsidy of EFS'H is nonetheless infructuous. Its only purpose is to improve the relative income of the producers *vis-à-vis* that of the consumers.

If the alternative assumption is made that the supply curve is normal beyond S', so that raising the producer's price to OE leads to a further increase in output, the implications of such a subsidy-induced expansion in production can also be seen from the diagram. With the supply curve taking the shape of SS'F', a producer's price of OE lifts production from OB to OB'. But consumers are now willing to offer only G'B' for a unit of the commodity, and the national exchequer has to carry the load of the subsidy EF'G'K'. If the Government takes monopsonistic control of the total supply, it could then recoup the subsidy by forcing up the price for the consumer. A phenomenon of this kind did in fact emerge in India in the late 1960s: as procurement, and hence issue, prices of wheat were set at inordinately high levels, consumers did not clear the entire output, and authorities had to fall back on stock-piling.

As the diagram makes obvious, irrespective of whether the actual market phenomenon resembles (a) or (b), or (c), there is a straightforward income distribution effect of the shift in prices in favour of farm products. In each of the cases, there is an addition to the income of the suppliers of surplus grains (or cash crops); at the other end, in so far as the subsidy and the cost of stock-policy operations are borne by the other classes in society, the latter experience a reduction in their level of earnings.

V

In view of the foregoing, it is of interest to explore who gains, even within Indian agriculture, from a rising spiral of farm prices. As mentioned earlier, there is a substantial segment of opinion which argues that by tilting the structure of relative prices against industry and in favour of agriculture, the nation is merely making partial amends for the ruthless exploitation the farming community had been subjected to in the past. The majority of the latter, however, consists of landless labourers and small farmers. In the case of both foodgrains and commercial crops, the benefits of higher prices hardly accrue to these groups; on the contrary, as a consequence of higher prices, they are called upon to pay more for meeting their consumption requirements. Admittedly, in areas covered by the New Agricultural Strategy, some improvement in the level of rural wages has taken place; this has however been more than neutralised in most instances by the all-round increase in prices, including the prices of foodgrains.[21]

An analysis based on the returns of the 18th round of the National Sample survey relating to the market dependence of rural households for their requirements of foodgrains sheds interesting light on the issue. The relevant data, relating to Andhra Pradesh, Maharashtra and Rajasthan, are reproduced in Table 3.

In the case of agricultural labour households not owning any land, the reliance on the market for cereals intended for domestic consumption, it will be seen, was as high as 99 per cent in Andhra Pradesh, 98 per cent in Maharashtra and 74 per cent in Rajasthan. For agricultural labour households in possession of less than 2.5 acres of land, the dependence on the market for cereal requirements was 81 per cent in Andhra Pradesh, 82 per cent in Maharashtra, and 87 per cent in Rajasthan. The pattern, there could be little doubt, is likely to be more or less similar for the entire country. A high level of foodgrain prices therefore militates not only against the interest of urban consumers, but also against those of the mass of landless labourers and small farmers, who form the bulk of the country's

TABLE 8:3

MARKET DEPENDENCE OF RURAL HOUSEHOLDS FOR FOODGRAINS

Class	Andhra Pradesh	Maharashtra	Rajasthan
Producer households	34.7	34.7	26.6
Agricultural Labour households possessing less than 2.5 acres of land	81.2	82.4	87.0
Agricultural Labour households without any land	99.4	97.6	74.0
All classes	53.5	49.4	29.3

Source: Agricultural Prices Commission, Government of India, *Report on the Price Policy for Kharif Cereals for the 1968–69 Season.*

population.[22] With regard to cash crops, too, whatever scattered data are available confirm the impression that small farmers by and large sell off the major part of their crop in the early part of the season either to the trader, or to the money-lender from whom they receive crop loans, or to the rich farmer who often doubles up as trader. Instances are not lacking where the poorer members of even co-operative societies dispose of their cash crops at low prices to the more substantial members of those societies; it is the latter who then reap the gains as market prices soar towards the close of the season.[23]

It should now be permissible to draw a few fairly tenable conclusions. We have shown that it is not possible to argue that, in India, the output of most of the principal crops has responded positively to the shift in terms of trade in favour of agriculture. Compared to the performance in the period preceding the induction of the so-called New Agricultural Strategy, both production and productivity appear to be declining. While the shift in terms of trade has implied a shift in real incomes in favour of the farming community considered as an aggregate *vis-à-vis* the rest of the nation, the resulting gains have been exclusively monopolised by the surplus-raising farmers and their trading partners; landless labourers and small farmers, who are net purchasers of grains from the market, have been as adversly affected by the rise in farm prices as the non-agricultural classes in general.

NOTES

1 *Report* of the Irrigation Commission, Government of India, 1972, Volume I, p. 82.
2 See Chapter 7 for a discussion of the issue.
3 The data are from the Reserve Bank of India *Bulletin,* March 1975, Statement No. 38.
4 This is in fact a continuation of a trend which had already developed in the preceding decade. See Ashok Mitra, 'Class Relations and Growth of Output', *Social and Economic Change,* edited by B. Singh and V. B. Singh, Asia, pp. 451-8. The tilt in the terms of trade has merely become more pronounced since the early 1960s; a major underlying cause must be the advance along the so-called 'learning curve'.
5 Government of India, *Economic Survey, 1974-75, p. 60.*
6 *Reserve Bank of India Bulletin,* March 1975, Statement No. 27.
7 R. Thamarajakshi, who has studied the terms of trade between the industrial and farm sectors in India for the period 1951-52 to 1965-66, arrives at a more cautious conclusion: 'During the period of the three five-year Plans, all prices received and paid by agriculture, irrespective of the nature of the product use, show an upward trend, though at differential rates. In general, prices received by agriculture have risen at a faster annual rate than those paid by agriculture, and yet the consequent secular improvement (in favour of agriculture) in the net barter terms of trade is

marginal. The income terms of trade have registered a significant rate of increase thus indicating the improved purchasing power of the agricultural sector for non-agricultural commodities. While the rate of rise in prices received by agriculture has compensated that in the prices that agriculture has had to pay for non-agricultural inputs, the cost of agricultural inputs for the non-agricultural sector has increased at a faster rate than the prices paid by agriculture for all non-agricultural products'. R. Thamarajakshi, 'Intersectoral Terms of Trade and Marketed Surplus of Agricultural Produce, 1951-52 to 1965-66', *Economic and Political Weekly,* Review of Agriculture, June 1969, p. A-99. As a consequence of developments since 1965-66, the shift in the barter terms of trade in favour of agriculture has however ceased to be 'marginal'.

8   In the United States, agriculture constitutes less than 10 per cent of national output and the labour force associated with agriculture hardly 4 per cent of the aggregate working population. A policy of subsidies pursued in respect of farm incomes does not therefore lead to any particular strain on the rest of the American economy, for its incidence is widely diffused. On the other hand, in the Indian case, since income accruing from agriculture is as much as nearly one-half of overall national income, and since nearly 70 per cent of the population are sustained through farm activity, attempts to stimulate farm growth by offering generous price incentives can raise a major problem for the other economic sectors. The burden of the problem is mitigated by the fact of per capita income being relatively low in the farm sector, but only partly. (It is of course an altogether different matter that the income subsidies in India have benefited only a minority of the farming population, and, as is argued later, made the position of the bulk of the agriculturists much worse.)

9   For a detailed discussion, see the various *Reports* of the Agricultural Prices Commission, Government of India, especially the *Reports on the Price Policy for Kharif Cereals for the 1967-68 and 1968-69 Seasons,* and the *Report on Price Policy for Rabi Cereals for 1968-69.*

10 See Chapter 9 for a more detailed discussion of the rationale of procurement price fixation in the case of rice and wheat.

11 See Ashok Mitra, 'Tax Burden for Indian Agriculture', *Administration and Economic Development in India,* edited by R. Braibanti and J. J. Spengler, Duke University Press pp. 280-303, and Government of India, Ministry of Finance, *Report of the Committee on Taxation of Agricultural Wealth and Income,* 1972.

12 Commenting on the developments with foodgrain prices in the 1973-74 season, the *Economic and Political Weekly* wrote: 'How are the higher market prices despite the larger crop to be explained? There is nothing to suggest that there has taken place an unusual rise in the consumption of foodgrains. On the contrary, various indicators such as the stagnation of industrial investment and production and the slow growth of employment would suggest a shift in the distribution of real incomes adverse to the poorer sections of the population, a rise in whose incomes could be expected to lead to a marked rise in the consumption of foodgrains. In the absence of a sharp rise in consumption, the present levels of prices of foodgrains can be explained only in terms of large-scale withholding of stocks from the market by producers and traders. The ability of these two groups to finance larger stocks in the expectation of bidding up prices further has been appreciably augmented in recent years by higher prices, by the larger flow of institutional finance to agriculture and by the overall increase of liquidity in the economy'. 'Farce of Procurement', *Economic and Political Weekly,* 26 January 1974, p. 81. Here is a further commentary on the influence of procurement prices on open market prices: 'The level of procurement prices is no longer a relevant factor . . . for actual procurement: by raising the government's purchase price, you do not necessarily improve your chances to procure, just as, by lowering tax

rates; you do not necessarily persuade more people to pay their taxes. It depends on the climate: if it is altogether permissive, if the government would not involve itself in the task and would leave it to the sense of patriotism of farmers and traders, little is likely to be procured, irrespective of how much you may decide to raise the level of procurement price. In the present context, the government's decision to increase its own purchase price actually provides the signal to the operators in the market to raise *their* prices. And the more they raise their prices, the more their holding power goes up, and therefore the more they are able to hold back stocks and further raise prices. This phenomenon of spiralling market prices has nothing to do with the cost of production; at current prices, the return over cost would be more than 100 per cent in a large number of cases. But, come the next season, the flop in procurement would be adduced as the reason for perhaps recommending a further rise in prices'. 'Food Policy: At the Traders' Mercy', *Economic and Political Weekly,* 11 May 1974, p. 743. True, the withholding of stocks cannot, other things remaining the same, continue indefinitely (even were warehousing capacity not regarded as a limiting factor), but intervention of climatic cycles takes care of the problem.

13   For comments on the relative rates of growth during these periods, see Ashok Mitra, 'Bumper Harvest Has Created Some Dangerous Illusions', *Statesman,* 14-15 October 1968, B. S. Minhas and T. N. Srinivasan, 'Food Production Trends and Buffer Stock Policy', *Statesman,* 14 November 1968, and T, N. Srinivasan, 'The Green Revolution or the Wheat Revolution?', *Agricultural Development in Developing Countries: Comparative Experience,* Indian Society of Agricultural Economics, 1971; also C. H. Hanumantha Rao, *Technological Change and the Distribution of Gains in Indian Agriculture,* Institute of Economic Growth, 1974, p. 4.

14   If worked out on the basis of three-year moving averages, these compound rates of growth show a marginal improvement, but they are still substantially below — by nearly as much as 50 per cent — the corresponding rates for the period 1949-50 to 1963-64.

15   Even in the case of wheat, a relative levelling off of output has been noticeable from 1971-72, despite the fact that both procurement and market prices for the grain have risen steeply since that year.

16   'Green Revolution: Halting in Mid-track?', *Economic and Political Weekly,* 1 September 1973, pp. 1591-3.

17   See Amit Bhaduri, 'A Study in Agricultural Backwardness Under Semi-feudalism', *Economic Journal,* March 1973; also by the same author, 'Towards a Theory of Pre-capitalistic Exchange', *Economic Theory and Planning,* ed. Ashok Mitra, Oxford.

18   It is worth quoting the following narration which concerns a money-lender in a village in Ludhiana, 'the core of the Green Revolution region of Punjab' 'The biggest money-lender in Manupur is Maghar Singh. The amount he has out on loan today comes to a total of nearly two lakh rupees. Although he has 35 acres of land, Maghar Singh does not wish to buy a tractor. Neither does he desire to purchase any more land. As he explained, an acre of land costs Rs.20,000. The gross yearly produce on it would be Rs.4-5,000. If one wishes to avoid management worries, one could lease it on a crop-sharing basis, on *katai.* The return would then be half the gross produce, that is, Rs.2-2500 a year. A far more attractive alternative, however, is loaning that Rs.20,000, and letting it fetch, even a low rate of, say, 20 per cent per annum, Rs.4,000. Unbelievable as it may sound to a Green Revolutionary, Maghar Singh put it this way: "As a tractor, money will turn into iron, lifeless and ossified; as a loan, it lives and grows" '. 'Arrested Green Revolution', *Economic and Political Weekly,* 21-28 June 1974, p. 945.

19 See 'Cult of Crash Programmes', *Economic and Political Weekly*, 2 November 1974, p. 1833.

20 In other words, in this case the income effect outweighs the price effect.

21 A. V. Jose ('Trends in Real Wage Rates of Agricultural Labourers', *Economic and Political Weekly*, Review of Agriculture, March 1974, pp. A-25–A-30) has shown that between 1956-57 and 1971-72, wage rates improved in real terms only in Haryana, Kerala, Gujarat, Tamil Nadu and Uttar Pradesh, that is for less than 30 per cent of the agricultural labour force in the country. According to an alternative estimate (Ashok Mitra, 'Domestic Terms of Trade and the Wage Structure', paper read at Conference on Wage Theory, Institute of Development Studies, University of Sussex, 1975), real wages during this period declined nearly everywhere in India, the only exceptions being Kerala, Uttar Pradesh and Tamil Nadu.

22 Such estimates derived from a single round of the National Sample Survey may not be considered as definitive. However, estimates developed separately by Pranab and Kalpana Bardhan substantiate the point that a majority of the rural poor are net purchasers of foodgrains. See their paper 'Problem of Marketed Surplus of Cereals', *Economic and Political Weekly*, Review of Agriculture, June 1969, Table 9, p. A-109, and also Pranab Bardhan, 'On the Incidence of Poverty in Rural India in the Sixties', *Economic and Political Weekly*, Annual Number 1973, footnote 8, p. 254.

23 These conclusions may appear to be at variance with the findings of Dharm Narain in the *Distribution of Marketed Surplus of Agricultural Produce by Size-level of Holding in India, 1950-51*, Institute of Economic Growth, 1962, which indicated a fairly high proportion of marketed surplus to total output in the case of small holdings. Dharm Narain's statistical conclusions have, however, been seriously questioned by Utsa Patnaik ('Development of Capitalism in Agriculture', *Social Scientist*, September, 1972 and 'Contribution to the Output and Marketable Surplus of Agricultural Products by Cultivating Groups in India, 1960-61', *Economic and Political Weekly*, Review of Agriculture, 27 December 1975), whose alternative estimates suggest that the marketable proportion of farm output is fairly low on the smallest holdings and increases more or less steadily with increasing average farm size.

CHAPTER 9

Farm Price Fixation: Two Cases of Asymmetry

I

In this chapter, we continue with the theme of class bias affecting Indian agricultural policy, and discuss two recent instances of inter-crop discrimination in pricing decisions. On the surface, it is the aspect of interregional discrimination which commands attention in the following narration. That, it will be maintained, is only a veil, and conceals the specificity of class alignments in the realm of polity.

The country's two principal cereals are rice and wheat. In respect of both production and consumption, while rice is the predominant grain in the south-eastern parts, wheat is the cereal of the north-east *par excellence*. Of late, a spectacular breakthrough in the production of rice has occurred in Punjab and Haryana, particularly of the newer varieties; similarly, in the traditional *kharif* belt, the cultivation of high-yielding varieties of wheat is being experimented with, by and large in the *rabi* season. These developments do not, however, diminish the significance of the fact that fluctuations in the levels of production and prices of rice have a greater relevance for the south-eastern States, just as movements in the prices and output of wheat have a more obvious economic consequence for the north-eastern States. The production of wheat has increased by more than 125 per cent since 1964-65: against a level of output of approximately twelve million tonnes in that year, it was close to twenty-seven million tonnes in 1971-72. In contrast, production of rice in the country has barely moved up from thirty-nine million tonnes in 1964-65 to forty-three million tonnes in 1971-72, an increase of barely 10 per cent.[1] Given this wide disparity in the rates of growth, the rise in the price level of rice during the decade, other things remaining the same, should have been much greater than that for wheat. This has hardly been the case. Inter-State variations in the trend do exist; however, in general, market prices of wheat have advanced at a faster pace than those of rice. In the decade between 1961-62 and 1971-72, the increase in the weighted wholesale price index for wheat outstripped that in the corresponding index for rice. If one concentrates on the period since 1964-65, the rise in the wholesale price index was, by 1971-72, around 70 per cent in the case of rice, but as much as 100 per cent for wheat.[2] This comparison too is somewhat misleading, for the weightage of price quotations for the inferior varieties of wheat in the composite price index has increased substantially in the more recent years, while the varietal composition of the rice crop has remained practically unaltered over the period.

The fact that the terms of trade between rice and wheat have shifted in favour of the latter, despite a near-stagnation in the output of the former and a spectacular increase in that of the latter, is largely a reflection of official policies discussed in the preceding chapter. This is confirmed by the drift in the levels of procurement prices for the two grains.[3] Between 1964-65 and 1972-73, the procurement price for the red and amber varieties of wheat — the varieties constituting the bulk of the procurement — advanced from Rs.48 per quintal to Rs.76 per quintal, an increase of the order of 60 per cent.[4] Table 9:1 indicates the shift in the level of procurement prices for the standard varieties of rice in the different States over the same period. The upward adjustment in the procurement price, it is evident, has everywhere been less than in the case of wheat, and markedly so for Andhra Pradesh, Kerala, Maharashtra, Orissa and Tamil Nadu. If one takes into account only the traditional rice-growing States in the south-eastern parts, the weighted increase in the procurement price of rice works out to only around 35 per cent.

TABLE 9:1

PROCUREMENT PRICES FOR RICE

(Rs. per quintal)

State	Variety	1964−65	1972−73	Percentage increase
Andhra Pradesh	Akkulu	63.00	83.30	32.2
Assam	Winter Sali	61.23	97.65	59.5
Bihar	Coarse	59.67	92.25	59.7
Kerala	Palghat Matta	71.76	85.88	19.7
Madhya Pradesh	Gurmatia	58.23	86.30	48.1
Maharashtra	Coarse	65.50	81.00	23.6
Orissa	Common	59.50	82.80	39.1
Punjab	Begmi	60.00	91.80	53.0
Tamil Nadu	Kattaisamba	64.45	75.75*	19.2
Uttar Pradesh	Grade III	63.00	92.00	46.0
West Bengal	Common	64.30	92.90	44.4

*Pertains to the 1971−72 season; no procurement prices were announced for 1972−73.

Source: Agricultural Prices Commission, Government of India.

A decade ago, the price of the standard variety of wheat, practically all over the country, was usually quoted at around three-fifths of the price of the standard variety of rice. This also more or less conformed to the conventional price parity between the two grains in the world market.[5] Consequent to developments in recent years, wheat is today being quoted in most States at prices which are at least four-fifths of, and in some instances the same as, the market quotations for rice.[6] This gain on the part of wheat echoes the trend in relative movements in the procurement prices for the two grains. If the policy of price incentives were intended exclusively to stimulate greater production and productivity, it is indeed curious that the bounty has been dispensed in a lesser measure in the case of a crop whose output was growing sluggishly than in the case of one which was expanding its production at a much more satisfactory rate.

Such a policy has manifold implications. If the price of wheat advances over that of rice, other things — including the nexus of inter-State trade for the two grains — remaining the same, the wheat-producing States experience a rise in their income relative to that of the rice-growing States even were the rate of growth of production of the two grains the same. Since, during the period under review, the rate of growth of output for wheat has been several times greater than for rice, divergent rates of income growth would in any case have emerged for the two categories of States. It is, then, of some relevance to enquire about the reasons considered necessary to aggravate the divergence by forcing, through official measures, the terms of trade in favour of wheat. A reversal of the trend towards widening disparities in inter-State incomes could have occurred provided the output — or prices — either in the other spheres of agriculture or in the other sectors of the economy increased in the rice-growing tracts at a pace faster than in the wheat-growing ones. It would be difficult to prove that this condition obtained in the past decade.[7]

There is a second factor affecting the interregional distribution of incomes worth noting. Apart from years of severe drought, the wheat-growing States in India have by and large been self-sufficient in foodgrains, and have not been dependent upon supplies from elsewhere: certainly they had no occasion ever to obtain rice from the other States. Whenever marginal deficits had arisen in these States in the post-Independence period, the gap was filled by lower-priced grains from abroad. In contrast, a number of States in the rice-growing belt, for instance, Kerala and West Bengal, have remained chronically deficient in food since the 1950s. This deficit has been mostly met by despatching wheat from Punjab, Haryana and other

States with a surplus in the grain. Because of the particular price policy pursued, Kerala and West Bengal, it is possible to suggest, have been compelled to make payments against these consignments of wheat that were substantially higher than would have been otherwise. These two States together imported wheat on the average to the extent of as much as three million tonnes annually from the north-eastern States between 1964-65 and 1972-73. On the assumption that the bias in official policy was responsible for the artificial increase in the price of wheat by at least Rs.20 per quintal, the consequential drain of resources from Kerala and West Bengal must have been of the order of Rs.60 crores per annum.

It may be considered somewhat illegitimate to draw absolute conclusions in this matter merely by studying shifts in relative prices of the two grains; an analysis of the unit cost of cultivation of the respective crops and of their profit margins is also no doubt called for. Firm data on the cost of cultivation of individual crops are generally scanty; they are certainly not available on a continuous basis, for the same crop or from the same area, for a number of years running. The Appendix to this chapter brings together some available estimates on cost of cultivation for wheat and paddy. The limitations of these data are not to be denied. They have nonetheless been used in Table 9:2 to present certain estimates of profit margins in wheat and paddy cultivation in a number of States. The conclusions which follow from the analysis of such isolated data need not be regarded as definitive; the range of States and years covered is too narrow, and the estimates provide no clue to the general trend in profit margins for the two crops. The scatter of observations would, however, indicate that farmers raising wheat have by and large tended to fare better than those engaged in paddy cultivation.[8]

II

Another instance of inter-crop discrimination in farm pricing policy is illustrated by the asymmetry in the fixation of minimum support prices for raw jute and raw cotton. Since purchases of either crop by Government agencies on the basis of a procurement price have been generally unknown, it is the level of minimum support price which has been crucial for influencing market expectations, and thus the earnings of producers.[9] This fact notwithstanding, and despite the official recognition of adequate price incentives to the farmer as one of the major means for raising output, there has been, over the past decade, intense resistance to attempts at raising the level of minimum support price for raw jute. Jute and jute manufactures, it has been argued, constitute one of the country's principal foreign exchange earners; any inordinate increase in the

TABLE 9:2
COST AND PROFIT MARGIN – PADDY AND WHEAT
Paddy
(Rs. per quintal)

State	Year	Total Cost	Procurement Price	Profit Margin (Percentage)
Uttar Pradesh	1967–68	38.45	56.25	42.1
	1968–69	39.59	56.25	40.6
Tamil Nadu (Samba)	1967–68	48.74	45.00	negative
	1968–69	46.66	45.00	negative
	1969–70	38.43	47.00	22.4
Orissa	1967–68	33.18	48.00	44.6
	1968–69	38.77	48.00	24.8
	1969–70	38.85	48.00	24.0
Assam	1968–69	43,54	56.25	29.2
	1969–70	54.10	56.25	3.7

Wheat
(Rs. per quintal)

State	Year	Total Cost	Procurement Price	Profit Margin (Percentage)
	1970–71	48.50	76.00	56.7
Haryana	1971–72	49.53	76.00	53.7
	1967–68	50.02	76.00 to 95.00	51.2 to 89.1
	1968–69	67.45	76.00	22.6
Punjab	1969–70	62.69	76.00	21.2
	1970–71	61.04	76.00	24.3
	1971–72	59.71	76.00	27.4
Uttar Pradesh	1967–68	49.13	80.00 to 85.00	60.1 to 71.0
	1968–69	44.19	76.00	70.2

level of support price for the fibre would adversely affect the unit processing cost and, therefore, the competitiveness of the industry in the export market.[10] Repeated representations for adjusting the support level to the rise in the price level and the general cost of living have met with but marginal response. The necessary consequence has been a forced reduction in the level of real earnings of the jute grower. Between 1961-62 and 1971-72, the minimum support price for, for example, the Assam Bottom variety of the fibre delivered at Calcutta moved up from Rs.30 per maund to Rs.43 per maund, and increase of less than 40 per cent; the rise in the wholesale price index for the fibre too was exactly of the same order.[11] In contrast, the all-commodities wholesale price index, however, nearly doubled over this period, and the working class consumer price index also rose by the same extent.[12]

Considerations of maintaining the viability of the export of cotton textiles[13] did not, however, deter authorities from steadily raising the support prices for the different varieties of raw cotton in the course of the past decade. In 1961-62, the level of support price for the Moglai Jorilla variety of raw cotton was Rs.495 per candy; this had been raised to Rs.1,050 per candy by 1970-71: the increase allowed for thus amounted to more than 120 per cent. The rise in the level of support prices for the other varieties was more or less of a similar order, and the wholesale price index for raw cotton had also increased by nearly 110 per cent over the period.[14,15]

It is of some relevance that, while between 1961-62 and 1973-74, the wholesale price index for cotton manufactures[16] moved up by 84 per cent, that for raw cotton advanced by 177 per cent, indicating a shift in terms of trade against the manufacturer in the cotton textile industry and in favour of the grower of raw fibre: this shift was in perfect conformity with the general movement in the terms of trade against industry and in favour of the farm sector. The case of raw jute and jute manufactures, however, stands out: the price index for jute manufactures rose by 103 per cent between 1961-62 and 1973-74, but that for the raw fibre increased by only 42 per cent: clearly, in this instance, the terms of trade had moved *against the producer* of raw jute.

In the course of the past twenty years, export subsidies have been developed as a standard device by which the competitiveness of Indian products is sought to be preserved and enlarged in foreign markets. With respect to cotton manufactures, these subsidies have included both cash assistance and import entitlement schemes.[17] The export of raw jute and jute manufactures has been consistently left out of the export subsidy schemes. Not only that, jute and jute manufactures have all along borne the burden of an export duty.[18] Of particular significance is the fact that the Indian Jute Mills Association, the representative body for jute manufacturers, has also not — until very recently — ever asked for an export assistance programme analogous to the one enjoyed by the cotton textile industry.[19]

There is only one hypothesis which satisfactorily explains the Government's discriminatory attitude with respect to the fixing of administered prices apropos of wheat and rice on the one hand, and cotton and jute on the other. It is not any specific regional political bias which has been at work, but the much more fundamental bias which stems from the operation of class forces. In the case of jute — and, to a large extent, rice — the majority of the cultivators are mostly small farmers and share-croppers, who are weak, unorganised, and have but little influence on the processes of the polity. In contrast, the bulk of the wheat crop — and certainly the overwhelming proportion of its marketed surplus — are raised in relatively large-sized holdings. The cultivation of cotton too is increasingly being organised on commercial and quasi-commercial scales in big holdings; besides, the relatively affluent amongst the farmers who raise the cotton crop have intimate links with trade and industry[20] and are accordingly in a position to bring a strong influence to bear upon the authorities in the matter of pricing policy. It is the inter-regional consequences of the discriminatory pricing policy which hit the eye, but the shifting terms of trade against rice and in favour of wheat, and against jute and in favour of cotton, is clearly the outcome of political arrangements having their roots in the antithesis of classes.[21]

Tables 9:3 and 9:4, based on the findings of the Twenty-sixth Round of the National Sample Survey, provide a substantial clue to the interregional variations in class realities. Table 9:3 provides the details on the percentage distribution of households and of area owned by size-class of ownership holdings, while Table 9:4 gives the corresponding details by size-class of household operational holdings, for four States, each from one region of the country, namely, Punjab, Gujarat, Kerala and West Bengal. In Gujarat, 9 per cent of the total households, either owning or operating holdings which are of more than 15 acres in size, controlled close to 55 per cent of the total land; in Punjab, similarly, nearly 45 per cent of the total cultivable area belonged to holdings of more than 15 acres in size, which were owned by 4 per cent, and operated by 5 per cent, of the households existing at the top. In contrast, in West Bengal, hardly 0.5 per cent of the total area covered belonged to holdings which were more than 15 acres in size; the situation was more or less identical in Kerala. It is the small-holders who predominate in both these two States: in West Bengal more than 70 per cent, and in Kerala more than 85 per cent, of the sown area seemed to belong to holdings less than 7.5 acres in size.[22]

Is it not these class realities which explain the varying pressures affecting official pricing decisions concerning agricultural commodities? Inter-crop and interregional discriminations in price fixation, it would seem are second-order manifestations: it is only because the relatively weaker elements predominate in the cultivation of certain crops and in certain regions and States that terms of trade have tended to move against them.[23,24]

TABLE 9:3

PERCENTAGE DISTRIBUTION OF HOUSEHOLDS AND OF
AREA OWNED BY SIZE-CLASS OF HOUSEHOLD OWNERSHIP HOLDING

Size-class of household ownership holding (acres)	Gujarat		Kerala		Punjab		West Bengal	
	Percentage of households	area	Percentage of households	area	Percentage of households	area	Percentage of households	area
Landless	24.97	–	43.97	–	21.06	–	22.62	–
0.01 – 0.49	23.69	0.18	43.96	16.99	47.78	0.77	36.24	2.97
0.50 – 0.99	3.87	0.57	5.04	10.76	1.84	0.51	7.82	4.66
1.00 – 1.24	1.91	0.47	1.13	3.93	1.83	0.82	3.83	3.09
1.25 – 2.49	8.20	3.36	2.00	10.25	4.12	2.92	12.42	17.25
2.50 – 4.99	11.74	9.80	2.35	24.25	6.28	9.19	9.61	25.30
5.00 – 7.49	7.02	9.60	1.20	21.48	5.68	13.26	4.12	18.27
7.50 – 9.99	3.78	7.34	0.19	4.36	3.28	11.06	1.47	9.27
10.00 – 12.49	4.13	10.18	–	–	2.42	10.28	0.99	8.10
12.50 – 14.99	1.96	5.93	–	–	1.72	9.12	0.34	3.44
15.00 – 19.99	2.99	11.57	0.16	7.98	1.24	8.21	0.37	4.61
20.00 – 24.99	1.86	9.08	–	–	1.08	9.04	0.14	2.37
25.00 – 29.99	1.33	7.85	–	–	0.74	7.80	0.03	0.67
30.00 – 49.99	2.13	18.08	–	–	0.72	10.73	–	–
50.00 and above	0.42	5.99	–	–	0.21	6.29	–	–

Source: Department of Statistics, Government of India, *National Sample Survey, Twentysixth Round: July 1971–September 1972, Tables on Land Holdings*.

TABLE 9:4

PERCENTAGE DISTRIBUTION OF HOUSEHOLDS AND OF
AREA OPERATED BY SIZE-CLASS OF HOUSEHOLD OPERATIONAL HOLDING

Size-class of household operational holding (acres)	Gujarat Percentage of households	area	Kerala Percentage of households	area	Punjab Percentage of households	area	West Bengal Percentage of households	area
Operating no land	48.38	—	53.45	—	70.75	—	47.81	—
0.01 – 0.49	1.10	0.06	34.86	16.99	0.71	0.06	9.09	1.34
0.50 – 0.99	3.63	0.51	4.85	10.71	0.50	0.11	6.33	3.12
1.00 – 1.24	1.82	0.44	0.99	3.61	0.75	0.30	3.19	2.40
1.25 – 2.49	7.77	3.15	1.97	10.10	1.68	1.16	13.59	18.08
2.50 – 4.99	10.95	9.09	2.32	25.00	5.61	7.45	11.76	28.91
5.00 – 7.49	7.84	10.63	1.20	20.99	4.81	10.43	4.78	19.76
7.50 – 9.99	3.70	7.15	0.19	4.44	4.94	15.15	1.86	11.09
10.00 – 12.49	3.89	9.30	—	—	3.01	11.87	0.84	6.39
12.50 – 14.99	1.92	5.77	—	—	2.14	10.24	0.28	2.60
15.00 – 19.99	3.24	12.41	0.17	8.16	2.38	14.31	0.30	3.50
20.00 – 24.99	1.72	8.29	—	—	1.14	8.69	0.14	2.23
25.00 – 29.99	1.32	8.05	—	—	0.61	5.77	0.03	0.63
30.00 – 49.99	2.29	19.13	—	—	0.77	10.04	—	—
50.00 and above	0.43	6.02	—	—	0.20	4.42	—	—

Source: Department of Statistics, Government of India, *National Sample Survey, Twentysixth Round: July 1971–September 1972, Tables on Land Holdings.*

APPENDIX TO CHAPTER 9

Data on Cost of Cultivation

Some data on the cost of production of wheat and paddy are presented in the three tables below. The estimates on the cost of production of wheat in Table 9:5 are on the basis of surveys conducted under the Comprehensive Scheme for Studying the Cost of Cultivation of Principal Crops launched by the Ministry of Agriculture, Government of India. The actual field-work under the Scheme is undertaken by non-official agencies such as agricultural universities or agro-economic research centres located in the respective

TABLE 9:5

COST OF PRODUCTION OF WHEAT BY SIZE-CLASSES
OF SAMPLE HOLDINGS, PUNJAB AND HARYANA
(Cost per quintal in Rupees)

Size-class (hectares)	HARYANA 1970–71	1971–72	PUNJAB 1970–71	1971–72
less than 2	59.44	47.53	66.93	78.93
2 – 3.99	48.11	53.96	58.07	60.43
4 – 5.99	49.27	51.00	62.28	58.10
6 – 7.99	51.98	47.14	59.63	58.52
8 – 9.99	45.41	50.88	65.10	59.62
10 – 11.99	40.43	48.42	57.94	64.97
12 – 13.99	42.26	49.50	62.82	57.74
14 – 15.99	45.81	51.63	53.13	43.13
16 – 17.99	45.91	41.33	61.17	75.03
18 – 19.99	37.02	} 39.84	70.23	} 60.32
20 – 21.99	39.63		77.09	
22 and above	40.72		60.04	
All classes	48.10	49.53	61.04	59.71

Note: According to surveys organised under similar lines in Uttar Pradesh and Rajasthan, the cost per quintal for wheat was Rs. 49.68 and Rs. 56.40 respectively in the two States in 1970–71.

TABLE 9:6

COST OF PRODUCTION OF PADDY
(Rs. per quintal)

State/District	1967–68	1968–69	1969–70
U.P., Muzaffarnagar	38.45	39.59	
Gujarat, Surat and Bulsar	52.87	49.82	
Tamil Nadu, Thanjavur			
ADT – 27	46.89	42.09	43.21
Samba Common – 25	53.61	43.06	55.29
Thaladi Common – 25	44.39	34.29	40.46
Samba local	48.74	46.66	51.44
Thaladi local	44.16	38.43	45.85
Andhra Pradesh, Cuddappah	62.14	61.32	67.33
Orissa, Cuttack	33.18	38.77	38.85
Assam, Naogong			
Sali		43.54	54.10
Bao		44.74	44.01
Ahu		60.61	63.77
Punjab, Ferozpore			
Local	53.47	44.74	44.66
IR – 8			36.28

States. The data in Tables 9:6 and 9:7 are culled from the Farm Management Studies carried out by the agro-economic research centres set up under the auspices of the Directorate of Economics and Statistics, Ministry of Agriculture.

The cost of cultivation in these estimates includes cash and kind expenditure on items such as human labour, bullock labour, seeds, manure, fertilisers, land revenue and cess, irrigation charges, depreciation charge for implements, machinery and buildings, interest on crop loans, rent paid for leased-in land, rental value of owned land, interest on owned fixed capital and imputed value of family labour. On a strict interpretation, the cost of

TABLE 9:7

COST OF PRODUCTION OF WHEAT
(Rs. per quintal)

	Uttar Pradesh	Punjab
1967–68	49.13	50.02
1968–69	44.19	67.45
1969–70		62.69

cultivation should not include the rental value of owned land and the interest
on owned fixed capital.

NOTES

1 The production of both crops fell in the following year, that of wheat declining to
   less than 25 million tonnes, and of rice to 39 million. By 1974-75, while wheat
   output had climbed back to 27 million tonnes, rice production was reported to be
   only 41 million. The source for the data quoted is the Directorate of Economics
   and Statistics, Ministry of Agriculture, Government of India.

2 There was a steeper rise in the price level of rice in 1972-73 and, during the last two
   years, the movements in the prices of the two crops have been relatively more
   uniform. But the shift in relative prices in favour of wheat over the decade
   remains pronounced.

3 The broad frame of official farm price policy has been briefly referred to in
   Chapter 8. Since the early 1960s, the Government of India has adopted a policy of
   minimum support prices for the major field crops, and, in addition, a policy of
   procurement prices for the principal foodgrains. The authorities announce, on
   the eve of sowing, a structure of minimum support levels for the different crops.
   These support prices are supposed to cover the expenses of production of all
   categories (including provision for domestic labour and depreciation of
   implements and other farm assets), as also normal profits. Irrespective of the size
   of output and trends in the market price, the Union Government is committed
   under the scheme to purchase, at the level of the announced support price,
   whatever quantities of a crop the farmer, *on his own initiative,* offers to sell. Thus
   even were market prices to crash, farmers could feel confident that, if the worst
   comes to the worst, they could dispose of their entire output — or their
   surplus — to the Government at the guaranteed minimum price. Since the latter
   is supposed to cover the cost of output, and also to provide for normal profit, it is
   in the nature of an insurance price.

   Under the support price policy, the authorities may or may not have to buy any
   quantities of the crop in question: it all depends upon actual market conditions.
   In contrast, under the programme of procurement, the Government announces *a
   priori* its intention to buy, at an indicated procurement price, specified quantities
   of the crop in question. The principal declared objective of procurement
   operations is to maintain a system of public distribution *cum* buffer stocks so as
   to even out inter-and intra-seasonal variations in the prices of important
   commodities, such as foodgrains: in addition, and perhaps more importantly, a
   regular system of public procurement and distribution is intended to cater to the
   needs of the more vulnerable sections of the community. It is the standard
   practice — although of late there have been exceptions — to announce the
   procurement price not on the eve of sowing, but on the eve of the harvest, when
   more or less precise information is available on the size of the crop. Since
   procurement takes place at the initiative of the Government, the procurement
   price is generally expected to be fixed at a level higher than that of the
   corresponding minimum support price. Obviously, the closer the procurement
   price is to the prevailing market price, the higher is the likely volume of
   procurement. But because a major purpose of procurement is to ensure supplies
   to the vulnerable sections, it would be self-defeating to have public purchases at
   or around the level of the market price, for then, unless subsidies could be
   arranged, the poor would find it beyond their means to lift the grain from the
   Government shops either. The general proposition namely, that while in a year of

good crop, the procurement price should move down closer to the support level, in a year marked by unsatisfactory harvest, it should be adjusted somewhat toward the direction of the market price, is well taken. Farmers with sizeable surplus as well as big traders, however, demur; according to their point of view, when market prices shoot up in a bad year, procurement prices too should be increased by an equal proportion. In a difficult year, reasons of expediency may suggest the need for a rise in the procurement price in conformity to market trends, otherwise there could be danger of relatively poor procurement. It is, however, equally difficult to brush off the argument that high market prices are more often than not the consequence of climatic vagaries, and that it would be less than ethical to permit surplus-producing farmers and traders to take undue advantage of it. If public distribution aims at reaching cheap grains to those sections of small farmers and landless labourers who do not raise any grain on their own or raise only a part of their total requirements, to increase inordinately the level of procurement prices would be tantamount to acting against the interests of the majority of the farming community.

In the past decade, minimum support prices announced for wheat and paddy have had little operational significance, for market prices have generally tended to be significantly higher than even the respective procurement prices. In the case of wheat, when market prices declined precipitately in 1968-69, the Government announced that all quantities offered for sale would be purchased, *not at the minimum support price, but at the substantially higher procurement price.* As a pace-setter in the market, therefore, it is the movement in procurement prices which has been of greater relevance. See, in particular, the *Annual Report* of the Agricultural Prices Commission, Government of India, 1969-70.

4 *Bulletin on Food Statistics,* Government of India, 1974.
5 In 1968, a metric tonne of wheat was quoted at $65, and of paddy at $100, in the U.S.A. In the same year, the price of a tonne of milled rice in Japan cost more than two-and-a-half times that of a tonne of wheat; so was the case in Pakistan. See Keith Griffin, *The Green Revolution: An Economic Analysis.* United Nations, 1972, p. 152.
6 This new domestic price parity between rice and wheat preceded the sharp rise in wheat prices in the international market following the 1972-73 season, and cannot therefore be attributed to the latter.
7 See Ashok Mitra, *'Population and Foodgrain Output in India: A Note On Disparate Growth Rates',* Economic Development in South Asia. ed. E. A. G. Robinson and Michael Kidron, Macmillan, 1970, pp. 21-8.
8 N. Krishnaji ('State Intervention and Foodgrain Prices', *Social Scientist,* Volume 3, Number 6/7) assembles the data given in the table from the various *Reports* of the Agricultural Prices Commission, and the *Report on Cost of Production of Wheat in Utter Pradesh during the 1971-72 Crop Season,* Directorate of Economics and Statistics, Ministry of Agriculture, Government of India, and comments: 'These data show that in the early seventies costs of production (excluding imputed values in respect of rent on owned land and interest on owned fixed capital) were in the neighbourhood of Rs.30 per quintal for both paddy and wheat, although we must concede that there are bound to be interregional as well as inter-farm differences in costs. But to the extent that such averages are meaningful they do conclusively show that the procurement price of Rs.76 per quintal of wheat offered during 1968-73 gave the wheat farmer in general, and more so the efficient large farmer, a significantly higher return than what the price of Rs.55 gave the rice farmer. The differences persist in the rates of return per hectare even after making allowance for possible differences in the yield rates of the two crops'. *op. cit.,* 55-6.

TABLE 9:8

COSTS OF PRODUCTION AND PROCUREMENT PRICES
(Rs. per quintal)

State	Year	Crop	Total Cost	Cost D*	Procurement Price
Haryana	1970–71	Wheat	48.10	30.78	76.00
Punjab	1970–71	Wheat	61.04	35.14	76.00
Uttar Pradesh	1971–72	Wheat	50.38	28.51	76.00
Andhra Pradesh	1971–72	Paddy	51.53	31.38	51.00
Orissa	1971–72	Paddy	44.47	27.64	55.00

*Excludes from total cost imputed value of rent from owned land and interest on owned fixed capital.

TABLE 9:9

RETURNS PER HECTARE
(Rs.)

State	Year	Value of Production including by-products per hectare	Cost D* per hectare	Net Returns per hectare
(1)	(2)	(3)	(4)	(5)=(3)−(4)
Haryana	1970–71	1,881.65	871.37	1,010.28
Punjab	1970–71	1,982.53	1,022.43	960.10
Uttar Pradesh	1971–72	1,940.76	935.89	1,004.89
Andhra Pradesh	1971–72	1,746.45	965.80	780.65
Orissa	1971–72	1,168.90	600.56	568.34

*Excludes from total cost imputed value of rent from owned land and interest on owned fixed capital.

9 Till the early 1970s, State intervention with the marketing of either fibre was limited to the power of the Textile Commissioner and the Jute Commissioner to requisition stocks in case of a bad crop or artificial scarcity. Such requisitioning never exceeded 1 to 2 per cent of the total availability in a year. The Cotton Corporation of India was established in 1970-71, and the Jute Corporation of India in 1972-73, both having the objective of evening out inter-and intra-season disparities in supply and ensuring a remunerative price to the growers. Of the

two bodies, the Cotton Corporation of India has been more active, more particularly because it has been less hamstrung by lack of liquid funds.

10   According to one body of opinion, the official reasoning on jute price policy was not only biased, but was also wrong from the point of view of export promotion, since relatively low prices for the fibre led to stagnant yields. See Deepak Nayyar, *India's Exports and Export Policies in the 1960s*, Cambridge University Press, 1976, Chapter 3.

11   These data are from the *Reports* of the Agricultural Prices Commission, Government of India.

12   Government of India. *Economic Survey, 1974-5*, pp. 91 and 93.

13   Cotton textiles have been, consistently since the 1950s, the third most important item of exports, coming immediately behind jute manufactures and tea.

14   Once again, these data are extracted from the *Reports* of the Agricultural Prices Commission.

15   What had been permitted with regard to the level of support price for the other major cash crop, sugarcane, is equally significant. The statutory minimum price for cane, which was Rs.4.02 per quintal for a recovery of 9.0 per cent or below in 1962-63, was raised to as much as Rs.8.00 per quintal for the same level of recovery in 1972-73, implying an increase of nearly 100 per cent.

16   Reserve Bank of India, *Report on Currency and Finance, 1973-74*, Statement 17.

17   Cash incentives for the export of cotton garments were 15 per cent of f.o.b.value of exports to so-called free foreign exchange areas and 7.5 per cent to so-called rupee payment areas and a standardised 5 per cent for exports of cloth above 80 counts. These incentives were withdrawn toward the close of 1974, but manufacturers have since been allowed to get off one square metre of the otherwise obligatory production of controlled cloth against the export of either Rs.5 worth of cotton textiles or Rs.7.50 worth of cotton garments. In addition, import replenishments are currently provided at the following rates: (a) ready-made garments made of cotton fabrics, and blended or mixed fabrics of cotton and rayon other than grey, 9 per cent: (b) mill-made cotton fabrics (other than grey). 6½ per cent; and (c) mill-made cotton yarn (other than grey), 6½ per cent. (Source: Ministry of Commerce, Government of India.)

18   The duty, which was Rs.900 per tonne on both carpet backing and hessian and Rs.600 on sacking in 1966, had been adjusted from time to time in response to developments in the foreign market. Even as late as March 1974, the export duty on primary and secondary carpet backing was Rs.650 and Rs.750 per tonne respectively, while it was Rs.600 on hessian and Rs.150 on sacking. Most of these duties have since been removed.

19   It is perhaps worth mentioning another anomaly. In 1967-68 as well as in 1973-74, market prices of raw jute crashed because of a sharp rise in output. During several weeks, jute prices in many centres for many varieties slipped below the specified support levels; official intervention in the way of price support purchases was feeble and ineffective. In stark contrast, when prices of certain varieties of cotton suffered a temporary break in the 1971-72 season, instructions were issued to the Cotton Corporation of India to start purchase operations not at the level of the minimum support prices, but at prices which were on the average 20 per cent higher than the ruling market prices in 1970-71.

20   A scrutiny of the lists of important office-bearers of the Indian Cotton Mills Federation — representing the textile manufacturers, the East India Cotton Association — representing the cotton traders, and apex co-operative cotton growers' societies in Gujarat and Maharashtra will reveal a considerable overlap of names!

21   A major increase in the procurement prices of paddy and wheat was announced in the 1972-73 season. It is tempting — and not at all unrealistic — to link this

change in official attitude with the fact that, in the more recent years, paddy cultivation has been taken up in a big way in the kharif season in Punjab and Haryana, where large-sized holdings dominate.

22 According to the Sixteenth Round of the NSS, these percentages were roughly around 60 per cent for West Bengal and 50 per cent for Kerala. Thus the results of the Twenty-sixth Round provide stark evidence of the progressive fragmentation of holdings which has occurred in the two States during the years between the two Rounds of the Survey.

23 Discussing the curious phenomenon that bank finance for price support operations in the case of jute has been generally niggardly, the *Economic and Political Weekly* commented on 12 October 1974 ('Untenable Asymmetry', p. 1721): '. . . while in the case of cotton, oilseeds and foodgrains, it is somehow always ensured that market prices do not come down, a different attitude gets reflected in government decision-making on jute. This simply cannot be because the price of raw jute has implications for the country's foreign exchange earnings. These implications hold no less for cotton. The major difference must lie in the fact that the cultivation of jute is still, by and large, carried on by small peasants, who do not constitute a powerful enough political lobby. This is, therefore, the only commodity whose market price the authorities can permit to fall with equanimity. There is also the other fact that, while the government can easily persuade the mills not to purchase stocks beyond three months' requirements, official capability visibly caves in in the reverse situation: i.e. when the mills ought to be ordered to purchase greater quantities so as to prevent a fall in the market price. Where it is a question of offering support to the weak and unorganised, the government's sense of symmetry collapses'.

24 It may seem paradoxical that the rich peasantry in the rice and jute belts did not assert themselves as much as their counterparts in the wheat and cotton belts. The answer must lie in the relatively small area under their control in the traditional kharif tracts, as can be seen in Tables 9:3 and 9:4. On the other hand, once paddy cultivation was taken up in an extensive manner in Punjab and other such *rabi* tracts in the early 1970s, the pressure for higher procurement prices mounted, obviously because the big farmers controlled a major segment of the area where paddy was being newly sown.

CHAPTER 10

Relative Price Movements and Industrial Growth

I

It is time for some stock-taking. The preceding chapters have dealt with an emerging principal reality in the Indian economic system. In recent years, the domestic terms of trade in the country have moved continuously in favour of farm products in general, and, within the agricultural sector, in favour of those specific crops that are marked by a relatively greater order of 'product dominance' on the part of the richer sections of the peasantry. This shift in terms of trade can be viewed as mirroring a political arrangement entered into by the urban bourgeoisie with the rural obligarchy. Its rationale can be easily explained. Given the frame of parliamentary democracy based on adult suffrage, urban industrialists, to maintain their control over political institutions, need to enlist support from amongst the rural electorate. The task is immensely facilitated by the understanding they reach with surplus-raising farmers and their trading partners, who are in a position to ensure the votes of major sections of small peasants and landless labourers. The fact that the latter are economically extremely vulnerable, and the rate of literacy amongst them is as low as ten to fifteen per cent, contributes to the process. It is not simply that — as generally argued — attempts to raise the level of productivity and income of the poorer farmers are adversely affected by the slow spread of elementary education. Their educational backwardness keeps the rural poor away from analysing the factors underlying their economic plight, and makes it difficult to mobilise them politically. Precisely because of their vulnerability, a kind of unequal exchange too gets established between them and the surplus-raising farmers and traders, who find the circumstances opportune for the exercise of a virulent form of monopsony power. The unequal exchange is reflected in the prices at which the poorer peasants are forced to sell their products to the rural oligarchs or traders at the beginning of the season or those at which they are forced to buy these back toward the close of the season, in the extortionary share which the share-cropper has to yield to the landlord, in the exorbitant interest charged by the surplus farmer-cum-moneylender-cum-trader from the poor, and in the low wages an agricultural labourer is fobbed off with by a big farmer. It is, however, also overwhelmingly reflected in the political pressures which the richer peasants and traders succeed in applying on the small farmers and farm workers. The threat to deny grain or lower wages or raise the lending rate or lower the proportion of the shared crop or eject from land can be — and is — held against the weaker sections so as to make them fall in line with the political wishes of the big farmers and the mercantile elements. The notorious 'vote banks' come to operate, and the urban bourgeoisie therefore find it altogether expedient to enter into an informal, quasi-contractual arrangement with the rural oligarchy. The arrangement, at least in part, is also helped by the fact of the urban bourgeoisie being closest to the rich peasants in terms of social alignments.[1]

A political alliance is a two-way relationship. The developing shift in the terms of trade in favour of the farm sector is the major price paid by the industrial bourgeoisie to cement their political coalition with the rural oligarchy. There have been, and are, other pay-offs, for instance, a large array of capital development projects for agriculture and fiscal and monetary transfers. A whole range of agricultural inputs have been sold at subsidised rates to the rich peasants at various times during the past two decades. These inputs have included not only the high-yielding varieties of seeds, but insecticides, pesticides and fertilisers. In addition, the authorities have conceded the demand of the affluent peasantry to keep the rates of power low and not to raise the rates for irrigation. Other indirect advantages have also accrued to the surplus-producing farmers: the direct tax on agriculture has remained inordinately low through the entire period. Suggestions for introducing a progressively graduated levy on cultivable holdings or for increasing the incidence of land revenue or for enforcing somewhat more rigorously the machinery for collecting these levies or the tax on agricultural wealth have been given short shrift. Proposals for enforcing a betterment levy on lands whose productivity has improved as a consequence of extensive State outlays have similarly been brushed aside.

Finally, as part of the implicit political contract, the bourgeoisie have been willing not to insist on the implementation of any meaningful measures for land reforms.[2] From time to time, declarations of intent have been made and legislations have been passed in the different States with the object of applying certain ceilings on land holdings, or allocating the crop between the landlord and the tenant or share-cropper, or protecting the wages of rural labour. Nearly each of these legislative measures has been honoured more in the breach. In a number of States, even such an apparently innocuous step as the maintenance of land records on a contemporary basis has been discouraged for obvious reasons.

Monetary quantification of these direct and indirect gains accruing to the richer farmers is not always easy. There can, however, be little doubt that the terms of trade effect apart, the net consequence of official policy has been to generate every year an additional flow of funds toward the direction of the more affluent sections of the farming community.[3] The fact that big farmers have increasingly benefited from certain other sources, namely, public financial institutions and the banking sector, has also to be taken into account. The flow of resources from such institutions as the Co-operative Credit Department of the Reserve Bank of India, the Agricultural Finance Corporation, the Agricultural Refinance Corporation, as well as the various agencies of the State governments has been rising with each year. Particularly following the nationalisation of the major commercial banks, both direct and indirect credit to agriculture has increased several-fold. The overwhelming proportion of these additional funds, including bank credit, intended for agriculture has gone to the surplus-raising farmers.[4]

All this constitutes the cost of the arrangement entered into with the rural oligarchy, of which a considerable part has to be borne by the bourgeoisie themselves. The contract must allow them to recoup this loss through compensatory gains registered elsewhere. These gains can be listed. To begin with, the political liaison enables the bourgeoisie to establish their complete command over the industrial and foreign trade policies of the Government. In a system dominated by administrative controls, the opportunity to influence State power ensures that, other things remaining the same, these controls are wielded in a manner that will maximise the economic benefits to the bourgeoisie. The latter are also allowed to scale the commanding heights of decision-making in matters pertaining to banking and foreign exchange. Bank finance normally follows their convenience; the foreign exchange earned by the country is allocated in accordance with their priorities. Special subsidies, too, such as for exports, are arranged.[5] In so far as fiscal resources are concerned, once provision has been made towards meeting the requirements of the affluent peasantry, the balance is by and large available to cater to the interests of urban industrialists. Spheres of influence are thus worked out. If, as a result, the bourgeoisie maximise their gains, the rural oligarchs feel equally happy with the arrangement, so much so that, unless exogenous factors intervene, the political alliance between the two classes could continue indefinitely.

But a shadow falls. It is not merely that — as stressed by Michal Kalecki in his description of the intermediate regime — the urban and rural proletariat, who form the majority of the nation, are left outside the arrangement. As we have seen in Chapter Eight, notwithstanding the marked shift in terms of trade in favour of farm products — and up to a point precisely because of it —, agricultural output tapers off, and the political alliance thus appears to be corrosive of growth in the major sector of the economy. The movement in the terms of trade — and the other gains which accrue to them through the instrumentalities of the State — without question lead to a secular increase in the rate of surplus generation on the part of rural oligarchs: the process is further helped by the monopsonistic manoeuvres they are able to launch *vis-à-vis* the poorer sections of the peasantry. None of these, however, has any significant positive impact on production.

What about profits and production in the industrial sector? To form a total picture, the economic advantages which flow in the direction of the bourgeoisie as a consequence of the political alliance need to be considered along with its impact on industrial profit-taking and on the rate of industrial growth. To an exploration of these issues we now turn.

II

One may begin at the very beginning. The shift in the terms of trade in favour of agriculture should, other things remaining the same, lead to a shift in income distribution in favour of the relatively richer 'farmers. In certain regions, the accretion of additional income with affluent rural sections may result in a rise in the level of money earnings of wage-labour as also to an increase in the incomes of small farmers. But this 'percolation' effect can have only a limited significance. A movement in the terms of trade in favour of farm products incorporates and reflects the fact of a rise in the price of foodgrains, and the additional outlay landless labourers as well as small farmers are now called upon to make for the purchase of their food requirements should in most cases outstrip the increase in their money earnings. Aside from this, the rise in farm prices contributes, either immediately or with a time-lag, to a corresponding increase in the price of industrial commodities too. In so far as the rate of rise in money earnings of small peasants and farm workers is over a period less than that in industrial prices, a further worsening takes place in their level of real incomes.[6] Thus the poorer sections of the rural community are caught in a pincer on account of the movements in relative prices: they are compelled to make a larger monetary outlay on foodgrains if they want to maintain their level of intake; simultaneously, they have to pay higher prices for a whole range of industrial goods.

The sequence is easily sketched. First, as the terms of trade improve for agriculture, the relative share of aggregate farm income going to small cultivators and agricultural workers declines. Second, a larger proportion of their earnings than before is now deployed for the purchase of foodgrains; alternately, they are forced to reduce their food consumption. If the quantity of food consumed is not cut back — or at least not cut back initially — the proportion of total income spent on food increases, so that a smaller proportion of the earnings than before is available for the purchase of industrial commodities. Accompanying this development is an across-the-board rise in industrial prices. Once the process works itself out, the demand for industrial commodities on the part of a preponderant majority of the rural community falls as a result of the shift in terms of trade.

This reduction in the demand for industrial goods on the part of the poorer sections of the farming population can conceivably be compensated in the event of a proportionately larger outlay on the part of the richer sections who experience major increases in their levels of income, in money as well as real terms. This is, however, unlikely to come about at least in the case of mass consumption goods, which attract the familiar Engel's Law. Even though a rise occurs in their absolute level of demand, the proportion of income spent by the affluent farmers on mass consumption goods actually declines. Most of their additional demand concentrates on a number of luxury consumer and capital goods.[7] It is an open question whether, overall, the loss of the market among the lower ranges of the rural population groups is compensated by the rise in demand on the part of the richer peasantry. An analysis by Ranjit Sau suggests the contrary.[8] On a rough reckoning, while between 1952-53 and 1964-65 the consumption of industrial goods in the rural parts of India went up by roughly Rs.1,000 crores, or by around 30 per cent, the rate of this rise was less than the rate of increase in the price level for industrial commodities over this period.[9] The problems of an appropriate price deflator and of lack of comparability between the compositions of the consumption basket in the different years should not be understated; even so, given the nature of Sau's findings, it appears unlikely that the real level of consumption of industrial goods in the rural sector moved up at all, or appreciably, over the period.

Equally noteworthy are his conclusions concerning the impact of the shift in terms of trade on the absorption of industrial goods in the urban sector. Between 1952-53 and 1964-65, urban consumption of industrial commodities increased by Rs.600 crores. Of this total, as much as one-third is attributable to the top 5 per cent of the urban population; for the other 95 per cent, the increase in the money demand for industrial goods was around 45 per cent, that is, more or less the same as the rise in the wholesale price index. Thus while in the aggregate there was some rise in the level of consumption of industrial goods in real terms, once the top 5 per cent are excluded, the order of this increase was negligible for the rest of the urban population. Here again, the slow rise in the level of demand is easily explained. During any period since 1947, the rate of rise in money wages for practically all categories of industrial workers, and in nearly each sphere of industrial activity — as also for other sections of urban employees, in each sphere of industrial activity — has been less than the rate of increase in general wholesale prices or in consumer prices. If the comparison is between the rates of increase in money wages and in foodgrain prices, the discrepancy is still wider.[10] Thus, over the years, a steadily rising proportion of money wages accruing to different segments of employees in the urban sector must have been spent to meet the requirements of food. The proportion of income intended for the purchase of industrial products could therefore increase only imperceptibly.

Sau's analysis carries the story forward only up to 1964-65. There is little reason to assume that the trend has been reversed in the subsequent period. The terms of trade have swung even more sharply in favour of agriculture and against industry in the past decade. Compared to 1964-65, the index number of agricultural prices had more than doubled by 1973-74, while industrial prices advanced on the average by around 70 per cent.[11] During this decade, since money wages continued to lag behind prices, the trend established between 1952-53 and 1964-65 must have emerged even more firmly, and the adverse consequences of the shift in terms of trade on the demand for industrial products following the shift in terms of trade more pronouncedly established. Output in the organised industrial sector of the country has been growing since the middle 1960s at a rate which is less than half of what it was in the preceding fifteen years.[12] As we shall see presently, while this decline in the rate of industrial growth is attributable to other factors as well, one major contributory factor must be the levelling off of industrial demand explicitly because of shifts in the terms of trade.[13]

III

What could be the effect of the shift in terms of trade on the supply conditions of Indian industry? Other things remaining the same, the unit cost of industrial output should rise over the years as a consequence of the movement in relative prices against industry; with farm prices, including prices of industrial raw materials, advancing all along the line, the unit cost of material input should increase for a wide range of industrial activities. On the assumption of a coalition of interests between the manufacturing bourgeoisie and the surplus-raising farmers, the rise in industrial costs on account of the increase in the cost of raw materials should be sought to be compensated by a rise in manufacturing prices. Were such a rise in product prices, however, to affect demand adversely, the modality of compensation for the increase in raw material cost would pose a problem. On the other hand, if the cost of living of employees were to go up as a consequence of the rise in food prices, this need not lead to any immediate rise in money wages in any industrial unit; the bourgeoisie could resist compensatory adjustments in wage rates. Whatever adjustments finally take place could take place only with a time-lag and need not be commensurate with the rise in the cost of living. According to Table 10:1, the share of wages as a proportion of value of output has fallen steadily since the 1950s; the compensation offered to the workers on account of the increase in food prices may thus appear to have been less than the increase allowed for in product prices. An alternative explanation could be that, taking the Indian industrial sector as a whole, a certain substitution of labour by other inputs, including capital, has occurred during this period, enabling entrepreneurs to reduce the proportion of the value of output going out as wages.[14]

An asymmetry could thus develop between the consequences of rising raw material prices and of rising foodgrain prices as far as the rate of industrial profits is concerned. What we are interested in is the net effect of the increasingly adverse terms of trade on the fortunes of the manufacturing bourgeoisie. It is in this connection that an examination of the trends in the rate of industrial profits during the past decade or thereabouts appears to be of considerable import. An analysis of this nature does of course bristle with difficulties. The Indian economy as a whole bears evidence of widely disparate developments; its industrial structure too is riven by similar heterogeneities. At any point of time, a compendium of old and new activities contributes to aggregate industrial output, and carries within their fold units whose capital structure is marked by widely differing characteristics; the technologies are diverse, the

TABLE 10:1

WAGE SHARE IN INDIAN INDUSTRIES

Year	Wages as percentage of value added by manufacture
1949	53.5
1952	51.6
1955	41.8
1958	39.8
1960	39.6
1961	39.2
1962	39.6
1963	37.6
1964	36.5
1965	36.6
1966	36.8
1967	38.9
1968	38.3
1969	34.7

Source: S. L. Shetty, 'Trends in Wages and Salaries and Profits of the Private Corporate Sector', *Economic and Political Weekly*, 13 October, 1973, Table 3, p. 1869.

methods of production and management vary from unit to unit, sales and purchase operations reflect marked discrepancies in cultural norms and institutional settings. The lack of availability of data, particularly of data which stretch over a reasonable number of years and enable inter-year and inter-industry comparisons, is also a major stumbling block in the way of detailed statistical analysis.[15]

The various deficiencies in basic data notwithstanding, the summarised presentation of the Reserve Bank of India's analysis of the profitability ratios in Indian industries in Table 10:2 tells a fairly consistent story for the period since 1960-61. While profits as a proportion of total capital employed have gone up in one or two organised industrial activities since 1960-61, the overall impression that is obtainable is one of general stagnation, if not of decline, in the rate of industrial profits. For the medium and large public limited companies, the rate of profit was 10.1 per cent in both 1960-61 and 1965-66, with but marginal shifts in the intervening years; although the coverage was different, there was little change in the position in the subsequent period up to 1970-71; if anything, the rate of profit would seem to have dipped a little for this group of companies in the late 1960s.[16] Profits after tax as a percentage of value added also showed a declining trend both during 1960-61 to 1965-66 and during

TABLE 10:2

PROFITABILITY RATIOS IN INDIAN INDUSTRY

	Profits before Tax as Percentage of Total Income	Profits after Tax as Percentage of Total Income	Profits as Percentage of Total Capital Employed
1259 Medium and Large Public Limited Companies			
1960–61	9.1	5.6	10.1
1961–62	9.0	5.1	10.0
1962–63	9.1	4.3	10.7
1963–64	9.3	4.6	10.5
1964–65	8.6	4.2	10.1
1965–66	7.7	3.8	10.1
1420 Medium and Large Public Limited Companies			
1965–66	8.2	4.1	10.1
1966–67	7.6	4.0	9.8
1967–68	6.2	3.2	8.7
1968–69	5.8	2.9	8.5
1969–70	6.8	3.9	9.7
1970–71	7.0	3.8	10.4
501 Medium and Large Private Limited Companies			
1960–61	5.4	2.9	11.3
1961–62	6.0	2.8	11.9
1962–63	6.2	2.2	12.1
1963–64	6.7	2.1	13.2
1964–65	6.4	2.4	13.1
1965–66	6.3	2.2	13.1
701 Medium and Large Private Limited Companies			
1965–66	5.7	2.0	11.7
1966–67	5.4	1.8	11.2
1967–68	4.4	1.4	10.2
1968–69	4.1	1.4	9.8
1969–70	4.4	1.6	10.2
1970–71	4.1	1.3	9.7

Source: S. L. Shetty, *op. cit.*, Table 2, p. 1867.

1965-66 to 1970-71. The story is hardly different for the private limited companies. Certainly during the late 1960s, profits both as a proportion of capital employed and as a proportion of value added fell, and this despite the fact that, aside from inflationary conditions, blanket exchange control provided nearly complete protection to domestic industries against the intrusion of foreign goods.

Even more revealing are the data in Table 10: 3 on rates of return of industrial units belonging to different size-groups of paid-up capital. The average rate of return on capital for public companies with paid-up capital of between Rs.5 to 10 lakhs, for instance, was 9.5 per cent in 1961-62, but 7.8 per cent in 1965-66; for companies with paid-up capital between Rs.10 and 25 lakhs, the rate of return declined from 9.7 per cent to 7.7 per cent between these two years; for units with paid-up capital of between Rs.25 to 50 lakhs, the decline was from 9.9 per cent to 7.9 per cent. For units with paid-up capital of between Rs.50 lakhs and 1 crore, however, the fall in the average rate of return was pronouncedly less, from 9.6 per cent to 9.2 per cent. And the picture is altogether different for companies with paid-up capital of Rs.1 crore and above; here the average rate of return seemingly went up from 10.2 per cent in 1961-62 to 11.2 per cent in 1965-66. The story is more or less repeated in the period 1965-66 to 1970-71. There was a fall in profitability for the relatively smaller-sized units, but those with more than Rs.50 lakhs of capital assets were able to register a moderate increase in the rate of profit. An hypothesis suggests itself. While the big units, by virtue of their commanding position in both product and factor markets, were, during the period under discussion, able to hold on to their own despite unfavourable trends in relative prices, this was not the case with the small and middle-sized firms; they were not able to pass on the rise in their unit material and wage costs to the product price.

A couple of different, but equally interesting conclusions follow from the data assembled in Table 10: 4. First, profits expressed as a proportion of total capital employed tended in both periods either to stagnate or to fall for most agriculture-based industries — such as sugar, jute and cotton textiles[18] — while this was not generally the case of the other industries. Second, the rate of profit in general was at a higher level elsewhere than in the industries heavily dependent upon the farm sector for inputs.[19] Both conclusions are in conformity with the expectation that, other things remaining the same, a shift in terms of trade in favour of the farm sector would affect the rate of return of the agriculture-based industries relatively more adversely.

Next comes another fact of some significance. In the case of the 1,259 large and medium public limited companies included in the RBI sample, profits after tax rose from Rs.130 crores in 1960-61 to Rs.140 crores in 1965-66, that is, by only 7.7 per cent (see Table 10: 5). Considering that the increase in the general price index during this period was of the order of more than 30 per cent, there was therefore an erosion of net real profits. The story is the same for

TABLE 10:3

PROFITABILITY RATIOS FOR PUBLIC LIMITED COMPANIES

Paid-up Capital *Rs. 5 lakhs – Rs. 10 lakhs*	Profits as percentage of total capital employed
I *Series*	
1961–62	9.5
1962–63	9.0
1963–64	9.0
1964–65	8.7
1965–66	7.8
II *Series*	
1966–67	6.8
1967–68	5.8
1968–69	4.2
1969–70	4.9
1970–71	6.2
Paid-up Capital *Rs. 10 lakhs – Rs. 25 lakhs*	
I *Series*	
1961–62	9.7
1962–63	8.5
1963–64	9.2
1964–65	8.8
1965–66	7.7
II *Series*	
1966–67	7.5
1967–68	5.9
1968–69	5.9
1969–70	6.4
1970–71	6.7
Paid-up Capital *Rs. 25 lakhs – Rs. 50 lakhs*	
I *Series*	
1961–62	9.3
1962–63	9.4
1963–64	10.0
1964–65	9.0
1965–66	7.9
II *Series*	
1966–67	8.2
1967–68	6.6
1968–69	6.9
1969–70	8.3
1970–71	8.0

TABLE 10:3 *(Continued)*

PROFITABILITY RATIOS FOR PUBLIC LIMITED COMPANIES

Paid-up Capital *Rs. 50 lakhs – Rs. 1 Crore*		Profits as percentage of total capital employed
I	*Series*	
	1961–62	9.6
	1962–63	10.7
	1963–64	10.6
	1964–65	9.8
	1965–66	9.2
II	*Series*	
	1966–67	7.7
	1967–68	6.6
	1968–69	7.3
	1969–70	8.6
	1970–71	8.8
Paid-up Capital *Rs. 1 crore and above*		
I	*Series*	
	1961–62	10.2
	1962–63	10.3
	1963–64	11.1
	1964–65	11.3
	1965–66	11.2
II	*Series*	
	1966–67	10.0
	1967–68	9.0
	1968–69	9.1
	1969–70	10.3
	1970–71	11.4
III	*Series*	
	1970–71	11.3
	1971–72	11.1

Note: I Series: 1,333 large and medium public limited companies
II Series: 1,501 large and medium public limited companies
III Series: 346 large companies

Source: S. L. Shetty, *op. cit.,* Table 8, pp. 1887–8.

TABLE 10:4
PROFITABILITY RATIOS FOR MEDIUM AND LARGE
PUBLIC LIMITED COMPANIES – INDUSTRY-WISE

Coal Mining	Profits as percentage of total capital employed
I *Series*	
1960–61	8.8
1961–62	8.4
1962–63	9.4
1963–64	8.3
1964–65	5.6
1965–66	6.0
II *Series*	
1965–66	6.3
1966–67	6.1
1967–68	6.4
1968–69	6.5
1969–70	7.3
1970–71	5.6

Edible Vegetables and Hydrogenated Oils

I *Series*	
1960–61	8.6
1961–62	7.1
1962–63	7.1
1963–64	6.5
1964–65	10.0
1965–66	9.6
II *Series*	
1965–66	11.3
1966–67	14.0
1967–68	7.0
1968–69	16.0
1969–70	14.5
1970–71	14.3

Sugar

I *Series*	
1960–61	8.4
1961–62	7.0
1962–63	7.1
1963–64	10.6
1964–65	10.4
1965–66	9.6
II *Series*	
1965–66	10.2
1966–67	8.2
1967–68	6.8
1968–69	13.0
1969–70	8.4
1970–71	4.9

TABLE 10:4 *(Continued)*

Cotton Textiles	Profits as percentage of total capital employed
I *Series*	
1960–61	11.7
1961–62	12.8
1962–63	7.8
1963–64	8.8
1964–65	8.7
1965–66	5.8
II *Series*	
1965–66	5.4
1966–67	7.8
1967–68	6.3
1968–69	5.3
1969–70	7.9
1970–71	7.9
Jute Textiles	
I *Series*	
1960–61	7.6
1961–62	3.4
1962–63	16.5
1963–64	10.9
1964–65	5.4
1965–66	6.6
II *Series*	
1965–66	5.8
1966–67	2.3
1967–68	1.3
1968–69	3.6
1969–70	3.0
1970–71	6.0
Silk and Rayon Textiles	
I *Series*	
1960–61	14.2
1961–62	12.1
1962–63	9.7
1963–64	10.8
1964–65	12.6
1965–66	18.2
II *Series*	
1965–66	17.6
1966–67	21.9
1967–68	19.9
1968–69	17.5
1969–70	18.1
1970–71	19.8

TABLE 10:4 *(Continued)*

Iron and Steel	Profits as percentage of total capital employed
I *Series*	
1960−61	7.2
1961−62	8.1
1962−63	9.9
1963−64	12.4
1964−65	11.8
1965−66	11.1
II *Series*	
1965−66	10.9
1966−67	6.6
1967−68	4.8
1968−69	6.3
1969−70	6.0
1970−71	7.4
Other Non-ferrous Metals	
I *Series*	
1960−61	11.6
1961−62	13.0
1962−63	13.1
1963−64	14.8
1964−65	18.3
1965−66	16.8
II *Series*	
1965−66	17.3
1966−67	10.3
1967−68	7.9
1968−69	5.0
1969−70	8.8
1970−71	13.1
Engineering	
I *Series*	
1960−61	10.7
1961−62	9.7
1962−63	11.4
1963−64	12.1
1964−65	12.7
1965−66	12.2
II *Series*	
1965−66	11.9
1966−67	10.0
1967−68	8.2
1968−69	7.3
1969−70	8.3
1970−71	10.0

TABLE 10:4 *(Continued)*

Chemicals	Profits as percentage of total capital employed
I *Series*	
1960–61	13.7
1961–62	12.7
1962–63	11.8
1963–64	12.1
1964–65	13.0
1965–66	14.2
II *Series*	
1965–66	14.9
1966–67	15.1
1967–68	12.6
1968–69	12.2
1969–70	14.9
1970–71	14.9
Mineral Oils	
I *Series*	
1960–61	13.0
1961–62	14.2
1962–63	14.4
1963–64	14.7
1964–65	12.3
1965–66	11.1
II *Series*	
1965–66	11.0
1966–67	12.0
1967–68	11.8
1968–69	17.8
1969–70	20.0
1970–71	24.2
Cement	
I *Series*	
1960–61	7.9
1961–62	8.7
1962–63	11.3
1963–64	10.0
1964–65	10.0
1965–66	11.2
II *Series*	
1965–66	11.0
1966–67	14.1
1967–68	11.8
1968–69	7.6
1969–70	8.7
1970–71	10.2

TABLE 10:4 *(Continued)*

Paper and Paper Products

I Series

1960–61	9.3
1961–62	8.2
1962–63	8.2
1963–64	7.8
1964–65	6.6
1965–66	7.9

II Series

1965–66	6.0
1966–67	7.0
1967–68	5.8
1968–69	6.9
1969–70	10.1
1970–71	12.5

Source: S. L. Shetty, *op. cit.,* Table 6, pp. 1875–85.

TABLE 10:5

PROFITS AFTER TAX OF THE CORPORATE SECTOR
(Rs. Crores)

	1259 large and medium public limited companies	501 medium and large private limited companies
1960–61	130	18
1961–62	127	18
1962–63	118	15
1963–64	137	15
1964–65	143	19
1965–66	140	19

	1420 large and medium public limited companies	701 medium and large private limited companies
1965–66	162	16
1966–67	177	15
1967–68	148	13
1968–69	149	14
1969–70	219	17
1970–71	248	15

Source: S. L. Shetty, *op. cit.,* Table 1, pp. 1865–6.

private limited companies: total net profits between the two years remained nearly static in money terms, implying a steep fall in the real level of profits. Similarly, between 1965-66 and 1970-71, profits after tax went up from Rs.162 crores to Rs.248 crores for the public companies, that is, by approximately 53 per cent, while, in the case of private limited companies, profits would actually seem to have shrunk even in money terms. The general price increase over this period was more than 90 per cent; in any event, real profits therefore once more declined in the case of both groups of companies.

The number of units covered in the two periods — 1960-61 to 1965-66 and 1965-66 to 1970-71 — was not the same; a moderately firm conclusion appears nonetheless to be in order. Between 1960-61 and 1970-71, over-all industrial output in the country rose by 80 per cent although, ever since 1965-66, the rate of growth has been generally sluggish. This considerable enlargement in the scale of industrial production did not, however, lead to any corresponding improvement in the scale of profits; in fact, in real terms, aggregate net profits seem to have declined since 1960-61. In individual industries as well as in individual units — particularly in the luxury consumer groups — both the rate of profit and its scale improved considerably over the period; but the general picture was one of retarded profits.

IV

To summarise, the profitability of the corporate sector has tended to stagnate during the past decade, and its own-account earnings have shrunk in real terms. This failure to generate resources for growth on the part of private industry can be causally related to the rise in input costs following the continuous shift in the terms of trade: wherever product prices could not be adjusted fully in response to increases in unit costs or economising was not possible in input use, savings to all appearances, fell.[20] The point is made rather convincingly by the data put together in Tables 10:6 and 10:7. In practically all industries, both between 1960-61 and 1965-66 and between 1965-66 and 1970-71, for public as well as private limited companies, profits after tax declined or, alternatively, the proportionate rise in profits was considerably less than the proportionate rise in the cost of material inputs and wages.[21] As a consequence, the corporate sector had to lean increasingly upon borrowings from outside to sustain its investment programmes. Tables 10:8 and 10:9, which detail the sources of finance for the private corporate sector in more recent years, are revealing. External borrowings constituted barely 20 per cent of the total funds invested by the public limited companies in 1961-62 (Table 10:8). By 1969-70, however, borrowings made up 40 per cent of the aggregate funds invested in the private corporate sector as a whole; in 1973-74, borrowed funds were on the verge of furnishing nearly one-half of the aggregate investments in the sector.[22] Most of these borrowed funds have come either directly from the Government or from various public financial institutions.

Table 10: 10 presents a synoptic view of the general trend of savings in the country. The inability of the corporate sector to

TABLE 10:6

PERCENTAGE INCREASE IN COST OF INPUTS,
WAGE COST AND PROFITS BETWEEN 1960–61
AND 1965–66 AND BETWEEN 1965–66 AND
1970–71 FOR PRIVATE LIMITED COMPANIES

		Cost of Inputs	Wage Cost	Profit After Tax
1.	Mining and Quarrying			
	I *Series*	50.0	39.7	−72.7
	II *Series*	53.5	63.0	−71.0
2.	Processing and Manufactures			
(a)	*Foodstuffs, Textiles, Tobacco, Leather and Products thereof*			
	I *Series*	52.7	60.1	10.0
	II *Series*	70.5	57.0	−42.6
(b)	*Metals, Chemicals and Products thereof*			
	I *Series*	80.9	107.2	39.0
	II *Series*	51.7	62.5	16.9
(c)	*Not Elsewhere Classified*			
	I *Series*	40.5	98.6	−47.1
	II *Series*	62.5	55.8	112.9
3.	Other Industries			
	I *Series*	22.2	49.9	−4.1
	II *Series*	18.8	22.5	−34.7

Note: Series I represents data from 501 companies, showing percentage increases in 1965–66 over 1960–61; Series II represents data from 701 companies, showing percentage increases in 1970–71 over 1965–66.

Source: S. L. Shetty, *op. cit.,* Table 5, p. 1874.

TABLE 10:7

PERCENTAGE INCREASE IN COST OF INPUTS,
WAGE COSTS AND PROFITS BETWEEN 1960–61
AND 1965–66 AND BETWEEN 1965–66 AND
1970–71 FOR PUBLIC LIMITED COMPANIES

	Cost of Inputs	Wage Cost	Profit After Tax
Coal Mining			
I *Series*	62.9	57.5	−19.5
II *Series*	40.7	50.4	− 5.1
Edible Vegetable and Hydrogenated Oils			
I *Series*	52.4	19.8	30.7
II *Series*	127.8	93.5	86.4
Sugar			
I *Series*	48.6	39.6	1.3
II *Series*	69.9	52.2	−102.6
Cotton Textiles			
I *Series*	51.8	45.4	−89.2
II *Series*	72.4	39.5	316.9
Jute Textiles			
I *Series*	48.5	66.8	−10.0
II *Series*	5.2	56.4	−45.6
Silk and Rayon Textiles			
I *Series*	187.5	110.9	95.1
II *Series*	78.7	80.0	118.5
Iron and Steel			
I *Series*	37.4	37.2	9.2
II *Series*	18.7	40.7	−28.3
Other Non-Ferrous Metals			
I *Series*	89.0	166.2	125.5
II *Series*	104.6	77.7	64.9
Engineering			
I *Series*	85.1	111.7	71.3
II *Series*	56.8	69.1	11.4
Chemicals			
I *Series*	97.8	100.6	43.9
II *Series*	109.2	96.7	82.2
Mineral Oils			
I *Series*	25.9	−7.5	−24.5
II *Series*	52.2	49.6	106.4

TABLE 10:7 *(Continued)*

	Cost of Inputs	Wage Cost	Profit After Tax
Cement			
I *Series*	74.2	71.0	80.0
II *Series*	93.9	42.6	81.6
Paper and Paper Products			
I *Series*	62.9	72.0	39.0
II *Series*	69.4	75.7	331.2

Note: Series I represents data from 1,337 companies, showing percentage increases in 1965–66 over 1960–61; Series II represents data from 1,501 companies, showing percentage increases in 1970–71 over 1965–66.

Source: S. L. Shetty, *op. cit.,* Table 4, pp. 1870–3.

TABLE 10:8

SOURCES OF FUNDS OF 1,333 PUBLIC LIMITED COMPANIES
(Rs. Crores)

	1961–62	1962–63	1963–64	1964–65	1965–66
Internal Sources	181.1	170.8	191.5	192.6	192.4
A. *Paid-up Capital*	6.7	13.2	6.9	0.9	9.2
B. *Reserves and Surplus*	52.8	45.2	63.0	67.8	58.6
C. *Provisions*	121.5	112.5	121.6	123.8	124.6
External Sources	147.4	174.1	182.3	222.0	237.6
D. *Paid-up Capital (Net Issues)*	38.2	29.3	28.8	24.0	22.3
E. *Borrowings*	67.8	91.2	100.6	126.0	152.8
F. *Trade Dues and other Current Liabilities*	40.9	53.8	53.7	70.9	62.2
G. *Miscellaneous Non-current Liabilities*	0.5	−0.2	−0.7	1.2	−0.2
Total	328.5	345.0	373.8	414.6	430.0

Source: Reserve Bank of India, *Financial Statistics of Joint-Stock Companies in India, 1960–61 to 1970–71.*

TABLE 10:9

PRIVATE NON-FINANCIAL CORPORATE SECTOR:
SOURCES OF INVESTMENT AT CURRENT PRICES
(Rs. Crores)

	1969–70	1970–71	1971–72	1972–73	1973–74
1. Capital Raised (including debentures)	77	71	70	106	90
2. Retained Profits	142	168	158	145	145
3. Borrowings	391	387	424	498	638
4. Depreciation Provision	349	380	396	425	469
Total	959	1006	1048	1174	1342

Source: Reserve Bank of India, *Report on Currency and Finance, 1973–74*, p. 13.

sustain its savings is fairly clearly brought out in the table, but what is equally revealing is the relative decline in *public* savings too as a proportion of national income. In fact, if account is taken of the price rise between 1969-70 and 1973-74, the volume of public savings shrank in real terms. Such a development not only inhibited private industrial expansion by affecting the flow of funds on the supply side; by the constraints it has enforced on public investments, it must also have had an adverse influence on the demand for the products of the private industrial sector. This atrophy in public savings can again be linked to the persistence of the drift in terms of trade in favour of agriculture. The additional income which concentrates in the

TABLE 10:10

DOMESTIC SAVINGS AT CURRENT PRICES
(Rs. Crores)

	1968–69	2969–70	1970–71	1971–72	1972–73	1973–74
1. Public Sector	584	682	747	724	749	859
2. Domestic Private Corporate Sector	62	121	210	191	143	164
3. Household Sector	1,778	1,854	2,496	3,166	3,442	3,977
4. Total	2,424	2,657	3,453	4,081	4,334	5,000

Source: Reserve Bank of India, *Report on Currency and Finance, 1973–74*, p. 6.

hands of the rural rich on account of the shift in terms of trade cannot be appropriated for purposes of the State, and for precisely the same reason which induces this shift in the first place. The apparent growth in the savings of the household sector in recent years reflects this fact of the gains registered by the affluent peasantry, but the rise in savings is largely made use of either in the form of increased consumption of durables or in stock-building: and the latter activity then becomes a major means for forcing a further tilt in the terms of trade toward the farm sector.

V

Now for a summing up. There has been a perceptible decline in the rate of Indian industrial growth since 1965-66, and signs of a quasi-stagnation are becoming markedly evident. This development we suggest is causally related to the continuous movement in relative prices against industry and in favour of agriculture. As argued in Section II, the shifting terms of trade have been instrumental in eroding the level of real incomes of the majority of the population in both urban areas and in the countryside; the demand for mass consumption goods has levelled off as a result. At the other end, by far the major part of the income additionally generated in the economy during the past decade has flown into the hands of a small fraction of the community; a number of luxury consumer goods industries have sprung up to satisfy their relatively sophisticated requirements. This has in turn called for a substantial demand for fresh capital funds, which have been generally under strain. In the case of most of these new industries, investments have also been disproportionately large in relation to the size of the market because of the high degree of built-in indivisibilities. To cover overheads, producers have been forced to fix prices at a relatively high level, a practice which has further inhibited demand. What has thus emerged is a syndrome of high capital intensity-large indivisibilities-high cost-high price-low demand-low output in the industrial sector.

Data on trends in industrial output for the past decade confirm this picture. The changes in the weighting pattern of the index for industrial production in the organised sector described in Table 10: 11 leave little doubt that since 1965, while the weight of the capital goods industries has been declining, that of the durable consumer goods has shown a sharp increase. What is equally remarkable, most of these consumer industries have also been marked by persistent

TABLE 10:11

WEIGHTING PATTERN FOR THE MAJOR INDUSTRIAL GROUPS

Major Groups	weights based on old classification, 1956=100	weights based on old classification, 1960=100	weights based on revised classification, 1960=100	weights based on revised classification for 1965	weights based on revised classification for 1970	weights based on revised classification for 1971	weights based on revised classification for 1972
(0)	(1)	(2)	(3)	(4)	(5)	(6)	(7)
Basic industries	22.33	26.01	25.11	25.66	30.79	31.54	32.02
Capital goods industries	4.71	10.70	11.76	18.66	14.61	14.10	14.36
Intermediate goods industries	24.59	26.34	25.88	23.60	22.73	22.31	22.21
Consumer goods industries	48.37	36.95	37.25	31.08	31.87	31.97	31.41
(i) durable goods	2.21	4.95	5.68	6.51	7.84	8.18	8.09
(ii) non-durable goods	46.16	32.00	31.57	24.57	24.03	23.79	23.32
Total	100.00	100.00	100.00	100.00	100.00	100.00	100.00

Source: Index Numbers of Industrial Production according to Alternative Classificatory Systems – A Methodological Note, Reserve Bank of India *Bulletin*, June 1970, for columns (1), (2) and (3); columns (4), (5), (6) and (7) separately computed.

excess capacity: the creation of capacity for the production of luxury goods has run way ahead of their actual demand.[23],[24]

On the supply side too, the terms-of-trade effect has emerged in the form of a steady rise in the unit cost of output over large segments of the industrial sector, substantially eroding industrial profitability. The rise in the price level of wage-goods and industrial raw materials has had an equally adverse effect on trends in public accounts: public expenditure has risen, but public revenue has not *pari passu*, thus affecting public savings and investments.[25] The latter were instrumental, both as a source of funds and a placer of orders, in stimulating private activity throughout the 1950s and the early 1960s; the deterioration in public savings has thus had a dampening effect on private investments too.[26]

The several aspects considered together, therefore, relative price movements in the Indian economy in the recent period have been a major factor contributing toward industrial retardation.

NOTES

1 See Chapter 7, p. 103.

2 This particular story is by now fairly well documented. See, for example, Wolf Ladijensky, 'Green Revolution in Bihar: A Field Trip in the Kosi Area', *Economic and Political Weekly,* Review of Agriculture, September, 1969 and also by him 'Land Ceilings and Land Reform', *Economic and Political Weekly,* Annual Number, February 1972.

3 This would be so even if transfers from agriculture to elsewhere were taken into account. For an estimate of *net* disbursements to the farm sector for an earlier period, see Ashok Mitra, 'Tax Burden for Indian Agriculture', *ibid.,* p. 295.

4 The following summary table provides an illustration of the steadily rising financial accommodation the farm sector has been receiving in recent years.

INSTITUTIONAL FINANCE FOR AGRICULTURE (DIRECT FINANCE ONLY)
(Rupees Crores)

Institution	Amounts of Credit Issued				
	1969–70	1970–71	1971–72	1972–73	1973–74
I. Co-operative	695.59	743.80	762.64	844.87	918.70
(i) Short-term	487.77	514.90	534.40	576.25	609.95
(ii) Term loans	207.82	228.90	228.24	268.62	308.75
II. Government	80.20	74.20	99.30	176.80	90.80
III. Total of I and II	775.79	818.00	861.94	1,021.67	1,009.50
(i) Short-term	567.97	589.10	633.70	753.05	700.75
(ii) Term loans	207.82	228.90	228.24	268.62	308.75
IV. Commerical Banks (Outstanding)	181.98	236.35	267.73	741.75	422.60
(i) Short-term	N.A.*	N.A.*	107.30	138.52	187.62
(ii) Term loans	N.A.*	N.A.*	160.43	203.23	234.98

*N.A. Not Available.

Source: Reserve Bank of India, *Report on Currency and Finance, 1973—74*, p. 128.

In the early 1950s, total institutional credit for agriculture was barely of the order of Rs.50 crores.

5   'Apart from the direct cash assistance programmes, exporters receive several other dispensations from the Government. These include import entitlements, subsidised credit, subsidised railway freight charges for both raw materials and finished products, drawbacks on excise, and, finally drawbacks on custom duty. If all these categories of assistance were to be added up, the Government's export promotion drive could indeed turn out to be one of the most uneconomic ventures ever launched anywhere — an aggregate export figure of Rs.2,800 crores might, for instance, have attached to it total subsidies worth around Rs.1,500 crores.' "Exports: Boondoggle of Cash Assistance", *Economic and Political Weekly*, September 7, 1974, p. 1511.

6   See the discussion in Chapter 8, as also A. V. Jose, 'Trends in Real Wage Rates of Agricultural Labourers', *ibid.,* and Ashok Mitra, 'Domestic Terms of Trade and the Wage Structure', *ibid.*

7   See Section V for a further discussion on this issue.

8   Ranjit Sau, 'Some Aspects of Inter-Sectoral Resource Flow', *ibid., Economic and Political Weekly,* Special Number, August 1974, pp. 1277-84. Relatively speaking, the market for industrial consumer goods in India, Sau concludes, is experiencing a secular shrinkage: the proportion of per capita consumer expenditure spent on industrial goods is declining over the years, rather sharply in the rural areas and mildly in the urban. Further, as between various fractile groups of the population, those at the bottom are increasingly withdrawing from the industrial market.

9   With 1952-53 = 100, the official index number of wholesale prices in April 1965 was 142.7 for manufactures, 157.9 for industrial products and 140.2 for finished products.

10   Government of India, *Report of the National Commission on Labour*, Volume I.

11   With 1961-62 =100, the index number of wholesale prices for agricultural commodities rose from 131 in 1964-65 to 231 in 1973-74; for machinery and transport equipment, chemicals and manufactures the rise was respectively from 112 to 183, from 117 to 219, and from 109 to 206.

12   With 1956 = 100, the index number of industrial production advanced from 73.5 in 1950 to 174.7 in 1964; in contrast, with 1960 = 100, between 1964 and 1973 it rose from 156.2 to 197.3. Of even greater basic significance in the present context, between 1960 and 1973, the output of consumer non-durable goods industries — despite availability of capacity — rose by only 40 per cent, reflecting — at least in part — the constraint of demand for mass consumption goods. See Reserve Bank of India, *Report on Currency and Finance*, 1973-74, Statement 11.

13   Compare Ranjit Sau, *op. cit.*, p. 1283: 'Could it be that, foodgrains being the first charge on a consumer's budget, the relative rise in foodgrain prices is eating into the market for industrial goods? Indeed, the close association between the upward movement of foodgrain prices and the slump in the demand for cotton textiles has been observed many a time. Secondly, there is the inequality of income distribution, which stands in the way of expansion of the market for industrial goods at the lower stratum of the population'. The 'upward movement of foodgrain prices' is itself a factor contributing to an aggravation of the inequality in income distribution.

14   It is, however, necessary to draw attention to the fact that the internal composition of the industrial sector changed considerably during the two decades 1949-69; some of the conclusions drawn from Table 10:1 may therefore be in need of modification.

15   Data with respect to the finance of the corporate units in the country are available from the official Annual Survey of Industries and from the Reserve Bank of India's studies on company finance. The most consistent set of data, spanning more or less the entire period since Independence, are provided by the analysis of

balance sheets and profit and loss accounts of joint-stock companies undertaken by the Reserve Bank. The basic source material for these studies can be compiled from the annual reports and accounts of companies. Such compilation is of course not free of problems. The companies do not follow a uniform accounting year; the number of companies covered in the RBI studies have also fluctuated. Till 1965-66, accounts of 757 medium and large *public* limited companies with paid-up capital for more than Rs.5 lakhs each were analysed. The number of such companies was increased to 1,001 for the study covering the period 1955-56 to 1960-61 and further to 1,333 for that for 1960-61 to 1962-63. In subsequent studies, the number of companies covered was raised to 1,501. For public limited companies, we thus have four different series for different sub-periods within the period 1950-51 to 1970-71. In each case, the coverage is around eighty per cent of the total paid-up capital of all companies belonging to the group; even so, since the number of companies vary, the comparison of results does present problems.

With effect from 1955-56, the scope of the studies was extended to medium and large private limited companies with paid-up capital of more than Rs.5 lakhs each. For the period 1955-56 to 1960-61, the accounts of 333 such units were studied. When the data for the years 1960-61 to 1962-63 came to be analysed, the number of units was increased to 501; the coverage was around 35 per cent of the total paid-up capital of all companies in the goup. The number of companies was enlarged to 701 in subsequent studies, but the paid-up capital covered declined to 23 per cent of that of all companies in the group.

The non-uniformity in nomenclature and in the method of presentation of accounts constitute other important hurdles. The Company Act of 1956 and its subsequent Amendments have gone some way to standardise the terminology and the mode of presentation; the problems have not, however, been altogether eliminated thereby. One particular limitation in comparability arises from differences in the basis of valuation of assets followed by the companies. In terms of the Companies Act, the gross value of fixed assets is shown at original cost in the annual accounts, but if the original cost is not available or cannot be ascertained, the value as indicated in the company's books is shown. Assets built by a company or acquired afresh are thus valued at their original cost, while used assets taken over as a result of amalgamation are generally shown at the written-down value. In cases involving revaluation of fixed assets, the original values are shown along with the re-valued amounts in the annual accounts for a period of five years; thereafter only the revised valuation is indicated. It is not always possible to segregate the cases of re-valuation or amalgamation from those of purchase of old assets, or to trace the original cost in each instance.

This problem of non-uniformity in valuation also arises in the case of two other items, namely, inventories and investments. Both categories are valued at cost or market value, whichever happens to be lower; it often becomes difficult to unscramble what is what. Differing methods are followed for estimating the cost of inventories too — for example, last in first out, first in first out, standard price, average cost, etc. — once more giving rise to the kind of complications already referred to.

By adjusting for Government companies and financial companies the data on paid-up capital for all non-financial, non-Government units, data can be tabulated separately for public limited and private limited companies. The overall estimates for all public limited companies are arrived at by multiplying the aggregates for selected companies under individual industries by the ratio of the paid-up capital of all non-financial non-Government companies to the total paid-up capital of selected units in the respective industries. This method of estimation is subject to one grave limitation: it assumes a linear relationship between individual items of company accounts and the size of paid-up capital.

There is, in addition, a set of general limitations arising out of the fact that data for companies having different activities are aggregated for purposes of analysis. Many companies are multi-activity units and, for the purpose of industrial classification, it is only their major activity as measured by the relative values of sales which is taken into account. Moreover, the composition of the organised industrial sector has undergone a considerable transformation between the early 1950s and the early 1970s; even the so-called traditional industries have experienced sweeping technological changes. A series of new industries have sprung up over the years; the value added by them currently constitutes perhaps as much as a quarter of the total industrial output in the country. In the case of some of these industries, profitability may be affected in the short period because of the phenomenon of latent indivisibilities. For certain luxury consumer goods industries, on the other hand, rigid exchange control and the consequent non-availability of imported goods has ensured almost instant success and a high rate of return.

Finally, the fact that the past two decades have been a period of almost continuously rising prices cannot but affect the estimates of profitability in one most significant way. The rate of profits as derivable from the RBI analysis is defined as profits in current prices expressed as a proportion of the capital stock which, as we have seen, is valued at historical prices. In a period of inflation, the rate of profit would accordingly appear to be higher than it really is.

16   In the context of the final point made in footnote 15 above, and given the fact that the period between 1965-66 and 1970-71 was one of fairly rising prices in the country, this conclusion would seem to be well warranted.

17   Many of these industries were recipients of wide-ranging export subsidies too during this period.

18   This proposition does not appear to hold good for the cotton textile industry during the period 1965-66 to 1970-71; the explanation possibly lies in the large role export subsidies assumed in the finances of this industry in the course of this period. The trend in profits for the vegetable oils industry seems to be more indeterminate; in so far as it caters to the demand of the richer sections, a part of the increased costs could — and possibly was — passed forward.

19   Basic industries, such as iron and steel and mining, were exceptions, obviously because of their capital-intensive nature and the low level of capital utilisation.

20   See S. Chakravarty, 'Reflections on the Growth Process in the Indian Economy', Foundation Day Lecture Series 7, Administrative Staff College of India, 1974.

21   And this despite the fact that the wage share in value added fell over the period.

22   It could indeed be that the nature of the *use* of funds too changed for the corporate sector as a whole during these years; for instance, inventory accumulation has come to constitute a larger component of investments than in the past. But, as will be argued in the next chapter, the propensity to hold larger inventories could itself be the consequence of a reduced rate of profit.

23   According to a recent official study, capacity utilisation in different groups of industries has declined from 78 per cent in 1968-69 to 70 per cent in 1973-74 on an average. The fall in the utilisation has been the highest in the consumer goods industries. *Financial Express*, Delhi, 12 June 1975.

24   'Even while the markets for traditional consumer goods industries were being saturated, new consumer goods industries catering to the needs of the richer sections of the population were growing up. Since the mid-sixties the relative importance of the markets for luxury consumer durables has increased, and this is reflected in the rate of growth of output of consumer durables. Taking 1960 as the base, while the general index number of industrial production in 1972 came to 199.4, the index number of production of consumer goods industries came to 168.2 and at the same time the index number of output of consumer durables

came to 284.2. However, even here, the small size of the market has quickly led to a falling off of the rate of growth of several industries (such as air-conditioners) and the emergence of excess capacity'. A. K. Bagchi, 'Some Characteristics of Industrial Growth in India', *Economic and Political Weekly*, Annual Number, February 1975, p. 159.

25 As a proportion of net national product, public savings were respectively 2.0 per cent, 2.2. per cent, 2.2. per cent, 2.0 per cent, 1.9 per cent and 1.7 per cent in 1968-69, 1969-70, 1970-71, 1971-72, 1972-73 and 1973-74 (Reserve Bank of India, *Report on Currency and Finance, 1973-74,* p. 6). It was close to 2.5 per cent of net domestic product in 1960-61.

26 For a slightly different analysis, see Prabhat Patnaik, 'Disproportionality Crisis and Cyclical Growth', *Economic and Political Weekly*, Annual Number, February 1972, pp. 329-36.

CHAPTER 11

The Political Economy of Atrophy

I

An impasse — in the sphere of farm as well as industrial output — is seemingly being reached in the Indian economic system. The explicit manifestations of this impasse are increasingly evident. Per capita national income has remained fairly static since the middle 1960s, and the rate of domestic savings has also levelled off.[1] Is this Indian experience altogether specific? Or can it be generalised into a broad economic prognosis for nations burdened by class formations analogous to those obtaining in India? The present chapter will attempt to supply at least some clues towards answering these questions.

It was suggested in Chapter 7 that the political coalition in India between the rural oligarchy and the industrial bourgeoisie is itself corrosive of growth; the mechanism of the coalition operates principally through adjustments and adaptations in the terms of trade between agriculture and industry, and through the instrumentality of the monopsony power exercised by the richer sections against the proletariat classes; certain inner tensions that are generated by the working of the mechanism have a perverse effect on production. The compendium of facts — which the last three chapters essentially are — has been aimed largely at supporting this contention.

The morphology of the political alliance, however, demands a closer analysis. To recapitulate, in terms of the trade-offs implicit in the arrangement between the industrial bourgeoisie and the rural oligarchy, the latter receive benefits in the form of higher product prices, subsidised inputs, special fiscal rebates, postponed land reforms and so on. In exchange, the bourgeois capitalists obtain the prerogative of exercising unfettered jurisdiction over industrial, trade and licensing policies, as well as over the management of foreign exchange and of the monetary and fiscal instruments. The rural poor, the urban working class and the fixed-income groups have to bear the brunt of the resulting economic cost of the alliance. The surplus-raising farmers expect to receive — and actually receive — the support of the bourgeoisie in suppressing the demands of the poorer peasants for higher wages or a larger share of the crop or reduced rent or land reforms. Political authority is massively ranged against the weaker sections of the peasantry. Outside agriculture, the industrial working class and the fixed-income groups are burdened with higher prices for foodgrains and for manufactures characterised by a large proportion of farm inputs. The shift in the terms of trade against industrial products also tends to increase the unit manufacturing cost; the bourgeoisie, however, try to muffle the effect of this rising cost by intensified use of monopsony power, such as through reducing in real terms the wage rate and the rate of earnings of the supervisory staff. The general direction of State policy turns increasingly anti-labour and anti-fixed income groups. Because of the nature of the political alliance, direct taxes on agriculture cannot be increased; and yet subsidies have to be arranged for the richer peasantry as well as to compensate the bourgeoisie for the loss suffered by them because of the tilt in terms of trade. A re-structuring of the fiscal system is therefore called for. The bourgeoisie naturally endeavour to lighten the incidence upon themselves, and the burden of the additional resource effort falls by and large on indirect taxes, which by their very nature are regressive and concentrated on commodities mostly consumed by the working class and the fixed income groups.

For the rich peasants and the urban bourgeoisie, all this could still be a worthwhile arrangement as long as no crisis intervenes. But it does, in both the farm and the industrial sectors. In agriculture, it is in any event somewhat optimistic to assume that output could be increased decisively despite the overwhelming majority of the farming community being excluded from the process. Particularly in areas where small-holders predominate, the denial to the latter of the right to the use of key resources merely confirms the trend toward stagnant output. As we have seen, there is, besides, an inexorable logic attendant upon the shift in terms of trade. As the cost of labour and raw materials rises in the manufacturing sector as a result of the change in relative prices in favour of agriculture, the cost of such important farm inputs as fertilisers too tends to move up. This increase in cost occurs in the first place at a given level of output; if the scale of production expands, calling for a larger supply of inputs, the rise in cost could be still higher. There is the apprehension of rising wage costs too with increased activity. The impact of a rising cost curve on the rate of profit tends to be somewhat indeterminate, particularly in cases where production is discrete, such as in agriculture. In the light of the circumstances, the availability of speculation and money-lending as parallel,[2] alternative modes activity proves most convenient for the rural oligarchy, since the surplus which eventuates in progressively larger order with each successive improvement in the terms of trade need not be ploughed back for expansion of farming activity, but deployed elsewhere.

In the industrial sphere too, as we have seen, the consequences of the shift in terms of trade are deleterious to growth. With the relative rise in the prices of raw materials and wage-goods *vis-à-vis* that of finished products, the unit cost of output rises in monetary terms in the industrial sector. Where prices are administratively determined, this rise in unit cost is compensated. In many other industries, however, the compensation is not adequate, or takes place with a time-lag, and thus the rate of profit-taking is affected adversely. The rise in the price level of wage goods and industrial raw materials has, in addition, an adverse impact on public savings and investment. Public savings were a major factor contributing to the sustaining of private industrial activity in India throughout the 1950s and the early 1960s;[3] the recent decline in public savings has led to a corresponding set-back to private investments. Moreover, a transfer of real income away from industry to the farm sector takes place as a direct consequence of the shift in terms of trade. According to most current evidence, the propensity to save is pronouncedly lower in rural than in urban areas; it is especially low for those sections of the farming community who benefit most from the changes in terms of trade. The over-all effect on aggregate savings is hence negative.

It is important in this context to consider the aspect of income distribution. The effect of income inequality on the demand for industrial products has been discussed at some length in Chapter 10. Such inequalities have yet other manifestations. For instance, the share of tertiary output in aggregate output is currently much higher in India than has been in the case of any other country at comparative stages of growth. The *rate* of expansion too in the tertiary sector is considerably higher than that in the secondary sector. The emergence of such a pattern is both a symptom and a cause. It is a symptom of the distorted pattern of income distribution in the economy. An inordinately large proportion of national income is concentrated in the hands of a relatively small proportion of the population. As a result, the demand for services increases more than in proportion to the demand for the output of other sectors.

This in turn also becomes the cause of retarded growth. An increase in service income and output implies that a portion of income which could otherwise have been saved is being deployed for direct consumption. The enlargement of service output is thus not only at the cost of commodity output; it also affects the level of savings and capital formation, and slows down the potential of overall growth.

The relationship between income distribution and the pattern of growth is therefore three-fold. First is the adverse effect of unequal income distribution as it operates from the demand side; efforts at raising the output of consumption goods fail because of inadequate demand on the part of the vast masses of the poor. Second, the excessive growth in service output weakens the capability of the economy to generate a high rate of savings. Third, the enlarged demand for service output leads to a diversion of even current savings from purely productive activities to those catering to services, that is to say, the capacity for material production is held back in order that the capacity for the production of services can grow.

The process is aggravated by the terms-of-trade effect on income distribution noted in the preceding chapter. The shift in the terms of trade itself depresses the rate of savings in the economy. Again because of the same factor, there is an aggravation of income inequalities, and the majority of the country's population experience little or no increase in their level of real income. Consequently, hardly any expansion in the demand for mass consumption goods is discernible, and the crisis on the demand side severely affects both plans for, and the actuality of, industrial growth. The predicament on the supply side is nearly as acute. With the shrinkage in savings, public investment levels off, and since such activity has been the major lever for private industrial capital formation, the latter too suffers heavily. At the other end, because of the shift in income distribution, a narrow section of the country's population at the top experiences a sharp rise in real income. This leads to the emergence of a new market reality, namely, the demand for a wide range of new consumer goods. A significant portion of the available savings in the economy is utilised for setting up a network of industries which could produce these goods; the policy of blanket exchange control helps the process. Given the limited demand for such commodities, however, the capacity utilisation is low. With overheads pitched at a relatively high level, prices tend to be high, which in turn further depresses demand. Little is thus yielded by these luxury consumer goods industries in the way of surplus which could be ploughed back for investment in other spheres of activity.

Yet this could not be and, indeed, is not, the whole story. The urban bourgeoisie must be keen to turn the political advantages stemming from the coalition into concrete economic ones. The shift in the crude terms of trade against industry, which causes a stagnation — and even a decline — in their apparent rate of profit-taking, could indeed make the bourgeoisie feel restless. Their ability to influence the fiscal, monetary, trade and exchange policies of the Government, as already mentioned, to an extent mitigates the adverse consequences of the movement in terms of trade. There is an additional element in the situation which partly restores the balance in favour of the industrial bourgeoisie. The shift in the terms of trade is a precursor of a spiralling inflation. Apart from the fact that the possibility of capital gains increases enormously in this situation, the scope for speculative profits does too. Many industrial houses, for example, have their trading counterparts. If the rate of industrial profits has not risen at the same rate at which the gains of the affluent farmers have gone up in the past two decades, perhaps that has not been a matter of much great concern to at least some industrial capitalists. They might have discovered that they too could participate in the sharing of spoils which rising prices allow to the affluent farmers by laying a claim to the gains from speculative profits. In many spheres of the economy, there is by now a fairly institutionalised relationship between the rich farmers, the traders and the industrialists. In some instances it may even help the industrialists to show in their books a lower rate of return, since to that extent they are able to deny the Government its due claim of direct taxes; to the extent profits are made to accumulate on the trading account, the scope for concealment and evasion of taxes is proportionately greater. As inflation develops in intensity, in any case the marginal propensity to invest in production declines and that for speculative ventures grows. Thus it is scarcely possible to pass judgment on the nature of viability of the present arrangement between the rich peasantry and the industrial bourgeoisie by reading off the apparent figures of returns from commercialised agriculture vis-à-vis those from organised industry. There are other elements of the given reality.[4]

Even so, it would be idle to pretend that all sections of the bourgeoisie partake equally of the fruits of trading and speculation. As observed in the last chapter, small firms in general tend to be affected more grievously by the rising spiral of wage and input costs that the big ones. If their share in trading profits is less than proportionate, they may certainly try to protect their flanks through other means. Thus a reluctance could develop within their folds to compensate workers to the full extent of the rise in cost of living, or attempts may be made, wherever feasible, to supplant labour by machinery, if the price level of the latter is lagging behind; depending upon circumstances, more extreme measures too could be thought of.

II

At this stage, we really move away from a description of the current economic atrophy in India to a prognostication of further developments. The ability of the industrialists to get by without compensating the workers to the full extent of the rise in prices and the cost of living would vary from sector to sector and economic activity to economic activity. There is in any case usually a time-lag in the adjustment of wages to prices; this time-lag can be there even were a standard formula available to link the adjustment of wages to variations in cost of living. The degree and speed of this adjustment are also a function of the speed of unionisation among the industrial working class. In any event, as inflation, sparked by the rise in foodgrain and other farm prices, begins to erode the real level of living of the workers, they may sooner or later begin to look around in search of devices through which this erosion could be stopped, or at least its rate slowed down. Sectors of production where a rise in money wages would, by raising unit cost, hamper export possibilities, or otherwise lead to a shrinkage in demand,[5] are likely to be the ones where the bourgeoisie would offer the greatest resistance to the demand for higher wages. After a while, the resulting tension could affect the entire industrial sector. While lags and leads in wage adjustments would inevitably continue as between the various sectors and units, the general feature would be a rising crescendo of demand for continuous revisions of money wages and corresponding attempts on the part of the industrial entrepreneurs to muffle it.

This is a situation full of chaotic possibilities. In a centralised system marked by stable arrangements, once a decision is taken to keep wages on leash, it is carried out in more or less a uniform manner in the different industries, and by the individual units within each industry. Similarly, a decision to raise wages is also generally implemented in a uniform manner — or in terms of an agreed norm of 'relativities' — in the various sectors and units. But given the circumstances engendered by a run-away inflation in a disorganised, under-developed economy, it is possible that the demand for, and the resistance to, higher wages would lead to a series of piecemeal, unintegrated developments in individual industries and units, whether in the private or in the Government sector. What may therefore emerge is a 'leap-frogging' of wages. The inevitable consequence would be a certain order of malfunctioning. In particular industries, wages may be adjusted to the rise in cost of living with a lag of six months; somewhere else, with a lag of only a few weeks. In some units, the rate of adjustment may be close to one hundred per cent; elsewhere it may be as low as twenty per cent. On account of such adjustments disparate in magnitude as well as time, the prospects of a dying down of tension could turn dimmer and dimmer. Disputes over 'relativities' as between different trades and skills, as also over the periodicity of adjustments, may continue interminably.

This could not but have a crippling impact on the processes of the economy. Since it would be impossible to prevent for long an across-the-board increase in wages, the fire of inflation would be further stoked, with attendant effects on the country's balance of payments and its rate of savings. At the other end, as resistance to the demand for higher remunerations continues, and often in an unco-ordinated manner, wage grumbles would spiral, and the industrial climate would be vitiated. We would thus enter a phase where bouts of inflation either are accompanied by, or alternate with, bouts of industrial strikes and lock-outs.

If the industrialists, given their economic strength and political prowess, refused to yield, so that lock-outs and lay-offs proliferated, the consequence could still be less than wholesome. With the fall in industrial employment, a further contraction in the demand for mass consumption goods is bound to ensue. Since the entrepreneurs would nonetheless want to maximise their aggregate net revenue, an attempt could be launched to counter the effects of the fall in demand by an increase in unit prices. While the demand for the necessities of life generally tends to be price-inelastic, this need not be so for all articles of mass consumption. Raising the unit price of essential consumer goods could actually further reduce the volume of demand, and thus intensify the crisis.

The possibility also remains open of an increasing trend towards the substitution of labour by machinery. In a general inflationary situation, the price level of machinery and equipment, it is true, should also rise along with the increase in wage rates. But, because of the specific nature of the cost inflation being discussed, namely, the shift in terms of trade in favour of agriculture and against industry, in the initial phase the rise in the price level of machinery and equipment may lag behind the rate of rise in money wages.[6] In such a situation, a switch from labour to equipment, provided technologically feasible, could be an attractive alternative course of action on the part of the bourgeoisie. Not that the urge for such a substitution would develop at all places and in all industries simultaneously. Technological possibilities for substitution may not be the same everywhere. Depending upon the strength of organised labour, trade union resistance to the replacement of labour would also vary from area to area and industry to industry. It is still difficult to brush aside the prospect of a gradual falling off in the marginal rate of absorption of labour. Those already in employment may not be laid off as substitution of men by machinery begins to take place, but the requirements for additional work force could peter out, and replacements need not be immediately looked for those who retire. While formally there may not be any retrenchment, the actual outcome could be the same as under a scheme of large-scale lay-off of labour, further intensifying the crisis in the industrial sector.

There is a direct — and immediate — implication of this progressive substitution of labour by equipment. Between two industries which are otherwise technologically identical and yield an identical stream of output against a given volume of investment, but one of which has a higher rate of labour utilisation than the other, the realised savings are likely to be different: other things remaining the same, the unit employing a lesser volume of workers would be featured by a higher rate of savings than the one where the number of men employed is larger. This higher rate of savings would obviously have some implications for the long-range growth of the economy. In the short run it may, however, be necessary to take equal, or ever greater, cognisance of the corresponding phenomenon of a further contraction in the demand for industrial goods which a reduction in the level of employment may bring about. The crisis is therefore not merely one stemming from the supply side. Difficulties would seem to be mounting even from the side of demand. The economic and political confusion would be compounded by the contraction of demand, the consequential further rise in unit prices and a further fall in demand for a whole range of industrial goods intended for mass consumption: inflation and declining output would dovetail into each other.[7]

III

A certain commentary by Marx in his Introduction to *A Contribution to the Critique of Political Economy* has been commissioned over the decades in support of diverse — and sometimes contradictory — ideological positions. It nonetheless retains an acute relevance till this day: 'At a certain stage of development, the material productive forces of society come into conflict with the existing relations of production, or — this merely explains the same thing in legal terms — with the property relations within the framework of which they have hitherto operated. From forms of development of the productive forces these relations turn into their fetters. Then begins an era of social revolution'.[8] As one surveys the Indian scene, it becomes evident that the circumstances described by Marx are almost upon us, that the relations of production, as defined by the existing class structure, are now proving to be major stumbling blocks in the way of the country's economic progress.

For, in both agriculture and industry,[9] the consequences of the political contract entered into by the two dominant classes — the rural oligarchy and the urban bourgeoisie — are, as we have noted, a gathering atrophy in production. Despite the enormous advantages they have come to enjoy as a consequence of the alliance — advantages which span from a continuously rising terms of trade to the postponement of land reforms, from immunity from bearing the burden of direct taxes to being beneficiaries of an array of fiscal and monetary subsidies — the rural oligarchy fail in their role as progenitors of agricultural growth. This is a role in which perhaps in any case they have been reluctant participants. By restricting output, and by purposely diversifying their outlay over money-lending, trading and speculation, they have succeeded in refining a short-period mechanism for profit maximisation whose narcissistic charm is yet to wear off. At the other end, the infra-structural arrangements underlying the alliance between the rich peasants and the bourgeoisie also enjoin that the small holders and landless labourers continue to be denied the use of resources needed to raise *their* output and earnings. The gradual deceleration of farm growth, certainly the most outstanding phenomenon in the Indian countryside in the past decade, is thus a direct consequence of the property-cum-political relations we have been alluding to.

A parallel development has occurred in the industrial sector. The pattern of income distribution implicit in the political arrangements — and which is reflected in the management of the terms of trade between agriculture and industry — has inhibited industrial growth. Because of the shift in terms of trade, both the urban working class and the rural proletariat are now forced to deploy a larger proportion of their money earnings on food articles;[10] there is, accordingly, a progressive shrinkage in the general demand for the products of industry, particularly for mass consumption articles. A crisis in the supply function is also gathering pace again, directly linked to arrangements mirroring the political alliance. The relative rise in the prices of basic raw materials and wage goods which the tilt in terms of trade has brought about has had a deleterious effect on savings,[11] a part of which, besides, has been pre-empted by the requirements of the highly capital-intensive industries producing articles of luxury consumption intended for the thin stratum of rich income-earners. While corporate savings have thus been placed under a squeeze, public savings too have tended to level off because of the same generic reason. The changing terms of trade are indicative of a persistent shift in income distribution in favour of the rural oligarchy, but the implicit conditions of the class alliance that are responsible for the movement in relative prices also thwart attempts at mopping up the rising incomes of the rich peasants for purposes of the State; there is little evidence of any massive deployment of these resources for productive activities through private channels either. On the other hand, since the rise in the price level of wage-goods and basic materials has had an unfavourable impact on the Government's income and expenditure accounts, the potential for additional public savings too has been reduced by the shift in terms of trade in favour of the farm sector.

The Marxian prognosis would thus appear to be starkly borne out by the developing Indian situation; the existing property and class relations, instead of liberating the forces of growth, are in reality acting as fetters, and holding back production. But, in the Marxian schematics, such a situation also heralds the 'era of social revolution': the contradictions latent in the given production relations are supposed to reach a point of nodality where new forces unleash themselves and the process of economic expansion is resumed. In India, have these contradictions, so basic for the 'social revolution', begun to stir toward the direction of the flash-point of crisis?

One dares say that they have. Consider developments in the rural sector first. As the terms of trade keep swinging in favour of farm products, the cost of living of the small cultivators, the share-croppers and the agricultural workers mounts. The adjustments in money wages for landless labour, and in the compensation received by the other categories, are, however, likely to lag behind. Even as the inflation induced by changing terms of trade grips the economy and makes the conditions of living increasingly difficult for the fixed-income groups and the economically weaker sections, the continuous shift in rural income distribution would thus leave the poorer elements amongst the farming community worse off to an even greater extent at each successive stage.[12] This is an unstable situation and cannot last indefinitely. Even though a simultaneous and synchronised revolt against the existing arrangements on a national scale seems improbable, rumblings of discontent may soon be heard at different points of the polity. Squeezed by the inflation, the landless cultivators may begin to ask for higher wages; the tenant may ask for a reduction in rent; the share-cropper may plead for a higher share of the crop; all of them may start asking for more intensive reforms in the existing structure of land distribution; the destitute agricultural worker or small-holder may even begin to mount a campaign demanding a reduction in the rate of interest charged against the advance of cash or grain by the merchant-moneylender-landlord.[13]

Such struggles launched by the poorer peasantry may not gather momentum immediately, nor would their momentum be evenly dispersed over different parts of the country. Up to a point, some correlation could be expected between the spread of literacy and the mobilisation of the poorer peasants for the defence of their economic and political rights. In the initial stages, the rural oligarchs would try their utmost to resist such pressures upon them by commandeering the use of the punitive instruments available to the State,[14] but beyond a point they are likely to acquiesce in marginal concessions. Whatever precise form or forms these concessions may take, other things remaining the same, they would lead to a lowering of the real level of income enjoyed by the rich peasantry. It would be uncharacteristic on their part to bear this loss without demur; their efforts may then be directed towards compensating themselves through either forcing a further tilt in the terms of trade in their favour or insisting upon additional fiscal and monetary subsidies from the State. But this could set up a self-defeating mechanism. The shift in terms of trade would further raise the cost of food and other agriculture-based consumption articles for the poorer peasants; were fiscal and monetary subsidies to involve inordinate credit creation, that too may lead to a further bout of inflation. As a consequence, landless labourers and small-holders would, with or without a time-lag, press with a newer charter of demands, which also would have to be conceded, sooner or later, in full or in part, and for which the rural oligarchs would seek fresh compensation either from the bourgeoisie or from the State exchequer. Inflation and rural tension would accordingly become endemic to the system.

As the terms of trade move continuously against industry, the crisis in the manufacturing sector would also intensify. The declining trend in profit-taking would, as we have suggested in the preceding Section, impel the bourgeoisie to try out, either severally or jointly, such modalities of defence as denying the industrial workers full compensation for the rise in the cost of living and increasing substitution of labour by automatised processes. These could hasten the confrontation between the industrial capitalists and the working class. Simultaneously, since the bourgeoisie, in order to compensate themselves for falling profits as well as for meeting the rising demands of the richer peasants, would increasingly take recourse to fiscal subsidies and liberal bank advances, inflation would gather further pace in the economy, and thus further squeeze the urban and rural proletariat.

The crisis is likely to affect unevenly the different industrial units.

The relatively bigger units would be in a somewhat stronger position to face the situation than the smaller ones; those with more intimate links with trade and speculation should be able to carry on with a shrunken level of profits for a longer while than those who possess no such links. Thus cracks could soon appear in the homogeneity of the industrial bourgeoisie, and more and more elements might be expected to start asking questions about the value of a political alliance whose economic gains were fast turning into a trickle. Once the mercantile bourgeoisie, for instance, begin to develop a distinct personality of their own and decide to cut their umbilical cords with the manufacturing bourgeoisie, the consequence could be an intensification of the self-doubt experienced by the latter.

Meanwhile, the spiralling inflation would have added a separate dimension to the crisis. In its advanced phase, inflation cuts athwart the processes of productive activity: the creation of goods becomes a matter of secondary concern, attention rivets upon their circulation. As the supply of goods contracts, and prices soar even more, the working class and, in addition, the lower strata of the urban bourgeoisie, who constitute the core of the *salariat*, are driven to the wall. Once that stage is reached, other considerations fall by the wayside; they ceaselessly engage in the battle for compensatory higher wages. Tension rends the air. Depending upon their own individual strength and the residual power of monopsony still wielded by the particular bourgeois groups they are facing, different sections of wage-earners succeed in wresting their demands only in varying proportions. This sets in its train a raucous controversy over 'relativities'. For a while, the bourgeoisie — or at least some sections from amongst them — may attempt to take control of the situation by making use of State power and riding roughshod over the demands of the working class. But such a strategy too involves a cost; the outlay on the police and the defence services mounts, ensuring a further draft on the availability of goods and services, and further exacerbating the forces of inflation. The erosion in the real level of living threatens to reach a critical point, so much so that strong-arm methods by themselves cease to be effective, and disaffection engulfs different segments of the economy. At that point, the manufacturing bourgeoisie may be persuaded to sit back and reassess the implications of the particular political alliance which is at the root of it all. For by now it is not merely their economic calculations which have been set at disarray by the developing events; stagnant production, spiralling prices and inadequate wage adjustments have also rapidly led to a total alienation of support, in the political sphere, of nearly the entire organised working class as well as of sizeable sections of the fixed-income-earning middle class. Till as long as the polity is made to rest on a framework of parliamentary democracy, the disappearance of such support would be the cause of the greatest concern for the ruling bourgeoisie.

The disintegration of the political arrangement is likely to be hastened by a parallel development in the rural sector. As the demand of the landless cultivators and small farmers grows in volume and pitch, the rich peasants keep offering marginal concessions to them. As already noted, the rural oligarchs endeavour to compensate themselves for this loss by transferring an additional load of demand — in the form of either even more favourable terms of trade or further fiscal and monetary subsidies or both — on the urban bourgeoisie. Sooner or later, the mounting economic burden may prove intolerable to the industrial capitalists. An additional consideration could also now begin to exercise their minds. The class alliance they entered into with the rural oligarchy had a concrete political basis, namely, the assurance that the latter would commandeer and deliver to them a majority of the rural votes in the parliamentary elections. As discontent over the erosion of living standards digs deep roots even in the countryside and the rural proletariat increasingly learn to mobilise themselves for political and economic struggles, their alienation from the rich peasants gradually emerges as an incontrovertible fact. The urban bourgeoisie, hemmed in from all directions, suddenly discover that they need no longer subjugate themselves to the yoke of the alliance: not only has its economic usefulness been reduced to negligible proportions, its political significance too has exhausted itself; the time has thus come to revoke the coalition and move in search of newer arrangements.[15]

IV

Since, in terms of our analysis, the coalition between the rural oligarchy and the urban bourgeoisie is mainly responsible for the crisis in production in the Indian economy, the collapse of the coalition must be regarded as a positive development toward reactivating the forces of growth. Objectively viewed, any factor which helps to accentuate the inner contradictions of the existing production relations therefore serves the cause of history. Not only the movement of the poorer sections of the peasantry for additional land or a greater security of tenure or a larger share of the crop or higher wages deserve to be welcomed on this ground; even the so-called 'economism' of the middle layers of the bourgeoisie, in so far as it adds to the strain of the existing system and nudges it towards the breaking point, fulfils a significant historical role in the given context.[16] Contrarily, any support proffered to the ruling classes by any element, whether endogenous or exogenous, could only prolong the phase of economic stagnation.[17]

A residual question. Assuming the continuation of a multi-party parliamentary form of democracy, what alternative class alignments are conceivable which could at the same time release the productive impulses in the economy,[18] and what are their implications for the terms of trade between the agricultural and industrial sectors? One can indeed indulge in endless speculation concerning the theme. It would, however, be idle to assume that the answer to the question is obtainable in the purely economic sphere. If the present study has one moral, it is that economic phenomena are determined by political categories and processes: to miss out their inter-action is to rob social analysis of its most fundamental content.

NOTES

1　Beginning with 1964-65 and ending with 1972-73, per capita net national product at 1960-61 prices was successively as follows: Rs.335.1, Rs.310.9, Rs.308.2, Rs.331.7, Rs.343.1, Rs.351.8, Rs.348.4 and Rs.337.4. The rate of domestic savings has wobbled around 10 per cent since 1960-61. See Central Statistical Organization, Government of India, *National Accounts Statistics, 1960-61-1972-73*, Tables 1 and 12.

2　See Chapter 8.

3　On the supply side, the State sector was an important source of capital funds for private industry; on the demand side, Government orders were crucial for the survival of many key private activities. See Chapter 10.

4　A formal economic link between the political allies in terms of a convergence of trading interests is not essential for the purpose of the present argument. Independently of each other, both the rural oligarchs and the industrial bourgeoisie might attempt to maximise their returns by increasingly moving away from production to mercantile operations. Till as long as they are able to come to an informal arrangement in regard to their respective spheres of activity, their commercial ventures need not be mutually harmful: both classes could, up to a point, gain at the expense of the other classes in society, namely, the rural poor and the urban workers and lower middle class.

5　Since the increase in money wages is to compensate for the rise in food prices, any positive income effect on industrial demand is unlikely to accrue.

6　This has certainly been the case in India during the past decade.

7　A final possibility remains. The industrial capitalists, in order to cope with the difficulties caused by the rising supply curve, could, wherever possible, endeavour to economise on basic materials purchased from agriculture, and take to utilising industrial synthetic products increasingly as inputs. In other words, to save themselves from the consequence of the shift in crude terms of trade, they may decide to swing the 'income' terms of trade in their favour by reducing their demand for farm products. But, once a move is afoot along these lines, the political alliance between the rural oligarchy and the urban bourgeoisie would immediately come under strain, and the crisis in production relations would threaten to assume an explosive form.

8   Karl Marx, *A Contribution to the Critique of Political Economy*, Moscow, 1970, p. 21.

9   It is the rates of growth in these sectors of material production which are crucial for over-all national growth; the circulatory processes are of secondary significance (even though, as argued earlier, they can affect developments in the goods-producing sectors).

10   The class bias in the Indian economic and administrative system is also made explicit by the manner in which procured and imported foodgrains are distributed through the public distribution system. Public procurement and distribution of foodgrains were originally intended to protect the vulnerable sections of the population from the ravages of high market prices. In practice, however, it has been deployed to provide relief to the urban bourgeoisie and a small section of the middle and working classes (with the obvious intention of quietening the wage grumbles voiced by the latter). Of the total number of ration and fair price shops in the country, close to three-quarters are in the urban areas, and, except in years of drought, not more than 5 per cent of the annually distributed foodgrains reach the countryside; small farmers and agricultural workers are therefore more or less totally excluded from the benefits of the public distribution system. The reluctance of the authorities to procure coarse grains — which constitute the staple cereal of the rural poor — is indicative of the built-in bias in official policy.

A few years ago, the Agricultural Prices Commission had proposed a scheme of differential issue prices for foodgrains to accord relief to the poorer classes: 'If the public distribution system is to be used for according relief to the vulnerable sections in the countryside, it may sometimes become necessary to supply grains, especially coarse cereals, to these sections at less than the economic issue prices. The resulting losses would be made good, to the extent prices in the free market permit, by charging a higher price for superior cereals issued to the better-off sections of the urban population'. (Agricultural Prices Commission, Government of India, *Report on the Price Policy for Kharif Cereals for the 1969–70 season*.) Commenting on the Government's unwillingness to accept the Commission's proposal, the *Economic and Political Weekly* ('Agricultural Prices: A Matter of Class Bias', 30 September 1972, p. 1994) observed: 'All through the relatively good years, the Government did not lift one little finger to increase the number of fair price shops in the rural areas. It did not do so because of its awareness that, at the fancy procurement prices paid out to the kulaks, there was scarcely any possibility of these grains being consumed by landless labourers and small cultivators, unless of course the issue price was heavily subsidised; but the subsidy for the poor was out — it spoils them'.

11   The stagnation of demand further reinforces the trend toward depressed savings.

12   A general point may be noted. Between 1964 and 1973, the annual rate of growth of both foodgrains and consumer non-durable goods has been less than 1.5 per cent, while the annual rate of population growth has exceeded 2 per cent. Even ignoring the factor of growing income inequalities over this period, it is therefore possible to form some judgment about the growing immiserisation of the majority of the population.

13   No doubt the time-scale is important here. Even growing misery need not lead to organised resistance in the short period, and certainly not everywhere. The role of chance events in sparking protest movements should not be under-rated either. Even so, the *possibility* of agitations is certainly greater under the circumstances described than would have been the case otherwise.

14   The implications of making excessive use of the punitive instrumentalities associated with State power can be far-reaching. The Government's fiscal burden is likely to go up as a result, and, if indefinite reliance is placed upon these instruments, this could contribute to the aggravation of the factors responsible for injecting inflationary trends in the economy. For instance, India's defence expenditure grew five-fold — from around Rs.300 crores in 1961-62 to roughly Rs.1,600 crores in 1972-73 — in the course of a bare dozen years (Ved P. Gandhi, 'India's Self-Inflicted Defence Burden', *Economic and Political Weekly*, 31 August 1974, p. 1485). The Indian Union Government's expenditure on the police increased from Rs.3 crores in 1950-51 to Rs.156 crores in 1974-75, that is by fifty-two times. ('In Lieu of Growth', *Economic and Political Weekly*, 5 October 1974, p. 1677.) (These increases are of course in money terms.)

15   On the other hand, if it is considered that a frontal attack on landlord property may rebound into an attack on bourgeois property as well, the industrial bourgeoisie could prefer the jettisoning of parliamentary democracy to a jettisoning of the alliance. See footnote 18.

16   Economists who favour a generalised frame of wage policy for an under-developed economy, and disapprove the demand of 'white collar' workers for higher wages as compensation for higher prices on the ground that there are other workers in the economy who are unemployed or under-employed (see, for example, A. K. DasGupta, 'Criteria for a Rational Wage Policy'; *Economic and Political Weekly*, 19 October 1974, pp. 1779–88, and Ashok Rudra, 'White Collar Workers', *Frontier*, May 17, 1975, pp 8–10), would thus appear to be somewhat off the mark; their analysis leaves out the social and political basis of an appropriate wage policy.

17   The prospect of economic assistance from the socialist countries, which Kalecki envisaged in the context of an 'intermediate regime', is of some relevance here. Such assistance might be offered with the expectation of promoting a preferred mode of 'non-capitalist' development; but, apart from the fact that it would only facilitate the further repression and exploitation of the working class, it would also fail — for reasons discussed above — to release the forces of growth.

For the same reasons, the import of private foreign capital, while likely to be eagerly sought by the domestic bourgeoisie as a way out of their predicament, would not by itself succeed in resolving any of the fundamental contradictions afflicting the economy, even though it may postpone the flashpoint of the crisis.

18   A possibility which need not be ruled out — particularly in view of recent developments — is the deliberate suppression of parliamentary democracy and the emergence of a variant of fascism, which seeks to maintain itself in power through increasing recourse to repressive measures; the subsequent movements in the terms of trade would then depend upon whether the industrial capitalists or the rural oligarchs succeed to a greater degree in influencing the processes of decision-making within the authoritarian regime. Whether such a regime would be able to activate the forces of growth is, however, very much open to question: for an inordinate share of the potential surplus might now have to be deployed to maintain the paraphernalia of repression.

CHAPTER 12

An Epilogue

The instrument of terms of trade, as we have described it in this work, belongs to the arena of class war. In a society torn by class divisions, it is sought to be used, remorselessly, by each of the contending classes to tilt the structure of asset and income distribution in its favour. It is not the only weapon deployed in class war, but certainly a principal one. And the significance of terms of trade policy is heightened by the fact that the manner in which it is wielded shapes in large measure the pattern of accumulation and growth for the economy as a whole.

The framework of analysis in this study, particularly in the later chapters, has been developed with reference to conditions obtaining in India. But its conclusions can have a wider significance. The nature of the problems India currently faces is common to several underdeveloped countries that are riven by hierarchies of classes in agriculture as well as industry, and where the rural oligarchy are advantageously situated by virtue of their total dominance over the countryside. The economic atrophy we prognosticate for India in the event of an elongation of the existing class relations could also be a prospect looming over other, similarly placed nations.

We, however, do see a silver lining. The alignment of class forces that now obtains in India carries the seeds of its own destruction. An excess of avarice on the part of the entrenched classes is likely to bring economic growth to a whimpering halt, and make inflation endemic. Beyond a point, the system is likely to break down: those classes which, bound by contract, have grown accustomed to the spoils of power, suddenly discover irreconcilable, antagonistic contradictions tearing them apart.

At that stage, a new social reality should take over. Not that, following the transition, the terms of trade problem would be resolved at one stroke. It would not, for the simple reason that the issue of 'town' versus 'country' is basically related to the phenomenon of division of labour, which in turn is an adjunct to the mechanics of economic progress.[1] Also, vestiges of the old class structure do not always immediately disappear with the introduction of new social arrangements; a cultural lag often persists. Depending upon the nature and extent of it, the issue of the terms of trade could emerge, as we have hinted, in an altered form. Whether economic growth will be helped or hindered by the new arrangements would also be determined by the quality of this lag.

Even a revolution which, on the face of it, liquidates all other social classes and establishes the rule of the proletariat, need not automatically succeed in rendering the problem of relative prices as between agriculture and industry more tractable. The Soviet procurement crisis of the 1920s brought this out rather starkly. It is not merely a question of specific elements refusing to abdicate their class interests; the issue has obviously wider ramifications, and is linked to the physical division of production between 'town' and 'country'. A certain modality was tried out in the Soviet Union for solving it; doubts, however, remain whether that was the optimal modality in a socialist system.

'The abolition of the antagonism between town and country is one of the first conditions of communal life . . .':[2] there is no mistaking the import of this challenge thrown at the ideologue. Perhaps more than anywhere else, in China, especially since the Great Leap Forward, an experiment is seemingly on to translate the Marxian edict into reality.[3] Provided it succeeds, the problem of the terms of trade between the industrial and farm sectors will fade away, and one of the major roadblocks to the nation's rapid economic growth will be removed. For many other nations the tasks still lie ahead.

NOTES

1 'The antagonism of town and country . . . is the most crass expression of the subjection of the individual under the division of labour, under a definite activity forced upon him — a subjection which makes one man into a restricted town-animal, the other into a restricted country animal, and daily creates anew the conflict between their interests'. Karl Marx, *The German Ideology*, Lawrence and Wishart, 1942, p. 44.
2 Karl Marx, *op. cit.*, p. 44.
3 For a discussion on the nature of the experiment, see Maria Antoinetta Macciocchi, *Daily Life in Revolutionary China*, Monthly Review Press, 1972, pp. 234–7, and Amartya Sen, *On Economic Inequality*, Clarendon Press, 1972, pp. 87–100.

Index